Critical Acclaim for other books from PC Learning Labs

PC Learning Labs Teaches WordPerfect 5.1

"Excellent keystroke-by-keystroke instruction is provided by this handsome book."

—*Computer Book Review*

"...a tightly focused book that doesn't stray from its purpose...it concentrates on the beginner, and it stays with the beginner."

—**William J. Lynott,** *Online Today*

PC Learning Labs Teaches DOS 5

"It's like having a personal teacher...you will emerge a confident user of personal computers...This book from an organization with 10 years of classroom teaching of personal-computer operation under its belt makes the learning process both easier and organized."

—**Hugh Anderson,** *The Gazette*

"[This] book is designed to help you attain a high level of DOS 5 fluency in as short a time as possible...a solid foundation of skills in DOS file management..."

—**Woody Liswood,** *MicroTimes Magazine*

PC LEARNING LABS TEACHES WORDPERFECT 6.0

z a b c d e

k l m n o p

q r s t u v

y z a b c a

PC LEARNING LABS TEACHES WORDPERFECT 6.0

LOGICAL OPERATIONS

Ziff-Davis Press
Emeryville, California

Curriculum Development	Logical Operations
Writer	Robert Kulik
Editor	Deborah Craig
Technical Reviewer	Mark Butler
Project Coordinator	Kim Haglund
Proofreader	Cort Day
Production Coordinator,	
Logical Operations	Tary Simizon
Cover Illustration	Ken Roberts
Cover Design	Carrie English and Ken Roberts
Book Design	Laura Lamar/MAX, San Francisco
Screen Graphics Editor	Dan Brodnitz
Technical Illustration	Steph Bradshaw
Word Processing	Howard Blechman, Cat Haglund, Allison Levin
Page Layout	Anna Marks and M.D. Barrera
Indexer	Elinor Lindheimer

Ziff-Davis Press books are produced on a Macintosh computer system with the following applications: FrameMaker®, Microsoft® Word, QuarkXPress®, Adobe Illustrator®, Adobe Photoshop®, Adobe Streamline™, MacLink® Plus, Aldus® FreeHand™, Collage Plus™.

Ziff-Davis Press
5903 Christie Avenue
Emeryville, CA 94608

ISBN 1-56276-105-6
Manufactured in the United States of America
10 9 8 7 6 5 4 3 2 1

CONTENTS AT A GLANCE

TABLE OF CONTENTS

INTRODUCTION

Welcome to PC Learning Labs Teaches WordPerfect 6.0. You are about to embark on a unique journey. When you come to the end of this journey, you will have learned all the basic skills necessary to use WordPerfect 6.0, one of the most popular and most sophisticated word-processing programs available today. You will then be able to take this knowledge and apply it directly to your own work—wherever you work and whatever you do.

This book is unique in that it incorporates what we at PC Learning Labs have learned from years of teaching WordPerfect in a classroom setting. We've used our experience in the classroom to create documents that will enable you to learn WordPerfect on a computer at your home or office. Unlike a class, this book encourages you to proceed at your own pace. Furthermore, we've carefully chosen the order of the topics to make sure you are always applying and reinforcing what you learned in earlier, more basic topics.

On this journey, you will be guided every step of the way, and you'll be shown landmarks so that you can chart your own progress and be confident in knowing that you're on a steady course. We hope that you find all the material in this book useful, informative, and fun.

WHO THIS BOOK IS FOR

This book starts you off with basic word-processing skills. For this reason, we assume that you have little or no experience with WordPerfect or even with computers. Even if you have been using WordPerfect or another word processor for some time, we trust that our systematic approach will provide you with a detailed, thorough, and practical knowledge of the program.

WHAT YOU NEED

This book assumes that your computer has a hard disk and that you have installed WordPerfect 6.0 on it. If you have not yet installed WordPerfect, see Appendix A for guidance. We will not assume that you have a printer, though readers who do have a printer will learn how to put it to work. We also will not assume that you have a mouse; everything you need to accomplish in WordPerfect 6.0 can be done easily through the keyboard.

WHAT THIS BOOK CONTAINS

Only the application, continued practice, and exploration of the material in this book will result in your eventual mastery of WordPerfect 6.0. This book facilitates and supports your initial and continued learning by including the following components:

- Carefully sequenced topics, designed to build on the knowledge you've gained from previous topics.

- Hands-on activities, through which you are guided step by step. In these activities, each step and keystroke is clearly given, and the results of performing that step are clearly explained.

- Illustrations that show how your screen should look at key points along the way.

- "Practice Your Skills" sections, which are challenging activities that apply the skills taught in one or more chapters. These activities, placed at strategically located points, help you to incorporate and apply many of your new skills in a broader context.

- Chapter summaries, which recap the major techniques covered in each chapter in a two-column format that's ideal for quick reference.

- A Data Disk, which contains all the files you will need to work through this course at a computer.

HOW TO USE THIS BOOK

This book is designed to be used as a learning guide, a review tool, and as a quick reference.

 AS A LEARNING GUIDE

Each chapter in this book covers one broad topic or a set of related topics. Chapters are arranged in order of increasing WordPerfect proficiency; skills you acquire in one chapter are used and elaborated on in subsequent chapters. For this reason, you should work through the chapters in strict sequence.

Each chapter is organized into explanatory topics and step-by-step activities. Topics provide the theoretical overview you need to master WordPerfect; activities allow you to immediately apply this understanding to specific, hands-on examples.

 AS A REVIEW TOOL

Any method of instruction is only as effective as the time and energy you are willing to invest in it. For this reason, we encourage you to review the more challenging topics and activities presented in this book.

 AS A QUICK REFERENCE

General features (such as printing a document) are presented as a series of bulleted steps; you can locate these bullets (•) easily by skimming through the book. In addition, at the end of every chapter you'll find a quick reference listing the mouse/keyboard actions needed to perform the techniques introduced in that chapter.

USING THE DATA DISK

 One of the most important features of this book is the Data Disk. This disk contains the sample files you'll retrieve and work on throughout this book. These are specially created documents, designed to give you a foundation that you will build upon as you acquire new skills. To perform most of the activities in this book, you will retrieve the original sample document file from this disk and make changes to it. When you save the file, you will rename it and save it to your computer's hard disk. (Word-Perfect will automatically direct it to C:\WPDOCS, a special directory that the program creates for storing WordPerfect documents.) The original document will remain intact on the Data Disk for future use.

Before you begin, you should make a copy of your Data Disk, so that you'll have a backup in case something happens to the original disk. To do this:

1. Turn on your computer. (Follow the instructions in your computer manual.)

2. After you see the screen prompt C>, C:>, C:\>, or something similar, type **diskcopy a: a:** (be sure to leave a space after the first colon) and press **Enter**. Note: If you are using drive B, substitute **b:** for **a:** throughout this book. You will see the prompt

   ```
   Insert SOURCE diskette in drive A:
   Press any key when ready . . .
   ```

3. Insert your Data Disk in drive A of your computer, close the drive door (if necessary), and press any key. You will see the prompt

   ```
   Insert TARGET diskette in drive A:
   Press any key when ready . . .
   ```

4. Remove the Data Disk from drive A, and replace it with a formatted blank disk. Close the drive door (if necessary).

5. Press any key. The contents of the Data Disk are now being copied to the blank disk. After the copying is completed, you see the prompt

```
Copy another diskette? Y/N
```

6. Press **N** (No).

7. Remove the disk and remember to label it and cover the write-protect notch. Use your copy to key through this book, and store the original Data Disk in a safe place, preferably one that is cool and dry.

A QUICK GUIDE TO THE KEYBOARD

Computers come with various styles of keyboards. These keyboards work in the same way, but the layout of the keys varies somewhat from keyboard to keyboard. Figures I.1, I.2, and I.3 show the three main styles of keyboard and how their keys are arranged.

WordPerfect 6.0 uses three main areas of the keyboard, as shown in Figures I.1 through I.3:

- The *function keys*, F1 through F10 or F12, enable you to use many of WordPerfect's features. On the PC- and XT/AT-style keyboards there are 10 such keys located at the left end of the keyboard; on the PS/2-style Enhanced Keyboard there are 12, located across the top of the keyboard. (Note: The function keys F11 and F12 are not necessary in order to use WordPerfect.)

- The *typing keys*, or *alphanumeric keys*, are located in the center of all keyboards. These are the letter, number, and punctuation keys, like those found on a common typewriter.

- The *numeric keypad* conveniently groups the numbers 0 through 9, which are also found across the top row of the typing keys, in one compact area for easier entry. The numeric keypad also contains the

Figure I.1   **The IBM PC-style keyboard**

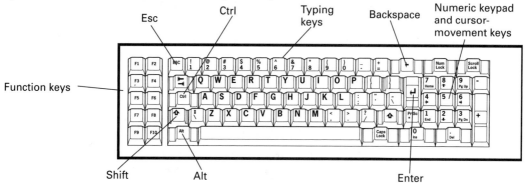

Figure I.2   **The PS/2-style Enhanced Keyboard**

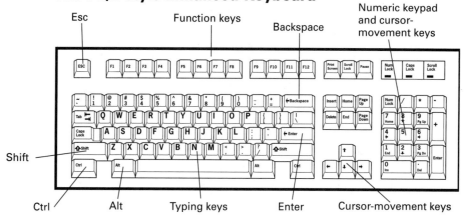

Figure I.3   **The XT/AT-style keyboard**

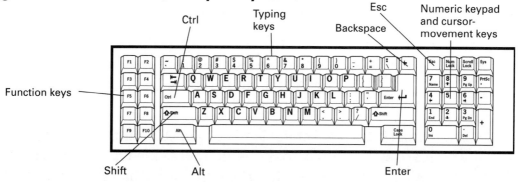

cursor-movement keys. Press the Num Lock key to switch between numeric entry and cursor movement. (For the use of the cursor-movement keys, see Chapter 1.) On the Enhanced Keyboard, there is a separate, additional cursor-movement keypad.

The typing keyboard includes the Ctrl, Shift, and Alt keys. To access WordPerfect's many features, you will use keys alone or in combination with one of these three keys. The Ctrl, Shift, and Alt keys don't do anything if you press them without pressing another key. If you are familiar with the use of a typewriter, then you'll already be familiar with the Shift key's most common use—creating uppercase letters and other special characters. You will become familiar with the uses of most of the individual keys as you progress through this book.

CONVENTIONS USED IN THIS BOOK

In activities that you are to perform at a computer, keystrokes, menu choices, and any characters you are to type are presented in boldface. Here's an example from Chapter 1:

1. Type **John Martinson**.
2. Press **Enter** to end the line and move the cursor to the beginning of the next line.
3. Type **2345 Industrial Circle** and Press **Enter**.
4. Type **Nashua, NH 03060** and press **Enter**.
5. Press **Enter** to add another blank line.

To help you distinguish between steps presented for your general knowledge and steps you should carry out at your computer as you read, we have adopted the following system:

- A bulleted step, like this, is provided for your information and reference only.

1. A numbered step, like this, indicates one of a series of steps that you should carry out in sequence at your computer.

Another convention in this book is the use of a plus sign (+) to show that you should press more than one key. For example, Ctrl+F3 means that you *press and hold* the Ctrl key, then press F3, then release them both. The plus sign is used in this way with the Ctrl, Shift, and Alt keys. In contrast, strings of keys that are pressed and released before the next key is pressed are separated by commas. For example *Home, Home, Home,* ↑ means to press and release Home three times, then press the Up Arrow key.

BEFORE YOU START

The activities in each chapter are designed to proceed sequentially. In many cases, you cannot perform an activity until you have performed one or more of the activities directly preceding it. For this reason, we recommend that you allot enough time to work through an entire chapter in one sitting.

You are now ready to begin. Good learning and...*bon voyage!*

CHAPTER 1: WORDPERFECT BASICS

If you've ever used a typewriter to create a document, you know that it's easy to make mistakes. Because letters are committed to paper as you compose the text, even simple typing changes like erasing a letter can become difficult. More extensive corrections generally require that you retype the entire document.

A *word processor* like WordPerfect provides you with a much more efficient way of creating, revising, and saving a document, because you can edit it and even make major adjustments, such as changing the margins or page breaks, in a single step or series of steps. Then, once you're satisfied with the appearance and content of your document, you can print it.

This chapter covers procedures that are essential to effective word processing. You will encounter most of them each time you use Word-Perfect. When you have finished this chapter, you will be able to:

- Enter text

- Use the Tab and Enter keys

- Edit a document by inserting, deleting, and replacing text

- Save, name, and print a document

- Clear the typing area

- Switch between text mode and graphics mode

- Exit a document

- Open and close menus and dialog boxes

Remember: the bulleted steps are provided for your information only, while the numbered steps should be carried out at your computer.

STARTING WORDPERFECT

Before you start WordPerfect, the program should be installed on your hard disk. See Appendix A if you need help installing the program. Also, you will be using this book's Data Disk. The Data Disk contains the prepared document files used throughout this book. Now, follow these steps:

1. Turn on your computer.

2. If prompted for the date, type today's date. (Skip to Step 4 if you are not prompted for the date.) Use the month-day-year format with dashes or slashes: *mm-dd-yy* or *mm/dd/yy*.

3. Press **Enter**. After typing a command, you must press Enter. Only then is the command actually carried out.

4. If prompted for the time, type the current time. (Skip to Step 6 if you are not prompted for the time.) Use the hour-minute format with a colon as separator, *hh:mm*.

5. Press **Enter**.

6. Type **cd wp60** and press **Enter**. If you installed WordPerfect in a directory other than WP60, use that directory name instead of WP60 in this step. Then type **wp**. This issues the command to start the program (WP).

7. Press **Enter**. After WordPerfect has loaded into the computer's memory, your screen should resemble the one shown in Figure 1.1.

Note: Elements of your screen might vary somewhat from those shown in the figures in this book, depending on the printer you have selected and the type of monitor you are using.

Figure 1.1   **The WordPerfect typing area**

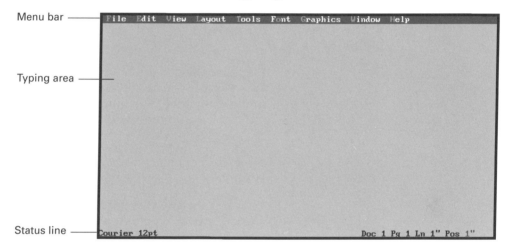

THE BASICS OF ENTERING TEXT

When you start WordPerfect, it displays a blank screen called the *typing area*, where the text you type appears. Formatting codes (which control text effects such as bold, underline, center, indent, and tab) are hidden from view unless you want to see them. Chapter 4 tells you more about codes.

Across the top of the screen is the WordPerfect menu bar. (You'll learn more about the menu bar later in this chapter.) Along the bottom of the screen is the status line.

 THE STATUS LINE

The *status line* at the bottom of the WordPerfect typing area is an information center that is always present while you are working in a document. Before you open a file, or save a document you are creating as a file, the left-hand side of the status line indicates the style and size of text that is currently selected. The right-hand side of the status line identifies the location of the *cursor*, the movable flashing line or rectangle that shows where the next character you type will appear on your screen. The status line summarizes your cursor's location, as shown in Table 1.1.

Table 1.1   **Status Line Indicators**

Status Line Indicator	Purpose
Doc	Identifies the document you are working in. In WordPerfect you can edit up to nine documents at the same time. The number after *Doc* will indicate which of the nine possible documents is displayed.
Pg	Indicates the page number within the active document.
Ln	Indicates the line your cursor is on, measured in inches from the top of the page.
Pos	Indicates the cursor's location on a line, measured in inches from the left-hand side of the page.

Follow these steps at your computer:

1. Notice that the position indicator, Pos, appears as a combination of uppercase and lowercase letters. The current cursor position should be *1"*, meaning that the cursor is located one inch from the left edge of the page.

2. Type your first name. Notice that all letters are lowercase.

3. Take another look at the Pos indicator. It indicates that your cursor has changed position.

4. Press **Caps Lock**. Now look at the position indicator. It should read *POS*—all uppercase letters—because you pressed Caps Lock.

5. With Caps Lock still turned on, type your first name. The position indicator should still read *POS*. The letters of your name now appear in uppercase. Note that pressing and holding the Shift key as you type produces *lowercase* letters, even though Caps Lock is turned on. Also note that the number—and therefore the cursor position—has changed again.

6. If the POS indicator is highlighted, press **Num Lock**.

7. Press ← on the *numeric keypad,* the group of keys on the right-hand side of most keyboards. The cursor moved one character to the left. Note that the position indicator reflects the cursor's new position.

8. Press → on the numeric keypad. The cursor moved one character to the right.

9. Press **Num Lock**. Notice that the POS indicator is now highlighted. This is WordPerfect's way of telling you that Num Lock is turned on.

10. With Num Lock still turned on, press ← on the numeric keypad. Then, press →. Instead of changing your cursor position, you typed the digits **46**. This happened because Num Lock activates the numeric keypad: Pressing those keys will now display numbers on the screen instead of moving the cursor.

11. Press **Backspace**. Notice that doing so deletes the character to the *left* of the cursor. Continue pressing the **Backspace** key until you have deleted all the text you have just typed. (Note that the Delete or Del key erases characters in the other direction, from left to right.)

12. Press **Caps Lock** *and* **Num Lock**. Caps Lock and Num Lock are *toggles*: They turn the respective features on and off. Press either key once to turn on the feature, and press again to turn it off. Also note that Pos (with a capital *P* and small *os*) is now displayed, and it is no longer highlighted. This tells you that both Caps Lock and Num Lock are turned off.

Here's a helpful hint: If your keyboard has a separate arrow keypad (often placed between the main key section and the numeric keypad), it's best to use that keyboard to move the cursor. That way, you won't accidentally type numbers with the numeric keypad.

USING THE ENTER KEY

In word processing, the Enter key is sometimes called the Return key, a term based on the similarity of the Enter key to the carriage *return* on a typewriter. In word processing, unlike typing, you do not press Enter at the end of each line. When text does not fit on a line, WordPerfect "wraps" words to the beginning of the next line. This feature is called *word-wrap*. Chapter 7 will show you how to control word-wrap by setting margins, and Chapter 8 will show you how to use WordPerfect's Hyphenation feature to fine-tune your control over where a line ends.

The only times you'll need to press Enter are

- To end a short line—a line that ends before the right margin is reached

- To end a paragraph

- To insert a blank line

On a clear WordPerfect screen, follow these steps:

1. Type **John Martinson**.

2. Press **Enter** to end the line and move the cursor to the beginning of the next line.

3. Type **2345 Industrial Circle** and press **Enter**.

4. Type **Nashua, NH 03060** and press **Enter**.

5. Press **Enter** to add another blank line.

6. Type **Dear Ted:** and press **Enter** *twice*, once to end the line and once more to skip a blank line.

Remember: If you make any minor errors while typing, you can always press Backspace to correct them.

 USING THE TAB KEY

Tabs, or tab stops, are positions that you can set on a line. Tabs make it easier to indent a line or whole paragraph, to create tables, and to position the cursor on a line. Pressing Tab moves the cursor to the next tab stop. In WordPerfect, tab stops are normally set at every half inch. (Chapter 6 will tell you how to adjust tab stops.)

Follow these steps at your computer:

1. Press **Tab** to position the cursor at the first tab stop.

2. Press **Tab** twice to move the cursor two more tab stops to the right.

3. Press **Backspace** twice to move the cursor to the left, erasing the two new inserted tabs.

4. Type the first sentence shown in Figure 1.2 and press **Space-bar** twice.

Figure 1.2   **A sample WordPerfect document**

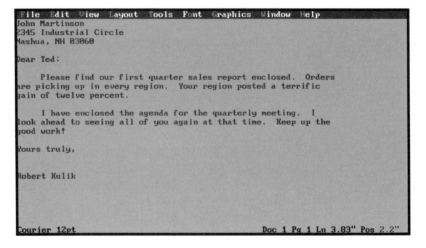

5. Type **Orders are picking up in every region**. You will notice that WordPerfect breaks to the next line automatically as you type, as a result of word-wrap.

6. Complete the letter as shown in Figure 1.2. When you come to the end of a paragraph, press **Enter** twice to end the paragraph and leave a blank line.

EDITING A DOCUMENT

You've already seen that word processing can make it easier to create and navigate your way through documents. Word processing is especially useful as an aid in editing documents. For example, on a typewriter, if you realize that you've omitted a word after typing a line of text, you can't go back and insert it—at least not without smearing White-Out on the page. It's also difficult to delete or replace text. With a word processor, you can easily insert, delete, move, and copy text. All text after your changes automatically adjusts to them.

Before you do any editing, let's get more experience using arrow keys to move around in a document. Using the same letter you were working on in the previous section, follow the next steps at your computer.

1. Press ↑ several times. Each time you press the key, the cursor moves up one line.

2. Press ↓ several times to move the cursor down one line at a time. Position the cursor on a line containing text.

3. Press → several times to move the cursor to the right one character at a time.

4. Press ← several times to move the cursor to the left one character at a time.

INSERTING TEXT

WordPerfect is normally in the *Insert* mode. As you type, text to the right of the cursor is pushed farther right, rather than overwritten (replaced). To insert text, use the arrow keys to position the cursor where you would like to begin inserting text in the document, and type.

Follow these steps at your computer:

1. Use the arrow keys to move the cursor under the *K* in *Keep*, in the last sentence of the second paragraph. This is where you will insert the new text.

2. Type **In the meantime,** and press the **Spacebar** to leave a space after the new phrase. The existing text was pushed to the right of the text being typed. While in the Insert mode, you don't have to press any special keys to insert text in the document. Compare your screen to Figure 1.3.

Figure 1.3   **Letter with inserted text**

```
File  Edit  View  Layout  Tools  Font  Graphics  Window  Help
John Martinson
2345 Industrial Circle
Nashua, NH 03060

Dear Ted:

    Please find our first quarter sales report enclosed.  Orders
are picking up in every region.  Your region posted a terrific
gain of twelve percent.

    I have enclosed the agenda for the quarterly meeting.  I
look ahead to seeing all of you again at that time.  In the
meantime, Keep up the good work!

Yours truly,


Robert Kulik




Courier 12pt                                    Doc 1 Pg 1 Ln 3" Pos 2"
```

DELETING TEXT

The Backspace key deletes the single character or code (such as a tab stop) immediately to the *left* of the cursor. The Delete key deletes the character directly *above* the cursor (that is, the character on which the cursor is blinking). You can use either of these keys to delete text one character at a time. Try not to get in the habit of holding down the Backspace key; otherwise you may delete too much text inadvertently.

Follow these steps at your computer:

1. Use the arrow keys to move the cursor under the *K* in *Keep*.

2. Press **Del** to delete the text at the cursor. Notice that the capital *K* in *Keep* is deleted.

3. Type **k** to change the word to *keep*.

4. Move the cursor so that it is under the space after the word *Circle*, in the second line of the address.

5. Press **Backspace** six times to delete the six letters of the word *Circle*. Backspace deletes the character to the left of the cursor.

6. Type **Parkway**. The inside address should now read *2345 Industrial Parkway*, as seen in Figure 1.4.

Figure 1.4   **Letter after deleting and inserting text**

```
File  Edit  View  Layout  Tools  Font  Graphics  Window  Help
John Martinson
2345 Industrial Parkway
Nashua, NH 03060

Dear Ted:

    Please find our first quarter sales report enclosed.  Orders
are picking up in every region.  Your region posted a terrific
gain of twelve percent.

    I have enclosed the agenda for the quarterly meeting.  I
look ahead to seeing all of you again at that time.  In the
meantime, keep up the good work!

Yours truly,


Robert Kulik



Courier 12pt                              Doc 1 Pg 1 Ln 1.17" Pos 3.3"
```

 TYPEOVER MODE

The alternative to using Insert mode, described in the previous section, is *Typeover* mode, in which new text overwrites, or types over, old text directly in its path. To activate Typeover mode, press the Ins key. *Typeover* appears on the left-hand side of the status line, and Typeover mode remains in effect until you press Ins again to return to Insert mode.

A word of caution: Despite its apparent convenience, Typeover mode should be used as little as possible, if at all. Because it's easy to forget that you've turned on Typeover mode, you might think that you're inserting text when you are actually overwriting text that you wanted to keep.

Follow these steps at your computer:

1. Move the cursor so that it is under the *p* in *picking up*, in the second sentence of the first paragraph.

2. Press **Ins**. The status line reads *Typeover*. You are now in Typeover mode.

3. Type the word **increasing**. Notice that *picking up* is replaced by *increasing*.

4. Press **Ins**. You are now back in Insert mode.

PRACTICE YOUR SKILLS

Use the skills you've just learned to complete the corrections listed below.

1. Delete *Ted* and type **John**.

2. Delete the word *our* in the first sentence of the first paragraph and type **the**.

3. Delete *ahead* in the second sentence of the second paragraph and type **forward**.

4. Delete *Yours truly* and type **Sincerely**.

5. Delete *terrific* in the third sentence of the first paragraph. Also delete the trailing blank space after *terrific*.

Check your work against the letter shown in Figure 1.5.

Figure 1.5   **The corrected letter**

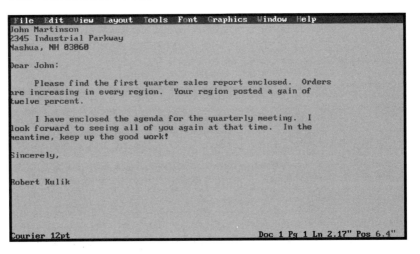

```
File  Edit  View  Layout  Tools  Font  Graphics  Window  Help
John Martinson
2345 Industrial Parkway
Nashua, NH 03060

Dear John:

     Please find the first quarter sales report enclosed.  Orders
are increasing in every region.  Your region posted a gain of
twelve percent.

     I have enclosed the agenda for the quarterly meeting.  I
look forward to seeing all of you again at that time.  In the
meantime, keep up the good work!

Sincerely,


Robert Kulik



Courier 12pt                              Doc 1 Pg 1 Ln 2.17" Pos 6.4"
```

SAVING, NAMING, AND PRINTING A DOCUMENT

Until you save a document, it exists only in computer *memory*, a temporary storage place that is available only as long as the power is on. When the power is turned off, your computer's memory empties; all your active files are erased. By copying all your files onto a disk (your computer's hard disk or a removable 3½- or 5¼-inch disk), you can later retrieve and alter them. You can think of a disk as a storage area more permanent than your computer's memory.

Get in the habit of saving your work frequently. That way, if something happens to the document in memory, you will have a recent copy of the document on disk, so that retyping will be kept to a minimum. Remember, if you make changes to a recently saved document, your changes will not be stored until you save the file with those changes.

Here are some helpful suggestions for saving your work:

- Save every 15 minutes.

- Save before printing.

- Save before spell-checking. (Chapter 8 tells you how to use WordPerfect's spell-checker.)

- Save from your hard disk to a removable disk at the end of a WordPerfect session.

In WordPerfect, as in other programs, you accomplish tasks by issuing commands. You can use either of two methods to issue commands: You can choose a command through the menu system, or you can use a keyboard shortcut.

 WORKING WITH THE MENU BAR

The WordPerfect menu bar allows you to issue commands by choosing them from a pull-down menu. The menu consists of a series of *submenus,* which branch out from the menu bar, much as roots spread out from a plant. Some submenu options lead directly to an activity (your command is executed), while others (followed by triangles) branch into additional submenus. When you choose a menu option that is followed by an ellipsis (...), a *dialog box* is displayed, in which you are offered another set of options.

To display, or open, one of the menus listed in the menu bar, press and hold down the Alt key, and then press the highlighted letter in the menu name. For example, to open the File menu, press Alt+F (the *F* is highlighted in the name *File*); to open the Font menu, press Alt+O (the *o* is highlighted in the name *Font*).

Note: In Graphics mode, these letters are underlined.

To choose an option that is displayed in an open menu, use one of the following methods:

- Use the ↑ or ↓ key to highlight the desired menu option.

- Press Enter.

Or:

- Press the highlighted letter in the desired menu option.

Note: If you would prefer to use a mouse in WordPerfect, see "Using a Mouse" later in this chapter.

 SAVE AS

When you are saving a document for the first time, you should use the Save As command. This command is also useful when you wish to rename an existing document and/or save it to another location.

To save a document using Save As:

- Press the F10 key; or press Alt+F, and then press *A* (the highlighted letter in Save As).

- Type a file name, specifying the desired drive and directory (if other than the current drive and directory).

- Press Enter.

When the document in the typing area has been saved, the file name and location (*path*) are displayed on the left-hand side of the status line.

 NAMING A DOCUMENT: SOME CONVENTIONS

If you are saving a document for the first time, you must name it. Later, you use this name to retrieve the document. To name a document, it is a good idea to follow these conventions:

- File names may contain up to eight characters.

- File names may include all letters or numbers, or a combination of both. Case is not significant.

- File names may not contain spaces or punctuation marks, except hyphen (-), underscore (_), and period (.).

- File names should be descriptive, so that a name reflects a file's contents.

- No two file names may be the same.

- An *extension* of one to three characters can be added to the file name, if you wish. Giving different files the same extension can help you keep track of your documents. If you add an extension, you must separate it from the file name with a period (for example, LETTER.LRN).

Follow these steps at your computer:

1. Press **F10** to save the letter you have been working on. The Save Document 1 dialog box is displayed. Notice that the cursor is positioned in the Filename box.

2. Type **myletter.lrn**. The file name is MYLETTER (eight characters), and the extension is LRN (three characters).

3. Press **Enter**. (The file is not saved until you press Enter.) The following message briefly appears

   ```
   Saving C:\WPDOCS\MYLETTER.LRN
   ```

   A copy of the file is written to the disk, yet the document remains in the typing area for you to work on.

4. Observe the file name and path display

   ```
   C:\WPDOCS\MYLETTER.LRN
   ```

   on the far-left of the status line. Notice that even though you typed the file name in lowercase letters, the name is automatically saved in uppercase.

 WORKING WITH DIALOG BOX OPTIONS

A dialog box contains a list of choices, or options, related to a function, such as formatting a page or printing a document. Figure 1.6 shows all the options available in the Print dialog box. In WordPerfect, there are two ways to choose dialog box options:

- Type the corresponding number of the desired option.

- Type the highlighted letter (often the first letter) of the feature.

Figure 1.6   **The Print dialog box**

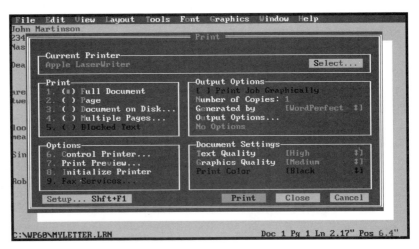

To get out of any dialog box (or menu) that you no longer want to use, press the Esc key. Any change you made in the dialog box will be canceled, and you will be returned to your last position—either the typing area or the previous menu.

You can also use the Exit key, F7, to leave a dialog box. Unlike the Esc key, F7 always returns you directly to the typing area. Also, while Esc cancels any menu selections you've made, F7 puts them into effect.

Note: Whenever you are using a two-key combination, it is important to *hold down* the first key (Shift, Ctrl, or Alt) while pressing the second key. Then release both keys. If you accidentally release the first key before pressing the second one, you will bring up the wrong menu or issue the wrong command. If this happens, press Esc to cancel the command, and start again.

Follow these steps at your computer:

1. Press **Shift+F7** (or press **Alt+F** to open the File menu, and press **P**) to open the Print dialog box (Figure 1.6). The printer name at the top of the Print dialog box will probably differ from the one shown in the figure. Also, you may see additional options if you are running WordPerfect on a network.

2. Examine the dialog box options. Remember that you can select an option by pressing either its number or the highlighted letter in its name.

3. Press **Esc** to leave the menu and return to the typing area.

 ## PRINTING A DOCUMENT

WordPerfect allows you to print in the *background:* You can continue editing documents while printing. You can even edit the same document that is printing, but the changes will not be reflected in that printout. However, when you edit or create while printing, the program responds more slowly.

To print a document, follow these general steps:

• Save the document.

• Press Shift+F7.

• Choose 1. Full Document from the dialog box. This will print the entire document.

• Press Enter or F7.

WordPerfect normally prints documents with full justification. (*Justified* text has an even right margin, rather than a ragged one.) WordPerfect is also set up to print with right, left, top, and bottom margins of 1 inch. Procedures for changing these settings are given in Chapters 3, 6, and 7.

Let's print our document:

1. Press **Shift+F7** to display the Print dialog box.

2. Choose **1. Full Document** (press **1** or **F**). Remember that you can continue working without waiting for the document to print. Compare your screen to Figure 1.6.

3. Press **Enter** (or **F7**) to accept your choice, close the dialog box, and print the document.

CLEARING THE TYPING AREA

Once you've finished working in a document, and before you start working in a different one, you should clear the typing area. Otherwise, WordPerfect will insert the new document into the current one (the one that has not been cleared), combining the two files in the typing area. (On occasion, you may want to combine short documents into a large one using this technique.)

Earlier, you learned to use the Save As command in the File menu (or F10) to save a document for the first time. Once the file has been saved, you can use the File, Exit command or press F7 to update the file in memory and clear the typing area. You can then begin typing a new document or retrieve an existing file to work on (as explained in Chapter 2).

To use File, Exit to clear the typing area:

- Press F7 (or press Alt+F and press E). The Document 1 dialog box opens and displays the prompt

      C:\WPDOCS\MYLETTER.LRN?

- Type Y.

- When WordPerfect prompts

      Exit WordPerfect?

  type N (or press Enter) to clear the typing area. If you type Y here, you will exit WordPerfect. At this point, you can press Esc if you do not want to close the document.

Follow these steps at your computer to save the document now on your screen:

1. Press **F7** (or press **Alt+F** and press **E**). The Document 1 dialog box opens and displays the prompt

       Save C:\WPDOCS\MYLETTER.LRN?

   Notice that the *Y* in *Yes* is highlighted.

2. Type **Y**. (If you typed **N** here, the file would not be saved.) The prompt

       Exit WordPerfect?

   is displayed.

3. Type **N** for *No* to remain in WordPerfect.

TEXT MODE AND GRAPHICS MODE

WordPerfect provides two different screen modes: *Text* mode and *Graphics* mode. By default, WordPerfect enters Text mode when you first start the program. In Text mode, the screen display does not accurately represent the document as it will appear when you print it. For example, in Text mode, if you underlined or italicized certain text, or changed its style or size—all of which you'll learn to do later in this book—these changes would not be visible as such.

In Graphics mode, the on-screen document is a more accurate representation of how the printed page will look. However, the program runs considerably slower in Graphics mode. Therefore, you should run WordPerfect in Text mode unless you prefer to use the program with a mouse. Graphics mode can also be helpful when you wish to view a more accurate representation of your document without printing (see also "Using Print Preview" in Chapter 3).

Note: Your computer and monitor must have graphics capability in order to run WordPerfect in Graphics mode. For more information, consult your computer and monitor reference manuals.

TURNING ON GRAPHICS MODE

To display Graphics mode, you can use either of two methods:

- Press Alt+V to open the View menu (see Figure 1.7).
- Press G to choose Graphics Mode.

Or:

- Press Ctrl+F3 to open the Screen dialog box.
- Press 3 or G to choose Graphics under Display Mode.

RETURNING TO TEXT MODE

To return to Text mode, you can use one of the following methods:

- Press Alt+V to open the View menu.
- Press 2 or T to choose Text Mode.

Or:

- Press Ctrl+F3 to open the Screen dialog box.
- Press 2 or T to choose Text Mode.

Figure 1.7   **View menu**

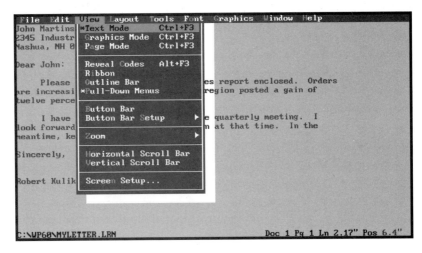

 USING A MOUSE

If you prefer to use a mouse rather than keystrokes to issue commands and move the cursor, you can do so. Here's a list of general procedures for using the mouse:

- To position the cursor, simply move the mouse to the desired location, and then click the (left) mouse button.

- To open a menu, click on the desired menu name in the menu bar.

- To choose an option from any menu or dialog box, click on the desired option.

- To close a menu, click again on the menu name in the menu bar.

- To exit the menu bar, click in the typing area.

It's important to note, however, that when you click on a menu name to close it, the name will remain selected even after the menu is closed. To "exit" the menu bar and reposition the cursor in the typing area, you must press the Esc key.

EXITING WORDPERFECT

As you've already seen, you can exit WordPerfect by choosing the File, Exit command, which is typically used to save and close a document. However, the program offers a command that's specifically designed for exiting the program: the File, Exit WP command.

To exit the program:

- Choose File, Exit WP from the menu (press Alt+F, X); or press Home, F7.

- In the Exit WordPerfect dialog box, press E (or press Enter or F7) to choose Exit.

Let's exit WordPerfect:

1. Choose **File, Exit WP** (press **Alt+F, X** or press **Home, F7**). The Exit WordPerfect dialog box opens (see Figure 1.8). Notice that the Exit option is currently selected, and that the cursor is positioned under the letter *E*. One way of issuing a command that is currently selected in a menu or dialog box is simply to press Enter.

2. Press **Enter** (or press **E** or **F7**) to exit WordPerfect and return to the DOS prompt.

Figure 1.8   **Exit WordPerfect dialog box**

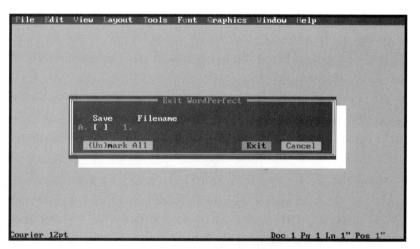

CHAPTER SUMMARY

Congratulations! In this first chapter, you've learned the essential procedures that you'll be using in the following chapters of this book and in your day-to-day experience with WordPerfect. You've learned the basics of entering text, reading and interpreting the status line, and using the Enter and Tab keys. You've also learned some important editing techniques: inserting, deleting, and replacing text; saving, naming, and printing your work; and clearing the typing area. Finally, you learned how to switch between Text and Graphics modes, how to use a mouse, and how to exit from WordPerfect.

Here's a quick technique reference for Chapter 1:

Feature or Action	How to Do It
Start WordPerfect	At the DOS prompt, type **c:\wp60\wp**, then press **Enter**
Type in uppercase letters	**Caps Lock**
Move the cursor left, one character at a time	←
Move one character to the right	→
Create a blank line	**Enter**
Move to the first (or next) tab stop	**Tab**
Move up one line at a time	↑
Move down one line at a time	↓
Erase the character above (at) the cursor	**Del**
Erase the character (or tab) to the left of the cursor	**Backspace**
Replace (overwrite) text	**Ins** (Typeover mode)
Save a document with a new name	**F10** or choose **File**, **Save As**, type the file name, and press **Enter**

Feature or Action	How to Do It
Update and close a document	**F7** or choose **File, Exit**, and press Enter
Display the Print dialog box	**Shift+F7** or choose **File, Print**
Print the entire document (from the Print dialog box)	**1. Full Document**
Cancel a command	Esc
Select Graphics mode	Choose **View, Graphics Mode**
Return to Text mode	Choose **View, Text Mode**
Exit WordPerfect	Press **Home, F7** or choose **File, Exit WP**, and press **Enter**

In the next chapter, you will learn the following skills: retrieving a document from a list of files; moving around in a document; deleting large portions of text; searching for text; and using WordPerfect's Search and Replace features.

CHAPTER 2: WORKING IN LARGE DOCUMENTS

Opening a
Document

Moving Around in a
Document

Deleting Larger
Blocks of Text

The Search Feature

The Replace
Feature

The basic skills you learned in Chapter 1 allow you to move around in a small document and do some minor editing. But on a larger document, you will need faster, more efficient ways to do your work. For example, suppose that you are working on a 23-page report and need to move quickly to page 22 and delete a large block of text. You could, of course, use the skills you have already learned and move a line at a time. However, with the shortcuts in this chapter, you'll be able to do your work in much less time.

By the time you are finished with this chapter, you will know how to:

- Open a document
- Move around in a large document
- Delete large portions of text
- Undelete (restore) something you have just deleted
- Search for specific information in a document
- Search for specific information and replace it with new information
- Save a document under a new name

OPENING A DOCUMENT

WordPerfect provides you with a few different ways to open a file that's been stored on disk. Each method is slightly different, and each has its own purpose. For example, there are times when you want to open a document from a disk but can't remember its file name. To solve this problem, WordPerfect provides a very useful feature, the *File Manager*.

 THE FILE MANAGER

The File Manager enables you to open a file from a disk and place the text in the typing area. It also lets you perform a variety of tasks by highlighting a file name and selecting an option. You'll be learning about these tasks in this and later chapters.

To use the File Manager, press F5 or choose File, File Manager (press Alt+F, F). This opens the Specify File Manager List dialog box. Then perform one of the following steps:

- To display the contents of the highlighted directory, press Enter.
- To open a file in another directory and/or drive, type the name of the desired drive and/or directory that contains the file that you wish to open in the Directory box, and press Enter.

If you are not currently running WordPerfect, please follow the steps listed in Chapter 1 under "Starting WordPerfect" to run the program.

Place the Data Disk in drive A (or B) and follow these steps at your computer:

1. With the typing area cleared, press **F5** or choose **File, File Manager** (press **Alt+F, F**). The Specify File Manager List dialog box is displayed. Notice the directory name that is currently displayed in the Directory box. If you have used the method of installation given in Appendix A, and started the program as instructed in Chapter 1, *C:\WP60*.** will be displayed.

2. Type **a:** to change to drive A, the drive containing the Data Disk. Compare your screen to Figure 2.1.

Figure 2.1

Specifying a different drive and directory

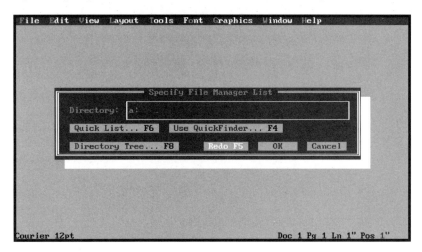

3. Press **Enter** to accept the displayed directory name (path) and display the File Manager screen (see Figure 2.2).

4. Use the Down Arrow key to highlight CHAPTER2.LRN.

5. Choose **1. Open into New Document** (Press **1** or the letter **O**). The CHAPTER2.LRN document appears in the typing area (see Figure 2.3).

A helpful hint: Files in the File Manager are listed in alphabetical order, making it easier for you to find a file name. Remember that the file you have retrieved is a *copy* of the original file, which remains unchanged on disk.

Figure 2.2 **The File Manager screen**

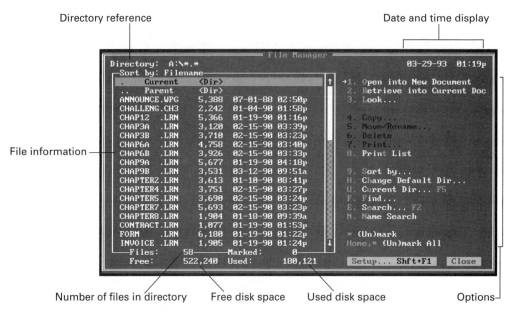

Directory reference

Date and time display

File information

Number of files in directory   Free disk space   Used disk space   Options

Figure 2.3 **The opened document**

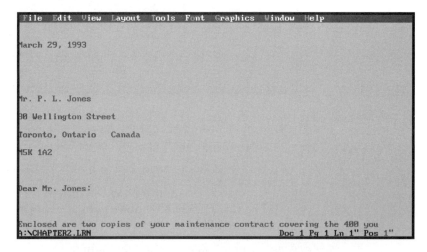

MOVING AROUND IN A DOCUMENT

The arrow keys help you get around in a document, but only one character or line at a time. To speed things up, other keys allow you to jump over large portions of text. These *cursor-movement* keys can take you to the end or beginning of a line, to the top or bottom of a screen, to the previous or next screen of text, to other pages in the document, and to the beginning or end of a document.

The cursor-movement keys are quite helpful, but you need not become overly concerned with memorizing them; you can always use the arrow keys. It is best to learn one or two keystrokes at a time, master them, and learn additional keystrokes as needed.

Table 2.1 lists some cursor-movement keystrokes and what they do. Keys joined by a plus sign are pressed *at the same time*. For example, while holding down the Ctrl key, press → to move to the beginning of the next word (Ctrl+→). As you've already seen, keys separated by a comma are used *in sequence*. For example, Home, Home, ↑ means press Home twice, and then press ↑ to move to the top of the screen.

Table 2.1   **Cursor-Movement Keys**

Keystroke	Moves the Cursor:
Ctrl+→	To the beginning of the next word
Ctrl+←	To the beginning of the previous word
End	To the end of a line (scroll right)
Home, →	To the end of a line (scroll right)
Home, ←	To the beginning of a line (scroll left)
Home, ↑	To the top of the current screen
Home, ↓	To the bottom of the current screen
+ on numeric keypad	Down one screen of text
- on numeric keypad	Up one screen of text
PgDn	To the top of the next page

Table 2.1   **Cursor-Movement Keys (Continued)**

Keystroke	Moves the Cursor:
PgUp	To the top of the previous page
Ctrl+Home, <Page #>, Enter	To the top of the page number you typed in (using Go To)
Home, Home, ↑	To the first character on the top of page 1 (the beginning of the document)
Home, Home, ↓	To the last character of the last page (the end of the document)

NAVIGATING ON ONE LINE OF TEXT

Table 2.1 shows five key combinations that allow you to move the cursor back and forth on a line of text:

- Ctrl+→
- Ctrl+←
- End
- Home, →
- Home, ←

To practice moving the cursor, follow these steps at your computer:

1. Use your arrow keys to move the cursor under the *E* in *Enclosed*, in the first sentence of the first paragraph.

2. Press **Ctrl+→** *twice* to move two words to the right.

3. Press **Home,** → to move the cursor to the end of the line.

4. Press **Home,** ← to move the cursor to the beginning of the line.

5. Press **End** to move the cursor to the end of the line.

6. Press **Ctrl+←** several times until the cursor is at the left margin. The cursor moves to the left one word at a time.

7. Press **Ctrl+←** again. The cursor moves to the last word of the previous line.

NAVIGATING THROUGH SCREENS OF TEXT

You may, at times, want to jump to a specific place in a long document. Table 2.1 shows four key combinations that allow you to move the cursor within and between screens:

- Home, ↑
- Home, ↓
- + (on the numeric keypad)
- − (on the numeric keypad)

To practice using these keys, follow these steps at your computer:

1. Press **Home,** ↑. The cursor moves to the top of the current screen.

2. Press **Home,** ↓. The cursor moves to the bottom of the screen.

3. Press **+** on the numeric keypad. The cursor moves to the next screen of text.

4. Press **-** on the numeric keypad. The cursor moves to the top of the screen.

5. Once again, press **-** on the numeric keypad. This time the cursor moves to the top of the *previous* screen.

NAVIGATING THROUGH A DOCUMENT

Table 2.1 also shows five key combinations that allow you to move the cursor one or many pages at a time:

- PgDn
- PgUp
- Ctrl+Home, <Page #>, Enter
- Home, Home, ↓
- Home, Home, ↑

The third key combination in this list begins with Ctrl+Home. The name for this command is *Go To*. The Go To command is an important one to learn, since it is the only one that allows you to specify the number of the page you want to move to. For example, to move to the top of page 5 of your document, you would press Ctrl+Home,

5, Enter. To use Go To from the menu, choose Edit, Go To (press Alt+E, G); then type the desired page number, and press Enter.

A helpful hint: Don't confuse a page with a screen! The text displayed on one screen can be more or less than one page; it is usually less.

To practice navigating, follow these steps at your computer:

1. Press **PgDn**. Examine the status line. The cursor moves to the top of page 2. Your screen should look like the one shown in Figure 2.4.

Figure 2.4   **The screen after Step 1**

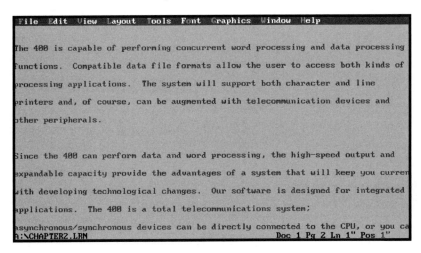

2. Press **PgUp**. The cursor moves to the top of page 1. (Examine the status line to verify this.)

3. Press **Ctrl+Home**. WordPerfect prompts:

   Go To:

   It is asking you what page you wish to go to.

4. Type **3** and press **Enter**. The cursor moves to the top of page 3.

5. Press **Home, Home,** ↓. Notice that the cursor moves to the end of the document.

6. Press **Home, Home,** ↑. The cursor moves to the top of the document. Your screen should once again look like the one shown in Figure 2.3.

DELETING LARGER BLOCKS OF TEXT

As you learned in Chapter 1, you can use either Backspace or Del to delete a single character. WordPerfect also has keystroke combinations that allow you to:

- Delete a word
- Delete from the cursor to the right margin
- Delete from the cursor to the end of the page

Table 2.2 lists keystroke combinations for deleting larger portions of text. Chapter 5 will show you how to highlight a block of text and then delete it.

Table 2.2   **Deleting Larger Portions of Text**

Keystroke	Result
Ctrl+Backspace	Deletes the word at the cursor
Ctrl+End	Deletes from the cursor to the end of the line
Ctrl+PgDn	Deletes from the cursor to the bottom of the page

 DELETING A WORD

In WordPerfect, you can delete a word using Ctrl+Backspace.

Follow these steps at your computer:

1. Move under any letter in the word *trained*, in the last sentence of the first paragraph on page 1.

2. Press **Ctrl+Backspace**. This deletes the word at the cursor, including the blank space *after* the word. The text shifts to accommodate the deletion.

DELETING TO THE END OF THE LINE

You can also delete text from the cursor to the end of the same line. Keep in mind that *line* refers to a line on the screen: all text of the same vertical position between the left and right margins. Don't confuse a line with a sentence. A sentence usually begins with a capital letter, spans several lines, and ends with a period.

Follow these steps at your computer:

1. Move to the space between the words *you* and *within*, toward the end of the first paragraph of the letter, on page 1.

2. Press **Ctrl+End**. The text is deleted from the cursor to the right margin.

3. Type . (a period) to end the sentence after the word *you*. Compare your screen to Figure 2.5.

Figure 2.5   **The screen after Step 3**

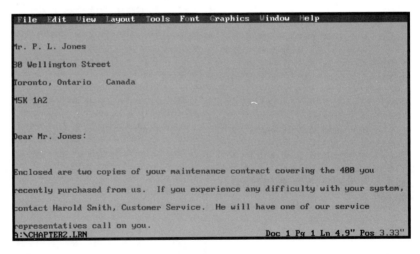

DELETING TO THE END OF THE PAGE

You can also delete text from the cursor to the end of the same page.

Follow these steps at your computer:

1. Move the cursor under the *I* that begins the second paragraph.

2. Press **Ctrl+PgDn**. The prompt

```
Delete Remainder of page?
```

is displayed.

3. Type **Y**, and look at your screen. The text is deleted from the cursor to the bottom of the page. (If you had typed N you would have canceled the command.)

You may have noticed that the three deletion methods you just learned all delete text forwards (down in the document) rather than backwards (up in the document). This means that you place the cursor at the *beginning* of the portion of text that you wish to delete, not at the end.

 ## THE UNDELETE FEATURE

Suppose you just realized that you made a mistake—you didn't mean to delete that text to the end of the page. In Chapter 1, when you issued a command, you used the Esc key if you changed your mind. Esc can also serve as the *Undelete* key, and pressing it restores deleted characters. (As you use WordPerfect more, you will find that many of the program's commands or menus have several purposes.) The Undelete feature lets you change your mind; you can restore deleted text from the last three deletions.

A *deletion* is any character or group of characters removed by any method *except* by using the Backspace key. Undelete restores text erased with Backspace unless you have since moved the cursor. There is no limit to the number of characters in each deletion.

There are three general steps for restoring deleted text:

• Position your cursor where you want the deleted text restored.

• Press Esc or choose Edit, Undelete (Alt+E, N).

• Choose 1 or R to restore the viewed text, choose 2 or P to view the *previous* deletion, or press Esc to cancel Restore. Press 1 after pressing 2 to restore a deletion you just viewed.

Now follow these steps at your computer:

1. Press **Esc**. Two options appear in the Undelete box, along with your most recent deletion (the one to the end of the page).

2. Choose **1. Restore** (press **1** or **R**). The text you deleted is now restored to the document beginning at the cursor's location.

3. Move the cursor to the beginning of the paragraph (*I have*) and press **Esc**. Notice that the same text that was just restored is displayed again (the *I have* paragraph). Compare your screen to the one in Figure 2.6.

4. Choose **2. Previous Deletion**. The deletion before the last one is now displayed on the screen (from the word *within* to the end of the line).

5. Choose **2. Previous Deletion** again. The single word *trained*, which you deleted earlier, is displayed on the screen.

6. Choose **2. Previous Deletion** again. The most recent deletion is once again displayed (the *I have* paragraph).

7. Press **Esc** to cancel the Undelete command.

A helpful hint: Position your cursor *before* pressing F1, because the text will reappear wherever the cursor is located.

Figure 2.6   **The Undelete feature (after Step 3)**

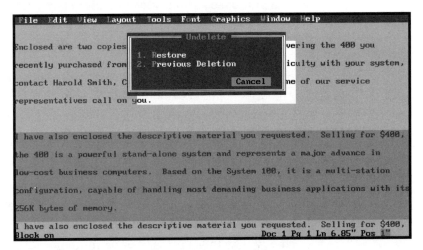

THE SEARCH FEATURE

Have you ever had to read through a document looking for a specific word, name, number, or series of characters? That's not a big problem if the document is a page or two long, but if it is any longer, your search could take much more time.

WordPerfect's Search feature helps you locate any series of characters or codes in your document. (You'll be learning about codes in Chapter 4.) The first step of a search is to define the *search string*, the series of characters you want WordPerfect to find. In the second step, WordPerfect automatically and quickly performs the search and shows you the results, saving you time and aggravation.

To perform a search:

- Position the cursor at the top of the document.

- Press the Search key, F2, or choose Edit, Search (press Alt+E, H).

- Type the string of characters you wish to find. Make sure to spell accurately.

- Press F2 again to begin the search. If a match is found, the cursor jumps to the first character *past* the first match.

- To repeat the same search, press F2, verify the text (the last search string is shown), and press F2 again.

You can press the Tab key to cycle through all the options in a dialog box, choosing or checking the options you want. (You can press Shift+Tab to move through the options in reverse order.) For example, if you want the program to search for the exact combination of uppercase and lowercase letters you've typed:

- Type your search string.

- Press Tab twice.

- Press the Spacebar to check the Case Sensitive Search option.

By default, the program does not look for whole words. For example, if you type *the* as the search string, the program will stop on words such as *their* or *there.* To tell the program to look only for occurrences of the word *the,* check the Find Whole Words Only option.

To uncheck a dialog-box option:

- Press the Tab key until the desired option is highlighted.

- Press the Spacebar.

Now follow these steps at your computer:

1. Move to the top of the document (press **Home, Home,** ↑).

2. Press **F2** to open the Search dialog box, shown in Figure 2.7.

Figure 2.7   **The Search dialog box**

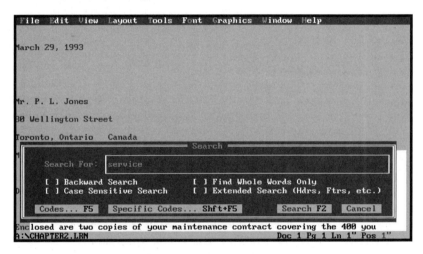

3. Type **service** as your search string, and compare your screen to Figure 2.7. Because the Case Sensitive Search option is not checked, your search string will find *service*, *Service*, and *SERVICE*.

4. Press **F2** to begin the search. The cursor jumps to the period after *Service*.

5. Press **F2** to reopen the Search dialog box. WordPerfect will search, by default, for the previous search string. You can press F2 to search for the next occurrence of *service*. (You could, of course, type a new search string, but for now use *service*.)

6. Press **F2** to continue the search. The second occurrence of the word is found.

7. Search for the third occurrence of *service*. When the third *service* is found, type an **s** at the position of the cursor to make the word *services*.

CHANGING THE DIRECTION OF THE SEARCH

Besides searching forward for a string (down in the document), you can also search backward (up in the document). Use Shift+F2 to search backward (from the cursor to the beginning of the document), with the cursor positioned at the bottom of the document.

THE REPLACE FEATURE

Wouldn't it be handy to be able to find a word in a document and automatically replace it with another one? For example, suppose that you just created a 30-page document with 12 references to *Consolidated Stuff, Inc.* After you finished the document, you found out that the company's name is *Amalgamated Stuff, Inc.* WordPerfect's Replace feature allows you to search for every occurrence of *Consolidated* and replace it with *Amalgamated*, either automatically or case by case.

USING THE HELP FEATURE TO LEARN ABOUT REPLACE

Like the Search key, the Replace keys, Alt+F2, move the cursor to a specific set of characters or codes. They also replace them automatically with other characters or codes—or delete them by replacing them with nothing. (You will learn about codes in Chapter 4.) You can also activate the Replace feature by choosing Edit, Replace (press Alt+E, L).

You can find out more about Replace by pressing the Help key, F1. You can press F1 for Help at any time. If you press F1 for Help after activating a function (such as Replace), the Help will be *context-sensitive*—the Help screen will tell you about the specific feature you are using. If you press F1 without activating a function, you can get information by following the instructions on the Help screen.

Follow these steps at your computer:

1. Move to the top of the document (**Home, Home,** ↑).

2. Press **Alt+F2**. The Search and Replace dialog box is displayed.

3. Press **F1** to display a help screen about the Search and Replace function. Read it to find out how to use Replace and the Confirm Replacement option.

4. Press **Esc** to exit Help and return to the Search and Replace dialog box.

USING REPLACE

One of the options listed in the Search and Replace dialog box is Confirm Replacement. With this option checked, *you* supervise replacements, sometimes replacing, other times not. With the Confirm Replacement option unchecked, replacement occurs *automatically*. We recommend that you always check this option before you use Replace, so that you control the entire process and avoid unwanted changes to your document.

To replace text:

• Position the cursor at the top of the document.

• Press Alt+F2 to display the Search and Replace dialog box.

• In the Search For box, type the characters you wish to find and *replace*. Make sure that the spelling is correct.

• Press Tab.

• Type the characters you wish to Replace With. Make sure that the spelling is correct.

• Press Tab, and press the Spacebar to check the Confirm Replacement option.

• Press F2 to start the Replace procedure. If you checked the Confirm Replacement option, you must type Y to make each replacement or N for no replacement. Otherwise, all replacements will be made automatically for you if you select Replace All.

Now let's use the Replace feature:

1. Observe the Search and Replace dialog box: The last search string, *service,* is still displayed.

2. Type **400** to specify a new search string.

3. Press **Tab** to move to the Replace With field.

4. Type **500 Model**.

5. Press **Tab,** and press the **Spacebar** to check the Confirm Replacement option. Compare your screen to Figure 2.8.

6. Press **F2** to find the first occurrence of the search string.

Figure 2.8   **Specified Search and Replace criteria**

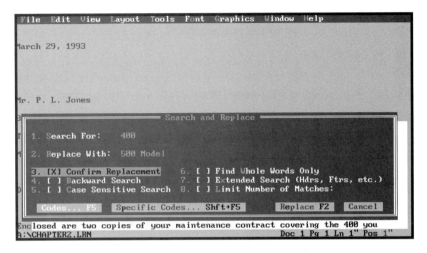

7. The Confirm Replacement message box prompts

   `Replace Match Number 1?`

8. Type **Y** to replace the first occurrence of *400* with *500 Model*. The Replace proceeds to the next occurrence, *$400*. We do not wish to change this.

9. Type **N** to leave the text intact and move to the next occurrence.

To replace from the cursor position backward (toward the beginning), follow the same steps for replacing forward, but check the Backward Search option in the Search and Replace dialog box.

PRACTICE YOUR SKILLS

1. Continue to replace *400* with *500 Model* for the rest of the document. When no other occurrences are found, the message

   `Search and Replace Complete`

is displayed, along with a tally of the number of occurrences found and replacements made.

2. Close the message box.

SAVING THE FILE WITH A NEW NAME AND EXITING

You've completed all the changes in your document. To retain the changes you've made, save the file. It's a good idea to keep your original file intact, so that you can review the skills you've learned any time you like. Saving the file under its original name would replace it with the changed file. In this case, it is best to save the file with a new name. That way, the original file remains intact.

Use the Exit key, F7, or choose File, Exit (press Alt+F, E) to save the document *and* clear it from memory, instead of using two procedures, Save As (Chapter 1) and Exit.

Let's save the document and clear the typing area:

1. Press **F7**. The prompt

        Save A:\CHAPTER2.LRN?

    is displayed.

2. Press **S** to choose Save As and open the Save Document 1 dialog box.

3. Type **mychap2.lrn** and compare your screen to Figure 2.9.

Figure 2.9   **Saving a document with a new name**

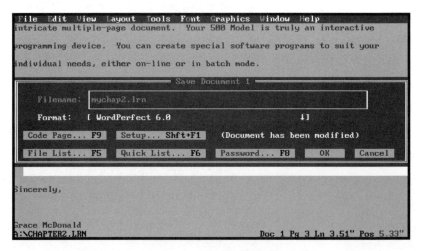

4. Press **Enter** to save the file.

5. At the prompt

```
Exit WordPerfect?
```

type **N** to remain in WordPerfect. Notice that the typing area is cleared.

THE QUICKLIST FEATURE

In the Specify File Manager List dialog box (Figure 2.1) and in the Save Document dialog box (Figure 2.9), you might have noticed the *QuickList* option. QuickList can be a useful way to organize your files, particularly if you find it difficult to work with (and understand) computer directory structures. To that end, QuickList allows you to group similar categories of files under categories, or *directories*, that you get to name. Furthermore, because category names can be much longer than file names and can include spaces, they can be much more descriptive of their contents.

To use QuickList:

- Open the Specify File Manager List dialog box, the Open Document dialog box, or the Save Document dialog box.

- Press F6 to display the QuickList dialog box (see Figure 2.10).

Figure 2.10   **QuickList dialog box**

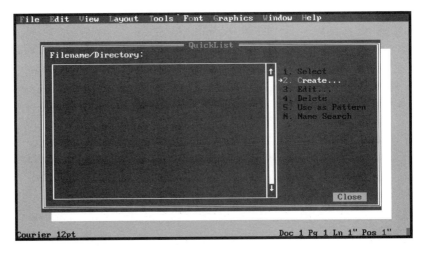

To create a QuickList directory:

- Choose 2. Create to open the Create QuickList Entry dialog box (see Figure 2.11).

Figure 2.11   **Create QuickList Entry dialog box**

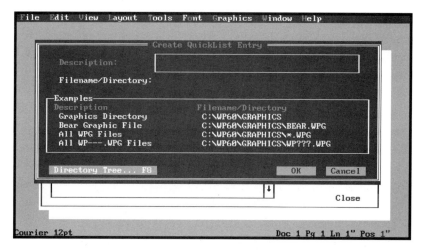

- In the Description text box, type a descriptive name; for example, *My learning files.* Then press Enter.

- In the Filename/Directory text box, type the drive letter and/or name of the directory that contains the desired files; for example, *a:\letters.* Then press Enter. If this directory is located on drive C, then you need not type the drive letter and colon (:).

- Press Enter to accept the changes and return to the QuickList dialog box.

To display the contents of a QuickList entry:

- In the QuickList dialog box, highlight the desired name.

- Choose 1. Select or press Enter. The File Manager opens, displaying the contents of the selected QuickList directory.

CHAPTER SUMMARY

In this chapter, you've learned some fairly sophisticated but easy-to-use techniques for getting around in a document as well as for editing it.

With the Data Disk you can practice the skills that you've learned at any time. Also, try using these techniques to create and edit your own documents. If you're concerned about making mistakes in your own documents, you might want to save them under new names and work on the new files. That way you can boldly try different techniques without being concerned about making irreversible changes.

Here's a quick technique reference for Chapter 2:

Feature or Action	How to Do It
Cancel	**Esc** (also **Edit, Undelete**)
List Files	**F5** or **File, File Manager**
Open a file (via File Manager)	**F5**, then **1. Open into New Document**
Move to beginning of next word	**Ctrl+→**
Move to beginning of previous word	**Ctrl+←**
Move to end of line (scroll right)	**End**
Move to end of line (scroll right)	**Home,** →
Move to beginning of line (scroll left)	**Home,** ←
Move to top of current screen	**Home,** ↑
Move to bottom of current screen	**Home,** ↓
Move down one screen of text	**+** on numeric keypad
Move up one screen of text	**–** on numeric keypad
Move to top of next page	**PgDn**
Move to top of previous page	**PgUp**
Move to top of page number typed in (using Go To)	**Ctrl+Home**, or **Edit, Go To**; *Page #*; **Enter**

Feature or Action	How to Do It
Move to first character in document	**Home, Home,** ↑
Move to last character in document	**Home, Home,** ↓
Delete word at position of cursor	**Ctrl+Backspace**
Delete from cursor to end of line	**Ctrl+End**
Delete from cursor to bottom of page	**Ctrl+PgDn, Y**
Undelete	**Esc** (same key as Cancel) or **Edit, Undelete**
Search (in forward direction)	**F2** or **Edit, Search**
Search (in backward direction)	**Shift+F2**
Replace	**Alt+F2**, or **Edit, Replace**
Help	**F1**

In the next chapter, you'll be learning methods for enhancing your text, such as aligning, emphasizing, and indenting. You'll also learn how to format and align text using the menu bar.

If you need to break off here, please exit from WordPerfect. (For help, see "Exiting WordPerfect" in Chapter 1.) If you want to proceed directly to the next chapter, please do so now.

CHAPTER 3:
TEXT ENHANCEMENT

Aligning Text

Emphasizing Text

Indenting Text

Text Enhancement
and the Menu
System

Whether you are preparing a long report or a short letter, you can usually improve its appearance. An enhancement can be as simple as making a heading bold or right-aligning portions of text. WordPerfect provides you with many ways to enhance text, and this chapter focuses on the most important of them.

When done with this chapter, you will be able to:

- Align text
- Emphasize text, changing fonts
- Indent text
- Enhance text using the WordPerfect pull-down menus

Figure 3.1 shows the document you will produce in this chapter.

ALIGNING TEXT

Text alignment determines how text is positioned between the left and right margins. There are three kinds of text alignment: flush left, centered, and flush right. This paragraph is an example of *flush-left* alignment. The lines of text are aligned evenly along the left margin. Examples of centered and flush-right text alignment are shown in Figure 3.1.

 CENTERING TEXT AS YOU TYPE

To center text on a manual typewriter, you must count the number of characters in the line of text to be centered, divide the number by two, and backspace *that* number of times from the center of the line to determine the point from which to type. On a word processor, centering, like all formatting, is a simple matter of correctly positioning the cursor and pressing one or more keys.

This is an example of centered text.
Each line of text is centered
between the left and right margins.
To center a single line,
press the Center keys,
Shift+F6,
and type the text.
To center several *single-line* paragraphs consecutively:
display the Format dialog box, press Shift+F8,
choose 1. Line,
2. Justification,
and 2. Center.

If you are not currently running WordPerfect, please start it now. With the typing area cleared, insert your Data Disk in drive A.

Figure 3.1   **The completed document**

```
                        Macco Plastics Inc.
                       Quarterly Sales Report
                           First Quarter

1.    General News

        Congratulations to all of you! An initial review of the sales figures for
the nation reveals a surge in sales in all of Macco's sales regions. Major new
clients have been added and many new products are on the way.

    Midwestern Region

    After several years of falling sales due to the slump in the auto
    industry, Blair Williams and his folks have something to celebrate. The
    recent boom in auto manufacturing has led to renewed demand for Macco
    products in Detroit.

    Northeastern Region

    Gene Davidson and his group are doing a great job in Nashua. They
    have secured major contracts for a wide range of new and existing
    products. Much of this business is coming from Computer Equipment
    Corporation (CEC), a major client of Macco's.

    Southern Region

    Mark Daley and his group have done a fine job of maintaining relations
    with XYZ's Product Development Division in London. They have been working
    closely with XYZ product people to develop new products to be used in
    XYZ's existing line.

    A companywide study will begin in March, under the direction of Cathy
    Donaldson and Bill Schuster in data processing, to determine how to most
    effectively implement automation in our firm. We will be making a large
    commitment to productivity gains via computerization sometime in the last
    quarter.

2.    Conclusion

        If the recovery continues at the current pace, this year should be a banner
    year for all of us at Macco. We want to thank all of you for the outstanding
    jobs you've done and, most important, for standing by Macco in hard times. Keep
    up the good work!


    John Smith
    Regional Coordinator
    Macco Plastics, Inc.
```

Let's open a file, and then center text in our document:

1. Press **F5** (or choose **File, File Manager**) to open the Specify File Manager List dialog box.

2. Type **a:** and press **Enter** to display a list of the files on the Data Disk.

3. Use the arrow keys to highlight the file CHAP3A.LRN, and choose **1. Open into New Document**. The file is retrieved into the typing area.

4. Move to the blank line directly above the paragraph numbered *1*.

5. Press **Shift+F6** to position the cursor at the center of the line.

6. Type **Macco Plastics Inc**. The text centers and adjusts itself as you type. Press **Enter** to end the line and return the cursor to the left margin of the next line. Each line must be centered individually.

7. Press **Shift+F6**. The cursor positions itself at the center of the line.

8. Type **Quarterly Sales Report** and press **Enter**.

If you wish to center text that you've already typed in the document, move the cursor under the first character of the line, and press Shift+F6.

PRACTICE YOUR SKILLS

1. Center and type the third line of the heading, **First Quarter**.

2. Press **Enter** to end the line and leave a blank line.

ALIGNING TEXT FLUSH RIGHT

This paragraph is aligned *flush right*. Lines of text are aligned evenly along the right margin. To right-align one line of text, press Alt+F6, and type the text. The alignment feature shuts off automatically when you press Enter to end the line.

To right-align several *single-line* paragraphs consecutively:

- Bring up the Format dialog box by pressing Shift+F8.

- Choose 1. Line.

- Choose 2. Justification.
- Choose 3. Right.

INSERTING THE DATE

The Date Text feature allows you to enter the current *system* date, which is supplied by your computer's built-in clock. To include *today's* date as a permanent part of the text, press the Format keys, Shift+F5, and choose 1. Insert Date Text. The 2. Insert Date Code option (press C or 2) adds a code to the document that inserts the *current* date whenever the document is retrieved. If you use the 1. Insert Date Text option, the date text never changes, while the date code always reflects the current date.

RIGHT-ALIGNING THE DATE

Let's right-align the date in our document:

1. Move to the top of the document (press **Home, Home,** ↑).
2. Press **Alt+F6**. The cursor moves to the right margin.
3. Press **Shift+F5** to open the Date dialog box.
4. Choose **1. Insert Date Text** (press **1** or **I**) to insert the date, in the format *Month dd, yyyy.* Today's date is inserted at the right margin.
5. Press **Enter** to end the line and advance the cursor to the left margin one line down. Compare your screen to Figure 3.2.

Remember to apply flush right to each *new* line of text to be right-aligned. If you wish to right-align text that you've *already* typed in the document, move the cursor under the first character of the line, and press Alt+F6.

JUSTIFYING TEXT

Text justification determines how paragraphs with several lines are positioned between the left and right margins. Each document requires the appropriate kind of justification. Newspaper columns, for

Figure 3.2   **Right-aligned text and centered text**

Right-aligned text ——
Centered text ——

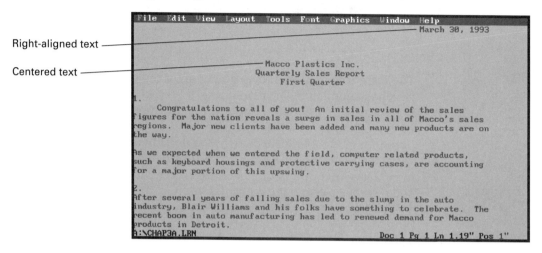

example, are typically fully justified; each line is flush with both margins.

WordPerfect has four justification settings: left, center, right, and full. Left, center, and right justification behave like left, center, and right alignment. Full justification, the default setting, produces text that is aligned evenly along both the left and right margins. (This effect is usually not visible in the typing area.) In WordPerfect, justification is a kind of line formatting, available from the Layout menu. (You'll learn more about line formatting in Chapter 6.)

Figure 3.3 shows a paragraph that is not fully justified. The right margin is uneven, or *ragged:* the space between words is the same from line to line. Figure 3.4 shows the same paragraph fully justified. The amount of space between words varies from line to line because the program automatically calculates the amount of space between words that is necessary to fill out, or justify, a line.

A helpful hint: To apply full justification, WordPerfect increases the space between words to justify text. Using left rather than full justification generally makes text more readable. If you do use full justification, try to hyphenate the text to reduce the irregular and sometimes large gaps between words. (You'll be learning about hyphenation in Chapter 8.)

In traditional typesetting and in some word processing and desktop publishing programs, *justification* refers only to what WordPerfect

Figure 3.3   **A ragged paragraph**

A companywide study will begin in March, under the direction of
Cathy Donaldson and Bill Schuster in data processing, to
determine how to most effectively implement automation in our
firm. We will be making a large commitment to productivity gains
via computerization sometime in the last quarter.

Figure 3.4   **The same paragraph with full justification**

A companywide study will begin in March, under the direction of
Cathy Donaldson and Bill Schuster in data processing, to
determine how to most effectively implement automation in our
firm. We will be making a large commitment to productivity gains
via computerization sometime in the last quarter.

calls *full justification:* aligning text evenly along both margins.
WordPerfect uses *justification* more loosely.

EMPHASIZING TEXT

One way to call attention to text is to apply text emphasis such as
bold, underline, double-underline, italic, and small caps. Although
WordPerfect gives you many options, try not to mix too many of
them in one document. Your document will look more attractive
and be more effective if you choose one or two options and use
them consistently. The Font dialog box (Ctrl+F8), shown in Figure
3.5, enables you to change the size, appearance, base font, and, if
you are using a color printer, color of text.

The 3. Appearance option in the Font dialog box (Figure 3.5) enables you to change the text *style.* Because bold and underline are
commonly used styles, they have their own separate function keys,
which you will learn about later in this chapter.

Figure 3.5   **The Font dialog box**

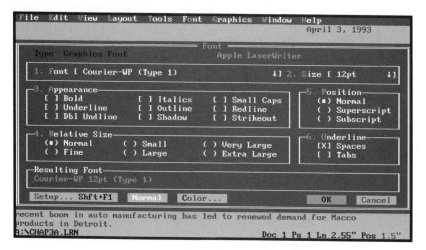

UNDERLINING FROM THE FONT DIALOG BOX

To underline, position your cursor and press the Font keys, Ctrl+F8. Choose 3. Appearance and 2. Underline, and then type the text. To turn the feature off, either press → once, or press Ctrl+F8, 3, 2 again. If the text is already typed, you can use the Block function (which you will learn about in Chapter 5) to highlight it and choose a font effect.

Note: In Text mode, you won't be able to view some changes in text emphasis in the typing area, although they may appear as a different color if you are using a color monitor. You can examine these changes in Print Preview or Graphics mode (see "Using Print Preview" later in this chapter).

Follow these steps at your computer:

1. Move to the space after *1.* on page 1.

2. Tab to Position **1.5"**. The cursor should be directly above the *C* in *Congratulations*.

3. Press **Ctrl+F8** to open the Font dialog box (see Figure 3.5).

4. Choose **3. Appearance** to activate the Appearance option.

5. Choose **2. Underline** to check the underline option.

6. Press **Enter** to turn underlining on. (The Pos measurement in the lower-right corner of your screen confirms that underlining is on: It is underlined or highlighted, depending on your monitor.)

7. Type **Introduction**. The text is underlined (or highlighted).

8. Press **Ctrl+F8** to open the Font dialog box again. Choose **3. Appearance** and **2. Underline** to turn underlining off.

9. Press **Enter** to end the line. (Actually, in this case, it wasn't necessary to turn off the underline option. You could have simply pressed Enter to end the line, which automatically turns off the option.)

UNDERLINING WITH THE F8 FUNCTION KEY

Instead of using the Font dialog box to underline text, you can use the shortcut key, F8. This key is a toggle. Press F8 to turn underlining on, and type the text; turn underlining off by pressing the key again.

Follow these steps at your computer:

1. Move to the space after *2.* on page 1.

2. Tab to Position **1.5"**.

3. Press **F8** to turn underlining on. (The Pos measurement once again confirms that underlining is on.)

4. Type **Regional Updates**. The text is underlined.

5. Press **F8** to turn underlining off. Pos returns to normal. When you use the F8 key to underline text, you must turn off underlining again *before* pressing Enter to end the line.

6. Press **Enter** to end the line.

PRACTICE YOUR SKILLS

Go through the rest of the document, typing and underlining the following subheadings for the paragraphs numbered 3, 4, and 5:

```
Computer Study
Quarterly Meeting
Conclusion
```

Remember, underlining might not be visible on your monitor.

MAKING TEXT BOLD AS YOU TYPE

You can use the Font dialog box to apply **bold** as well as underlining. To do this, open the Font dialog box by pressing Ctrl+F8, choose 3. Appearance, and choose 1. Bold.

F6 is the shortcut for applying bold. Simply press F6 and type the text. Then toggle bold off by pressing F6 once more. To apply bold to text that you've already typed, you can also use the Block feature (which you'll learn about in Chapter 5) to highlight the text, and then press F6.

Follow these steps at your computer:

1. Move the cursor under the *A* in *After several*, in the first paragraph under *2. Regional Updates*.

2. Press **Tab**.

3. Press **F6** to turn bold on. (The Pos measurement reflects that bold is active: It becomes brighter or changes color.)

4. Type **Midwestern Region**.

5. Press **F6** again to turn bold off. The Pos measurement returns to normal.

6. Press **Enter** twice to end the line and place a blank line under the subtitle. Compare your screen to Figure 3.6.

PRACTICE YOUR SKILLS

1. Using the preceding steps as a guide, create the bold subtitle **Northeastern Region** for the paragraph beginning *John Martinson and his group*.

2. Create the bold subtitle **Southern Region** for the paragraph beginning *Mark Daley and his group*.

MAKING TEXT LARGER AS YOU TYPE

Relative Size refers to a character's height or position on a line. In the Font dialog box, the Relative Size option enables you to select from several sizes of characters. The Position option enables you to

Figure 3.6   **Making text bold**

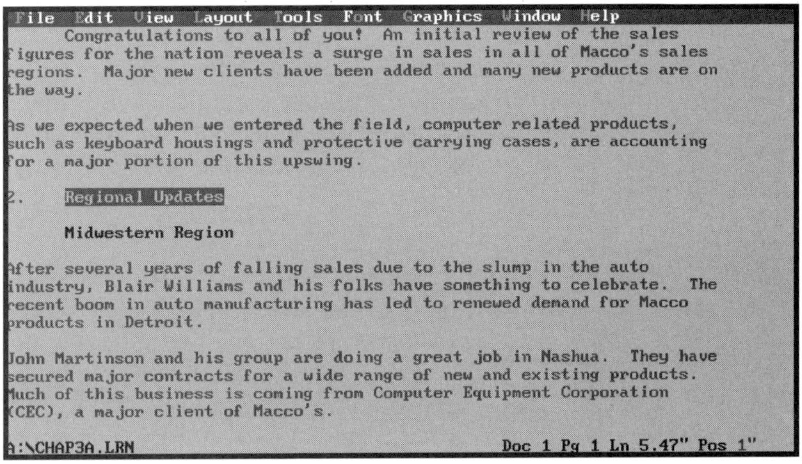

```
File  Edit  View  Layout  Tools  Font  Graphics  Window  Help
        Congratulations to all of you!  An initial review of the sales
figures for the nation reveals a surge in sales in all of Macco's sales
regions.  Major new clients have been added and many new products are on
the way.

As we expected when we entered the field, computer related products,
such as keyboard housings and protective carrying cases, are accounting
for a major portion of this upswing.

2.    Regional Updates

     Midwestern Region

After several years of falling sales due to the slump in the auto
industry, Blair Williams and his folks have something to celebrate.  The
recent boom in auto manufacturing has led to renewed demand for Macco
products in Detroit.

John Martinson and his group are doing a great job in Nashua.  They have
secured major contracts for a wide range of new and existing products.
Much of this business is coming from Computer Equipment Corporation
(CEC), a major client of Macco's.

A:\CHAP3A.LRN                              Doc 1 Pg 1 Ln 5.47" Pos 1"
```

format characters as subscript or superscript. This can be useful in texts dealing with mathematical or scientific subjects.

Follow these steps at your computer:

1. Move to the top of the document (**Home, Home,** ↑).

2. Press **Caps Lock** to turn capitalization on. The position indicator changes from Pos to *POS*.

3. Press **Ctrl+F8** to display the Font dialog box.

4. Choose **4. Relative Size**.

5. Choose **6. Extra Large**, and press **Enter** to accept the change and close the dialog box.

6. Type **INTERNAL MEMO**, the text to be formatted as extra large.

7. Press **Ctrl+F8**, choose **4. Relative Size**, and choose **1. Normal**, to restore normal fonts. Then press **Enter**.

8. Press **Caps Lock** to turn capitalization off. Pos returns to normal.

9. Press **Enter** to end the line.

Like changes in appearance, changes in size cannot all be viewed in the typing area. They may, however, appear as a different color if you are using a color monitor. You can examine these size changes in Graphics mode or Print Preview (see "Using Print Preview" just ahead).

A note on printing: The way text appears when printed depends on which fonts your printer supports. If you select extra-large type, but the text is printed in the normal size, your printer probably does not offer a font larger than the one you're already using.

USING PRINT PREVIEW

You may want to see how your changes affected your document, or you may just want to get an idea of how your document will look. The Print Preview feature simulates printed output on the screen. To view your document before printing it, choose File, Print Preview; or press Shift+F7, and choose 7. Print Preview.

Your document will then be shown in the *Print Preview* area. By default, this area shows the document at 100% view. You can magnify a portion of your document to 200 percent by choosing View, 200% View from the menu; or you could use the View menu to zoom in or out, or view the document in full or facing pages. You can also use the Pages menu to view the page of your choice. Press F7 or choose File, Close to leave the preview area and return to the document.

A note to mouse users: When you enter Print Preview, a button bar is displayed across the top of the Print Preview area, directly below the menu bar. The button bar provides you with most of the choices that are available through the menus. To use the button bar, simply click on the desired button.

Follow these steps at your computer:

1. Press **Shift+F7** to display the Print dialog box.

2. Choose **7. Print Preview**. The first page of the document appears in the Print Preview area. A menu bar appears at the top of the screen.

3. Choose **View, 200% View**. The extra-large text is clearly visible.

4. Choose **View, 100% View** to return to 100% view.

5. Press **F7** to return to the typing area.

INDENTING TEXT

Indenting lines is a way of setting them off from surrounding text. In WordPerfect, *indenting* moves every line of a paragraph away from the left or right margins, or from both at the same time. Since WordPerfect lets you do this with keystrokes, you do not have to change margin settings for every paragraph you want to indent. Indentation creates a new temporary left, right, or left-right boundary, while the left and right margins remain unchanged.

COMPARING TABS AND INDENTS

Many people confuse tabs and indents. A tab indents *one* line. If you insert a tab before the first word of a paragraph, only the *first line* is indented; the other lines remain at the left margin. An indent moves the *entire paragraph* away from the left or right margin, or from both.

> Left-indent a paragraph to move it away from the left margin. As in this paragraph, left indent creates a new left boundary.

To indent before you start typing text, press F4 for Left Indent, and type the text. Pressing Enter to end the paragraph also ends the indent. Indenting must be turned on for every paragraph you wish to indent. To indent existing paragraphs, move the cursor under the first character of the paragraph, and press F4.

Let's left-indent some text in our document:

1. Move the cursor under the *A* in *As we expected*, in the second paragraph under *1. Introduction*.

2. Press **Tab** to indent the first line of the paragraph. Notice that the first character moved to the first tab stop, the first line moved away from the left margin, and the rest of the paragraph remained aligned with the left margin.

3. Move the cursor under the *A* in *After several*, under *Midwestern Region*.

4. Press **F4** to indent the paragraph. Notice the difference between the paragraph with the tab and the one with the indent.

PRACTICE YOUR SKILLS

Using F4, indent the paragraph underneath the subtitle *Southern Region*. Compare your screen to the one shown in Figure 3.7.

Figure 3.7   **The document with left indents**

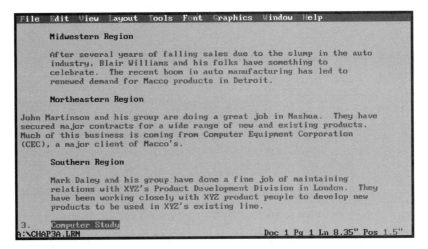

INDENTING MORE THAN ONCE

You can indent a paragraph even farther from the left margin. To increase an indent, press F4 two or more times. The indent positions are based on tab stops. Because tab stops are set by default at every half inch, every indent moves the text one-half inch away from the margin.

Follow these steps at your computer:

1. Move under the letter *J* in *John Martinson*, under *Northeast Region*. (To compare different types of indents on one screen, position your cursor so that all three paragraphs are visible at once.)

2. Press **F4** twice, to indent the paragraph twice. It moved one inch (two tab stops) away from the left margin. Compare this paragraph to the one above.

3. If necessary, move the cursor under the *J* in *John Martinson.* Press **Backspace** twice to un-indent the text. You will be indenting it differently in the next activity.

A helpful hint: If you indent too far, you can always press Backspace to un-indent the text by deleting the Indent code. (Chapter 4 will introduce codes.)

INDENTING A PARAGRAPH FROM BOTH SIDES

Just as you can move an entire paragraph away from the left margin, you can also move it away from both the left and right margins. Left/Right Indent changes both the left and the right boundaries, as in this paragraph.

To indent before you start typing text, press Shift+F4 for Left/Right Indent, and type the text. Pressing Enter turns off indenting. Indenting must be turned on for every paragraph you wish to indent. To indent an existing paragraph, move the cursor under the first character of the paragraph, and press Shift+F4.

Follow these steps at your computer:

1. Move the cursor under the *J* in *John Martinson*, if it is not already there.

2. Press **Shift+F4** to indent the paragraph from the left and right. The right margin has increased as well as the left margin; there's more space between the text and both margins. Compare your screen to the one shown in Figure 3.8.

You can indent more than one tab stop by pressing Shift+F4 twice or more. Keep in mind that because the paragraph is being indented from *both* sides *each* time you press Shift+F4, the lines of text can become very short. Therefore, you should use the Left/Right Indent with care.

CREATING HANGING INDENTS

In a *hanging indent*, the first line of a paragraph extends to the left of the margin set for the rest of the paragraph. This paragraph has a hanging indent. This can be useful in numbered or bulleted lists in which you want the text to line up to the right of the number or bullet. Figure 3.9 shows a numbered list using hanging indents.

Figure 3.8   **Paragraph with left and right indents**

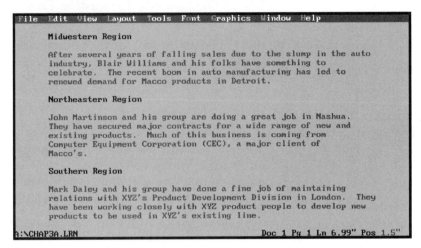

Figure 3.9   **Paragraphs with hanging indents**

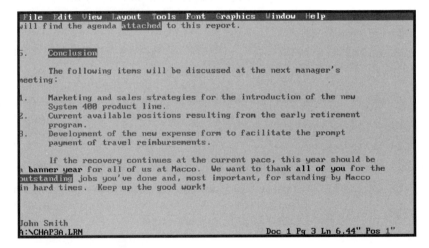

To produce a hanging indent for a paragraph:

- Position the cursor on the first character of the paragraph.

- Press the Left Indent key, F4, or the Left/Right Indent keys, Shift+F4.

- Press the Margin Release keys, Shift+Tab, to create a hanging indent.

Follow these steps at your computer:

1. Move under the number *1* in *1. Marketing and Sales* (the first numbered paragraph on page 2, under *5. Conclusion*).

2. Press **F4** to indent the paragraph.

3. Press **Shift+Tab** to create a hanging indent. The first line of the paragraph moves to the left, while the second line begins at the first tab stop.

PRACTICE YOUR SKILLS

Using the preceding steps as a guide, create hanging indents for the paragraphs numbered *2* and *3* under *5. Conclusion*. Compare your screen to Figure 3.9.

SAVING THE FILE WITH A NEW NAME AND CLEARING THE TYPING AREA

Throughout this chapter, you've been making changes to the document CHAP3A.LRN, but you have not yet saved your changes. By saving the revised document as a file with a different name, you leave the original file intact and can practice your skills as often as you like.

Let's save our file with a new name:

1. Press **F10** (or choose **File, Save As**) to open the Save Document 1 dialog box. The current file name is displayed in the Filename box.

2. Type **mychap3a.lrn** as the new file name. The previous drive letter and file name are automatically replaced.

3. Press **Enter**. The path and file name C:\WP60\MYCHAP3A.LRN are now displayed on the status lines.

4. Press **F7** (or choose **File, Exit**).

5. At the prompt

    Save C:\WP60\MYCHAP3A.LRN?

   press **Enter** (or **N**) to choose No. (We already saved the file.)

6. At the prompt

```
Exit WordPerfect?
```

press **Enter** (or **N**) to choose No. The typing area is now cleared.

TEXT ENHANCEMENT AND THE MENU SYSTEM

Up to now, you've been using the function keys to enhance text. You can do the same things by using WordPerfect's menu system.

USING MENUS

In Chapter 1, you learned that there are two ways to choose a menu option:

- Highlight the option by using ↑ or ↓, and press Enter.

- Type its highlighted letter.

Menu choices with arrows next to them have submenus that appear to the *right* of the menu choice. Figure 3.10 shows a typical submenu (Layout Justification).

Figure 3.10   **The Justification submenu**

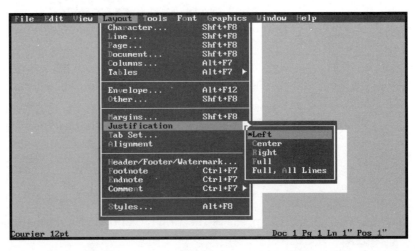

Follow these steps at your computer:

1. Open the Layout menu (press **Alt+L**).

2. Press ↓ to move down to Justification.

3. Press **Enter** to display and activate the Justification submenu.

4. Press **Esc** to return to the Layout menu.

5. Press **Esc** again to return to the menu bar.

6. Press **Esc** to return the cursor to the typing area.

 USING THE STLYE MENU TO MAKE TEXT BOLD

Earlier in this chapter, you learned how to make text bold with F6 or the Appearance option in the Font dialog box. You can also bold-face text by using the Font menu directly.

Let's open a new document file; then, we'll use the Font menu to make text bold:

1. Choose **File, File Manager** from the menu bar to open the Specify File Manager List dialog box.

2. Type **a:** and press **Enter** to display the File Manager screen.

3. Highlight and open the file CHAP3B.LRN (choose **1. Open into New Document**).

4. Move the cursor under the *M* in *Mark Daley*, under *2. Regional Updates*.

5. Press **Tab** to move the first line of the paragraph to the first tab stop.

6. Open the Font menu (press **Alt+O**). Notice the Bold choice; its highlighted letter is *B*.

7. Press **B** to choose **Bold**. The position indicator shows that bold is on; everything you type will appear in bold until it is turned off.

8. Type **Southern Region**.

9. Choose **Font, Bold** to turn bold off.

10. Press **Enter** twice to end the line and create a blank line.

A helpful hint: In Step 9 above, you could also have pressed F6 to turn bold off. If you turn a feature on using a menu, you can use that feature's corresponding function key to turn it off, and vice versa. Function keys and menus offer you different ways to do the same thing.

USING THE LAYOUT MENU TO INDENT TEXT

You can also use the Layout menu's Alignment submenu, shown in Figure 3.11, to indent text.

Figure 3.11   Alignment submenu

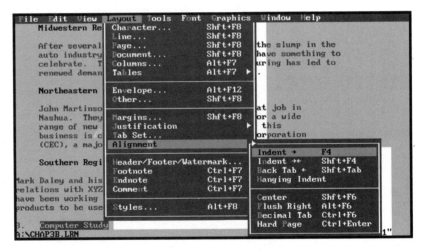

- To left-indent a paragraph, choose Layout, Alignment, Indent →.

- To indent a paragraph from the left and right sides, choose Layout, Alignment, Indent →←.

- To create a hanging indent, choose Layout, Alignment, Hanging Indent.

Follow these steps at your computer:

1. Move the cursor under the letter *M* in *Mark Daley,* under the heading *Southern Region.*

2. Open the Layout menu (type **Alt+L**).

3. Choose **Alignment** (highlight it and press **Enter**, or press **A**).

4. Choose **Indent** → to left-indent the paragraph. You can see that it is now indented. Compare your document to the one shown in Figure 3.12.

Figure 3.12   **Paragraph indented using Layout Alignment**

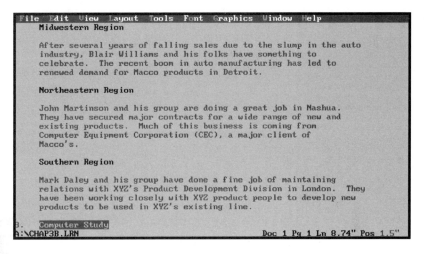

USING THE FILE MENU TO SAVE THE DOCUMENT AND CLEAR THE TYPING AREA

Earlier you learned that you can use F7 to save your document and either exit WordPerfect or clear the typing area. You can also use WordPerfect's File menu to save and exit.

Follow these steps at your computer:

1. Choose **File, Exit**. The same prompt that you get when you press F7 appears:

        Save A:\CHAP3B.LRN?

2. Choose **Save As** (press **S**) to save the file with a new name. The Save Document 1 dialog box is displayed.

3. Type **mychap3b.lrn** and press **Enter**. The message

```
Saving C:\WP60\MYCHAP3B.LRN
```

is displayed briefly. Next you see the following prompt:

```
Exit WordPerfect?
```

4. Type **N** (or press **Enter**) to remain in WordPerfect and clear the typing area.

PRACTICE YOUR SKILLS

In the first three chapters of this book, you have learned how to create, edit, save, and print a document. You have also learned how to scroll through a document and delete, replace, and enhance text.

The following activity gives you the opportunity to practice these skills.

This is the first such activity in this book, and there will be several others. Think of it as an opportunity to sharpen your skills. Only through repetition will you absorb what you have learned. Feel free to review the previous chapters at any time.

In this activity, you will retrieve a document from your Data Disk and then edit it to produce the final document shown in Figure 3.13.

Follow these steps at your computer:

1. Clear the typing area (Chapter 1). Open the file PRACTICE.CH3 (Chapter 2).

2. Search for the name *John Martinson* (Chapter 2).

3. Delete *John Martinson*. In its place type **Gene Davidson** (Chapter 1 or Chapter 2).

4. Position the cursor on the 2 near the bottom of page 1. Delete the text from the cursor to the end of the page (Chapter 2).

5. Undelete the text deleted in Step 4 (Chapter 2).

6. Move the cursor to the top of the document (Chapter 2).

7. Center the three lines at the top of the document as they appear in Figure 3.13.

Figure 3.13   The corrected document

Macco Plastics Inc.
Quarterly Sales Report
First Quarter

1.   <u>General News</u>

Congratulations to all of you! An initial review of the sales figures for the nation reveals a surge in sales in all of Macco's sales regions. Major new clients have been added and many new products are on the way.

Midwestern Region

After several years of falling sales due to the slump in the auto industry, Blair Williams and his folks have something to celebrate. The recent boom in auto manufacturing has led to renewed demand for Macco products in Detroit.

Northeastern Region

Gene Davidson and his group are doing a great job in Nashua. They have secured major contracts for a wide range of new and existing products. Much of this business is coming from Computer Equipment Corporation (CEC), a major client of Macco's.

Southern Region

Mark Daley and his group have done a fine job of maintaining relations with XYZ's Product Development Division in London. They have been working closely with XYZ product people to develop new products to be used in XYZ's existing line.

A companywide study will begin in March, under the direction of Cathy Donaldson and Bill Schuster in data processing, to determine how to most effectively implement automation in our firm. We will be making a large commitment to productivity gains via computerization sometime in the last quarter.

2.   <u>Conclusion</u>

If the recovery continues at the current pace, this year should be a banner year for all of us at Macco. We want to thank all of you for the outstanding jobs you've done and, most important, for standing by Macco in hard times. Keep up the good work!

John Smith
Regional Coordinator
Macco Plastics, Inc.

8. Create and underline the following numbered titles:

```
1. General News
2. Conclusion
```

9. Use keystrokes to left indent the paragraph under the heading *Southern Region.*

10. Save the document as CORRECT.CH3 (Chapter 1).

11. Print your document (Chapter 1), and compare it to the one shown in Figure 3.13.

You may wish to enhance your skills by continuing to practice the techniques you have learned so far. If so, you can do the following activity. Refine the document you just worked on, but this time use the menu system.

Follow these steps at your computer:

1. Clear the typing area. Use the File Manager to open the file CHALLENG.CH3.

2. Search for *John Martinson* (Chapter 2).

3. Delete the name, and type **Gene Davidson** (Chapter 1 or Chapter 2).

4. Move the cursor to the top of the document (Chapter 2).

5. Create and center the heading at the top of the document (see Figure 3.13), using the Alignment submenu.

6. Create and underline the following numbered titles:

```
1. General News
2. Conclusion
```

7. Left-indent the paragraph under the heading *Southern Region.*

8. Save the document as CORRCHAL.CH3.

9. Print your document (using the **File** menu), and compare it to the one shown in Figure 3.13.

10. Clear the typing area.

CHAPTER SUMMARY

In this chapter, you learned a number of ways to enhance your documents, including methods for aligning, emphasizing, and indenting text. With WordPerfect, you can enhance text using either function keys or the menu system.

Here's a quick technique reference for Chapter 3:

Feature or Action	How to Do It
Center	**Shift+F6**
Align Flush Right	**Alt+F6**
Insert current date	**Shift+F5**, choose **1. Insert Date Text** or **2. Insert Date Code**
Extra Large type	**Ctrl+F8** (Font), **4. Relative Size, 6. Extra Large**
Bold	**F6**; or **Ctrl+F8** (Font), **3 Appearance, 1 Bold**
Underline	**F8**; or **Ctrl+F8** (Font), **3 Appearance, 2 Underline**
Print Preview	Press **Shift+F7** and choose **7. Print Preview**; or choose **File, Print Preview**
100% view	Choose **View, 100% View** from the Print Preview Area
200% view	Choose **View, 200% View** from the Print Preview Area
Left Indent	**F4**; or choose **Layout, Alignment, Indent** →
Left/Right Indent	**Shift+F4**; or choose **Layout, Alignment, Indent** →←
Hanging Indent	**F4, Shift+Tab**; or choose **Layout, Alignment, Hanging Indent**

Remember: You've been saving your files under a new name to keep the originals intact. At any time, feel free to retrieve any unchanged file and go over the skills you have learned. Don't feel that you have to complete this book (or any number of chapters, for that matter) before practicing what you've learned.

In the next chapter, you'll learn about WordPerfect's formatting codes. Understanding codes will make it easier for you to edit documents and take advantage of WordPerfect's powerful formatting capabilities.

If you need to break off here, please exit from WordPerfect. If you want to proceed directly to the next chapter, please do so now.

CHAPTER 4: CODES

The Reveal Codes
Area

Editing Codes in
Reveal Codes

Deleting Codes in
the Typing Area

Printing with Draft
Quality

Until now, you've been making a number of changes to documents. For example, you've enhanced text by underlining it or making it bold. While you've been making these enhancements, WordPerfect has been implementing them behind the scenes by inserting special codes. These codes tell your printer how to handle your changes. To print a word in bold, for example, WordPerfect inserts codes telling the printer to print bold.

When done with this chapter, you will be able to:

- Read and interpret codes
- Move around in the Reveal Codes area
- Edit and search for codes in the Reveal Codes area
- Edit codes from the typing area

THE REVEAL CODES AREA

Whenever you underline or indent text, end paragraphs, or make any changes to how your document looks, WordPerfect inserts codes. To keep the typing area clutter-free, these codes appear in the *Reveal Codes area*. WordPerfect makes it possible for you to move between the typing area and Reveal Codes area and to edit codes in either place.

INTERPRETING CODES

Ordinarily, you need not be concerned with the Reveal Codes area when you are typing. But when you need to go back and undo formatting—underlining, for example—you must delete the code that tells the printer what and how to format. You can insert and delete codes and move around in the Reveal Codes area just as you would within the typing area.

To display the Reveal Codes area, press F11 or Alt+F3, or choose View, Reveal Codes. With codes revealed, your screen is divided into three parts, as shown later in Figure 4.1:

Top	Text in the typing area. When you use Reveal Codes, less of the typing area can be viewed.
Tab ruler	Under the typing area's status line is the tab ruler, also known as the separator line. It shows the current margin and tab settings, where { represents the left margin, } represents the right margin, and ▲ represents a tab stop.
Bottom	Reveal Codes area. Displays the same text as the top portion of the screen, but includes the codes.

F11 and Alt+F3 act as toggles. To leave the Reveal Codes area and return to the typing area, press the key or keys again.

Place the Data Disk in drive A and follow these steps at your computer:

1. Use the File Manager to open the document CHAPTER4.LRN (press **F5** or choose **File, File Manager**, type **a:**, press **Enter**, highlight the file name, and choose **1. Open into New Document**). The top of the document is the part for which you would like to see codes.

2. Press **Alt+F3** to display the Reveal Codes area. Compare your screen to Figure 4.1.

Figure 4.1   **The Reveal Codes area**

Typing area —

Tab ruler —

Reveal Codes area—

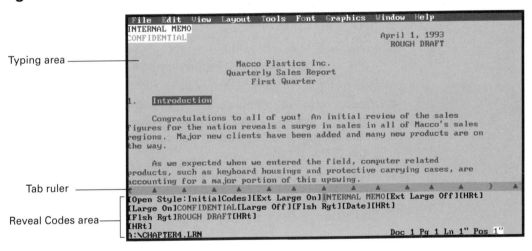

3. Examine the three areas of the screen. Text from the top also appears in the bottom, but codes appear only in the bottom, in bold, embedded in the text. Try to identify codes for Extra Large, Center, and Flush Right. (If necessary, press ↓ to view all these codes.)

4. Press **Alt+F3** again to return to the typing area.

MOVING AROUND IN THE REVEAL CODES AREA

Before using Reveal Codes, position your cursor in the part of the document whose codes you would like to see. Once you go into the Reveal Codes area, you can move the cursor just as in the typing area. As you move the cursor in the Reveal Codes area, the same text is displayed in both the top and bottom parts of the screen, with the position, line, and page indicators in the status line adjusting accordingly. Keep an eye on these indicators while you're moving around in Reveal Codes.

Follow these steps at your computer:

1. Move to the top of the document if you are not already there. This is the part of the document for which you will reveal codes.

2. Choose **View, Reveal Codes** to display the Reveal Codes area. Notice that the cursor is positioned in both the typing area and the Reveal Codes area.

3. Press →. The cursor in the Reveal Codes area moves one character or code to the right, highlighting the character or code it is on. The cursor in the typing area moves in the usual way.

4. Press ↓ to move the cursor down one line. Notice that in the Reveal Codes area, the cursor does not move down, as it does in the typing area; instead, the codes (and text) scroll up to "meet" the cursor.

5. Press ← to move the cursor one character or code to the left.

6. Choose **View, Reveal Codes** again to turn off Reveal Codes and return to the typing area.

MOVING TO THE VERY TOP OF A DOCUMENT

In WordPerfect, a code affects the document from the point at which it is inserted to any code later in the document that cancels it. If, for example, the first line of text in your document is centered and you would like to precede it with a line of flush-left text, you must position the cursor *before* the code that tells WordPerfect to center text. Otherwise, a new line of text typed after the code would also be centered.

In Chapter 2, you learned to move the cursor to the beginning of the document by pressing Home, Home, ↑. But pressing Home, Home,

↑ moves the cursor only to the beginning of the *text* in the document, not to a position before any *codes* preceding the text. To move the cursor to the very top of the document (before all text and codes), press Home, Home, Home, ↑. Use these keys whenever you need to position the cursor at the very top of the document. Likewise, press Home, Home, Home, ↓, to move the cursor to the bottom of the document, beyond all text and codes.

Follow these steps at your computer:

1. Press **Alt+F3** to display the Reveal Codes area.

2. Press **Home, Home,** ↑, and examine the cursor position in the typing area. The cursor appears to be at the top of the document, on the first character of *INTERNAL MEMO*.

3. Examine the cursor position in the Reveal Codes area. The cursor is on the *I* of *INTERNAL MEMO*. The [Ext Large On] code is *before* (to the left of) the cursor.

4. Press **Home, Home, Home,** ↑ to move the cursor to the top of the document, before all codes. Notice that in the typing area, the cursor appears to be at the top of the document, on the *I* in *INTERNAL MEMO,* just as it was when you pressed Home Home, ↑. In the Reveal Codes area, the cursor is highlighting the code, which has now become the [Ext Large On:Courier-WP; 24pt] code. This means that the cursor is truly at the top of the document. (Note that your text style (Courier-WP) and size (24pt) might vary, depending on the type of printer you are using.)

5. Press **Alt+F3** to return to the typing area.

EDITING CODES IN REVEAL CODES

The main reason for using Reveal Codes is to remove an enhancement by deleting its code. You can also delete codes in the typing area. By deleting codes in the Reveal Codes area, you reduce the margin for error because you can see exactly what you are doing.

DELETING CODES

Each code is treated like a single character. When the cursor is positioned on a code, the entire code is highlighted; you cannot move the cursor inside the brackets. To delete a code, highlight it with the cursor in the Reveal Codes area and press Del.

Codes for certain features are *paired*; the first code turns the feature on and the second one turns it off. For example, underlining is turned on with [Und On] and off with [Und Off]. To delete a paired code, delete only one code; its partner is deleted automatically.

Follow these steps at your computer:

1. Move under *b* in *banner year*, in the last paragraph on page 2.

2. Press **F11** (or **Alt+F3**) to display the Reveal Codes area.

3. Position the cursor on the [Bold On] code. The cursor expands when it highlights the code in the bottom part of the screen.

4. Press **Del** to delete the code the cursor is on. When you delete the [Bold On] code, the [Bold Off] code is also deleted; *banner year* is no longer bold.

5. Press **Alt+F3** to return to the typing area.

PRACTICE YOUR SKILLS

Using the preceding steps as a guide, remove the underline from the word *attached* (in the section titled *4. Quarterly Meeting*) by deleting the [Und Off] code. Then compare your screen to the one shown in Figure 4.2.

 ## ADDING CODES

You can add text as well as codes in the Reveal Codes area. Position the cursor where you want to add text and enhancements. Then simply type and format the text as usual; your formatting changes appear as codes.

Follow these steps at your computer:

1. Move to the bottom of the document, under *Regional Coordinator*.

2. If you are not already in the Reveal Codes area, press **Alt+F3**.

3. Press **F6** to turn bold on. Both the [Bold On] and [Bold Off] codes appear in the Reveal Codes area. The cursor is on the [Bold Off] code.

Figure 4.2   **The Reveal Codes area after completing Practice Your Skills**

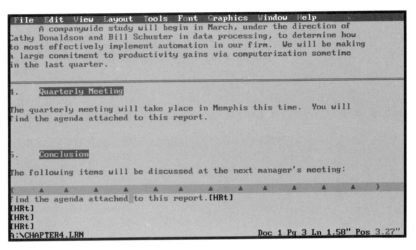

4. Type **Macco Plastics Inc**. The text is inserted between the [Bold On] and [Bold Off] codes.

5. Press **F6** to turn bold off. Notice that the cursor has moved beyond the [Bold Off] code. You could also have pressed → to move past the code.

6. Press **Alt+F3** to return to the typing area.

SEARCHING FOR CODES

Because the Reveal Codes area is so dense, you may find it difficult to get around. To find codes more easily, you can use WordPerfect's Search feature (F2 or Edit, Search), which you learned about in Chapter 2.

Follow these steps at your computer:

1. Move to the top of the document by pressing **Home, Home, Home,** ↑.

2. Press **F2** to open the Search dialog box.

3. To search for the Italic On code, press **F5** to open the Search Codes list box. The Search Codes list box contains a list of all the codes used in WordPerfect.

4. Type **ital** (the first four letters of *italic*). Notice that the list has scrolled to find a code that matches the text you have typed; *Italc Off* is highlighted.

5. Press ↓ once to highlight *Italc On* in the list. Then compare your screen to Figure 4.3.

Figure 4.3   **Finding a specific code in the Search Codes list box**

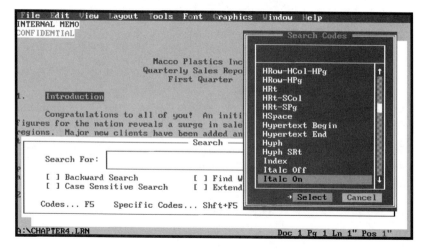

6. Press **Enter** to accept the selection and close the Search Codes list box. Notice that the [Italc On] code is now entered as the search string in the Search dialog box.

7. Begin the search (press **F2**), and examine the screen. The Search feature has found italic text, the phrase *all of you*.

8. Turn on Reveal Codes (press **Alt+F3**) to verify that the italic text has been found (see Figure 4.4). Just as in any search, the cursor is positioned directly to the right of text that matches the search string; in this case, to the right of the [Italc On] code.

9. Highlight [Italc On] and press **Del**, or just press **Backspace**, to delete the code.

Figure 4.4   **Italic text found using the Search feature**

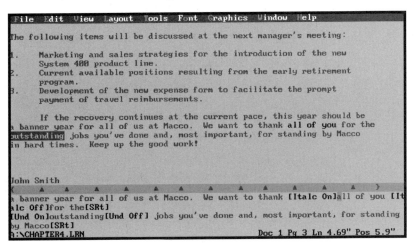

10. Turn off Reveal Codes (press **Alt+F3**).

DELETING CODES IN THE TYPING AREA

Although you can edit codes in the typing area, this technique can be tricky, because you must guess where the code is. Codes that indent, tab, and turn underlining on and off can be detected because the screen gives away their location. For example, if the *first* line of a paragraph is indented, there is probably a tab preceding it.

Some codes are tougher to edit. For example, the codes for a hanging indent are not paired; they consist of a [Lft Indent] code and a [Back Tab], or margin-release, code, followed by a [Lft Tab] code. To delete the hanging indent from the typing area, you must delete both codes. If you do not delete both codes, the text does not return to normal. That's why it is easier to delete codes in the Reveal Codes area.

Note: WordPerfect enables you to delete certain codes without displaying the Reveal Codes area. For example, you can press the Tab key to move text to the next tab stop, and then press Backspace to delete the tab (and, of course, its code). However, codes such as those for making text bold or underlining text cannot be deleted from the typing area. Such codes must be deleted in the Reveal Codes area. In any case, a good rule of thumb to follow is to delete only the most obvious codes from the typing area. This will prevent you from accidentally deleting the wrong code.

In the Reveal Codes area, Backspace deletes codes to the *left* of the cursor; Del deletes codes *at* the cursor.

Follow these steps at your computer:

1. Move the cursor to the beginning of the line that contains the word *outstanding*, in the paragraph under *5. Conclusion*. (Press **Ctrl+→** until the cursor is positioned under the *o* in *outstanding*.)

2. Press **Backspace**. Notice that the underlining (shown by text that is highlighted or in a different color) has not been removed. Instead, the space between *the* and *outstanding* has been deleted; because the Reveal Codes area was not displayed, the program, in effect, skipped over the [Und On] code. WordPerfect employs this tactic as a safeguard to help you avoid deleting a code unwittingly.

3. Press the **Spacebar** to reinsert the space you deleted in step 2.

4. Display the Reveal Codes area (press **Alt+F3** or **F11**).

5. Place the cursor on the [Und On] code to highlight it, and press **Del**. The [Und On] and [Und Off] codes have been deleted; *outstanding* is no longer underlined.

6. Press **F10** (or choose **File, Save As**).

7. Type **mychap4.lrn** to save the file with a new name.

8. Press **Enter** to save the file as MYCHAP4.LRN.

9. Turn off Reveal Codes.

Remember: Despite the program's safeguards, and because it is difficult to figure out where codes are in the typing area, try to use the Reveal Codes area to delete them.

PRINTING WITH DRAFT QUALITY

If you have a printer available, you may wish to see a *hard copy* (printout) of your document at this point. To print your document:

- Press Shift+F7 or choose File, Print.

- Press Enter.

By default, the program automatically prints the full document. To print a specific page or range of pages, choose 2. Page under Print, in the Print dialog box.

Follow these steps at your computer:

1. Press **Shift+F7** to display the Print dialog box.

2. Choose **Text Quality** (press **T**) to change the quality of the printed text. The Text Quality pop-up list is displayed (see Figure 4.5). The default setting is High.

Figure 4.5   **Text Quality pop-up list**

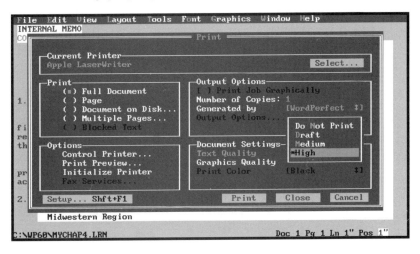

3. Choose **Draft** (press **D**) to print in draft quality. Notice that, under Print, 1. Full Document is currently selected.

4. Choose **Print** (press **Enter** or **F7**) to begin printing. Compare your printout to Figure 4.6.

5. Press **F7**.

6. At the prompt, type **N** or press **Enter**. The document has already been saved; you don't have to save it again.

7. At the

       `Exit WordPerfect?`

Figure 4.6   **The completed document MYCHAP4.LRN**

INTERNAL MEMO
CONFIDENTIAL   April 2, 1993
                                                     ROUGH DRAFT

                        Macco Plastics Inc.
                        Quarterly Sales Report
                        First Quarter

1.   Introduction

      Congratulations to all of you! An initial review of the sales
figures for the nation reveals a surge in sales in all of Macco's
sales regions. Major new clients have been added and many new
products are on the way.

      As we expected when we entered the field, computer related
products, such as keyboard housings and protective carrying cases, are
accounting for a major portion of this upswing.

2.   Regional Updates

      Midwestern Region

      After several years of falling sales due to the slump in the
auto industry, Blair Williams and his folks have something to
celebrate. The recent boom in auto manufacturing has led to
renewed demand for Macco products in Detroit.

      Northeastern Region

      John Martinson and his group are doing a great job in
Nashua. They have secured major contracts for a wide
range of new and existing products. Much of this
business is coming from Computer Equipment Corporation
(CEC), a major client of Macco's.

      Southern Region

      Mark Daley and his group have done a fine job of maintaining
relations with XYZ's Product Development Division in London.
They have been working closely with XYZ product people to
develop new products to be used in XYZ's existing line.

3.   Computer Study

      A companywide study will begin in March, under the direction
of Cathy Donaldson and Bill Schuster in data processing, to
determine how to most effectively implement automation in our firm.
We will be making a large commitment to productivity gains via
computerization sometime in the last quarter.

Figure 4.6   **The completed document MYCHAP4.LRN (Continued)**

4.   <u>Quarterly Meeting</u>

The quarterly meeting will take place in Memphis this time. You will find the agenda attached to this report.

5.   <u>Conclusion</u>

The following items will be discussed at the next manager's meeting:

1.   Marketing and sales strategies for the introduction of the new System 400 product line.
2.   Current available positions resulting from the early retirement program.
3.   Development of the new expense form to facilitate the prompt payment of travel reimbursements.

     If the recovery continues at the current pace, this year should be a banner year for all of us at Macco. We want to thank all of you for the outstanding jobs you've done and, most important, for standing by Macco in hard times. Keep up the good work!

John Smith
Regional Coordinator
Macco Plastics Inc.

prompt, type **N** or press **Enter** to remain in WordPerfect but clear the typing area (and memory). Because *No* is the default choice, pressing Enter has the same effect as pressing **N**.

Looking at your printed document (or Figure 4.6), notice the bold and underlined text, and the large font used at the top of the document.

A helpful hint: When you are printing final documents, use high-quality print by pressing 4 High in the Text Quality pop-up list. When you are printing drafts, choose 2 Draft for draft quality, which decreases the time the document takes to print.

PRACTICE YOUR SKILLS

In this chapter, you have learned skills for using the Reveal Codes area to delete codes. The following activity gives you the chance to practice what you've learned in the last few chapters. The document you will be editing contains several misplaced codes for you to find and delete (Figure 4.7).

1. Clear the typing area (Chapter 1). Retrieve the file PRAC-TICE.CH4 (Chapter 2).

2. Move your cursor to the first superscripted number in the document, using Figure 4.7 as a guide.

3. Turn on Reveal Codes, find the erroneous code, and delete it.

4. Move to the second error. Find the offending code and delete it.

5. Continue until you have corrected all ten errors.

6. Save the file as CORRECT.CH4.

7. Print the document (Chapter 1), and compare your printout to Figure 4.8.

If you have finished the above activity and would like to try another one that requires similar skills but provides a bit less guidance, try the following activity. Edit the document PRACCHAL.CH4, removing 20 erroneous codes from the typing area. Figure 4.9 shows what the document looks like with the misplaced codes. This exercise does not include any superscripted numbers to help you find the misplaced codes.

1. Clear the typing area (Chapter 1). Retrieve the file PRAC-CHAL.CH4 (Chapter 2).

Figure 4.7 **PRACTICE.CH4 with misplaced codes**

```
                        Macco Plastics Inc.
                       Quarterly Sales Report
                           First Quarter

     Congra   [1]tulations to all of  you!   An initial review of the
              sales figures   for  the  nation  reveals a surge in
              sales in  all  of  **Macco's sales re**[2]gions. Major new
              clients have been  added  and many   new products are
              on the way.

         As we  expected when we  entered the  field,  computer  related
     products, such   as  keyboard  housings   and  protective   carrying
     cases, are accounting for a major portion  of this upswing.

     Midwestern Re[3]gion

     After several years of falling sales due to the slump in the
     auto industry, Blair Williams  and his  folks have something
     to celebrate.  The recent boom in auto manufacturing has led
     to renewed demand for Macco products in Detroit.

     Northeastern Region

     John Martinson and his group are  doing a  great job in
     Nashua.  They have secured major con   [4]tracts   for  a
                                            wide  range  of
                                            new         and
                                            e x i s t i n g
                                            products.  Much
                                            o f   t h i s
                                            business     is
                                            coming    from
                                            C o m p u t e r
                                            Equipment
                                            Corporation
                                            (CEC),  a major
                                            client       of
                                            Macco's.

     Southern Region

     Mark Daley and his group have done a fine  job of  maintaining
     relations with  XYZ's Product  Development Division in London.
              [5]They  **have  been worki**[6]ng closely with XYZ product people
              to  develop  new  products  to be  used in XYZ's existing
              line.

         A companywide study will begin in March, under the direction
     of  Cathy  Donaldson  and  Bill  Schuster  in data processing, to
     determine how to most  effectively  implement  automation  in our
     firm.  We will be making a large commitment to productivity gains
     via computerization sometime in the last quarter.

         If  the  recovery  continues  at the current pace, this  year
```

Figure 4.7   **PRACTICE.CH4 with misplaced codes (Continued)**

```
should be a banne[7]r  year for all of us at Macco.  We want to thank
all of  you  for   the   outstanding jobs   you've  done  and, most
important, for standing   by Macco in hard times.  Keep up the good
work!


[8]John Smith
  Reg  [9]ional Coordinator
  Macco[10] Plastics, Inc.
```

2. Look carefully at Figure 4.9 to determine where the erroneous codes are. (Mark or number them in your book, if you wish.)

3. Move your cursor to the first item to correct. Place your cursor directly to the right or left of where you believe the code is.

4. Delete the incorrect code. Check the screen to be sure that you are deleting codes and not the text.

5. Replace any text deleted by mistake.

6. Continue until you have deleted all 20 errors.

7. Save the file as CORRCHAL.CH4 (Chapter 1).

8. Print the document (Chapter 1), and compare your printout to Figure 4.8.

Figure 4.8   **Corrected PRACTICE.CH4**

```
                         Macco Plastics Inc.
                        Quarterly Sales Report
                           First Quarter

        Congratulations to  all of  you!   An initial  review of the
    sales figures for the nation reveals a surge  in sales  in all of
    Macco's sales  regions.   Major new  clients have  been added and
    many new products are on the way.

        As we expected when we entered  the field,  computer related
    products,  such as  keyboard housings  and  protective carrying
    cases, are accounting for a major portion of this upswing.

    Midwestern Region

    After several years of falling sales due to the slump in the
    auto industry,  Blair Williams  and his folks have something
    to celebrate.  The recent boom in auto manufacturing has led
    to renewed demand for Macco products in Detroit.

    Northeastern Region

    John Martinson  and his  group are doing a great job in
    Nashua.  They have secured major  contracts for  a wide
    range of  new  and  existing  products.   Much of this
    business is coming from  Computer Equipment Corporation
    (CEC), a major client of Macco's.

    Southern Region

    Mark Daley and his group have done a fine job of maintaining
    relations with XYZ's Product Development Division in London.
    They have  been  working  closely with XYZ product people to
    develop new products to be used  in XYZ's existing line.

        A companywide study will begin in March, under the direction
    of Cathy Donaldson  and  Bill  Schuster  in  data  processing, to
    determine how  to  most  effectively implement automation in our
    firm.  We will be making a large commitment to productivity gains
    via computerization sometime in the last quarter.

        If  the  recovery  continues  at the current pace, this year
    should be a banner year for all of us at Macco.  We want to thank
    all  of  you  for  the  outstanding  jobs you've  done and, most
    important, for standing by Macco in hard times.  Keep up the good
    work!


    John Smith
    Regional Coordinator
    Macco Plastics, Inc.
```

Figure 4.9   **More misplaced codes (PRACCHAL.CH4)**

```
                        Macco Plastics Inc.
                                    Quarterly Sales Report
                        First Quarter

     Congratulations to  all of  you!   An initial  review of the
sales figures for the nation reveals a  surge in sales in  all of
                                        Macco's    sales  regions.
                                        Major   new  clients have
                                        been  added and many  new
                                        products  are on the way.

     As we  expected when  we entered the field, computer related
products,  such as  keyboard  housings and  protective carrying
cases, are accounting for a major portion of this upswing.

                        Midwestern Region

     After several
years of  falling sales  due to  the slump  in the auto industry,
Blair Williams and his  folks have  something to  celebrate.   The
recent boom  in auto  manufacturing has led to renewed demand for
Macco products in Detroit.

     Nor   theastern                                     Region

     John Martinson and his group are  doing a  great job in
Nashua.    They have  secured major contracts for a wide
range of  new and  existing  products.    Much  of this
business is coming from  Computer Equipment Corporation
(CEC), a major client of Macco's.

                                        Southern Region

Mark Daley and his group have done a fine job of maintaining
relations with XYZ's Product Development Division in London.
          They have been working  closely with XYZ product
people to develop new products  to be used in XYZ's existing
line.

               A companywide study will begin in March,
          under  the  direction  of Cathy Donaldson and
          Bill  Schuster   in   data   processing,   to
          determine how  to most effectively implement
          automation in our firm.  We will be  making a
          large  commitment  to productivity  gains via
          computerization sometime in the last quarter.

     If  the  recovery  continues  at the current pace, this year
should be a banner year for all of us at Macco.  We want to thank
all of  you  for the  outstanding jobs you've  done and, most
important, for standing by        Macco in hard times.   Keep up
the good work!
```

Figure 4.9   **More misplaced codes (PRACCHAL.CH4) (Continued)**

```
John Smith
Regiona   l Coordinator
                                    Macco Plastics, Inc.
```

CHAPTER SUMMARY

In this chapter, you learned to interpret the Reveal Codes area and to move your cursor within it. You also learned how to edit codes in both the Reveal Codes area and the typing area.

Here's a quick technique reference for Chapter 4:

Feature or Action	How to Do It
Reveal Codes (On/Off)	**Alt+F3** or choose **View, Reveal Codes**
Very top of document	**Home, Home, Home, ↑**
Very bottom of document	**Home, Home, Home, ↓**
Print draft quality	**Shift+F7, Text Quality, 2 Draft, Enter**
Print full document	**Shift+F7, 1. Full Document, Enter**

In the next chapter, you'll be learning some valuable techniques for formatting, copying, and moving blocks of text.

If you need to break off here, please exit from WordPerfect. If you want to proceed directly to the next chapter, please do so now.

CHAPTER 5:
BLOCK, MOVE, AND
SWITCH

Opening a
Document with File
Open

Defining and
Working with
Blocks

Switching between
Two Documents

As you write and edit, you can usually clarify your ideas by moving words around. Sometimes, moving just one word will do the trick. Sometimes, you have to move a phrase, sentence, paragraph, or even several pages to communicate as clearly as possible. When you have polished your ideas, you may want to make them stand out—to enhance them by applying bold, underline, uppercase, different letter sizes, or a combination of effects.

In this chapter, you will learn about WordPerfect's Block feature, which simplifies the process of editing and enhancing text. This feature allows you to define a block—any character or consecutive characters—and to edit, enhance, copy, and move a block as your work requires. You will also learn about the Switch feature, which allows you to toggle (switch back and forth) between two open documents.

This chapter shows you how to:

- Retrieve a file by keystroke

- Define a block

- Edit and enhance blocked text

- Move and copy blocked text within a document

- Edit two documents at once

- Move and copy blocked text between documents

OPENING A DOCUMENT WITH FILE OPEN

Let's start by opening a document. In Chapter 2, you learned how to do this using the File Manager (F5); you can also use the File Open keys, Shift+F10, or File, Open. To open a file, you have to know the name of the document you wish to work with and type it correctly.

To use File Open:

- Press Shift+F10 or choose File, Open.

- Type the name of the file you wish to open (include the path if the file is not in the current drive and/or directory).

- Press Enter.

This method is helpful in that it, in effect, bypasses the File Manager. Remember, you can use File, Open whenever you know the location and name of the file you wish to open. However, if you display the Open Document dialog box but can't remember the name of the file you want to open, you can still open the File Manager by pressing F5.

If you are not currently running WordPerfect, please start the program now.

Let's use the File Open technique to open a document:

1. With the typing area cleared, press **Shift+F10** or choose **File, Open**. The Open Document dialog box is displayed (see Figure 5.1). Notice that the cursor is in the Filename box. In the Method portion of the dialog box, the Open into New Document option is currently selected. (We'll discuss the Retrieve into Current Document option in Chapter 7.) This command has the same function it has in the File Manager.

Figure 5.1   **Open Document dialog box**

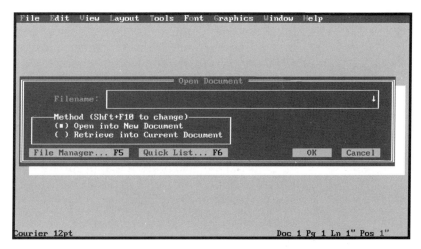

2. Insert your Data Disk in drive A. Then type **a:\chapter5.lrn** and press **Enter**. The document is now displayed in the typing area.

DEFINING AND WORKING WITH BLOCKS

A *block* is made up of any number of consecutive characters; you determine where the block starts and where it stops. A block can be as small as a character or as long as a document. Once you *define* a block, you can:

- Enhance it (for example, by underlining it or changing it to uppercase)

- Delete it

- Save it as a separate file

- Append it to the end of another file

- Move or copy it to another place in the same document

- Move or copy it to another place in a different document

DEFINING AND ENHANCING A BLOCK

To define a block, press the Block keys, Alt+F4, or choose Edit, Block, and highlight, or *select,* the desired text by using the arrow or cursor-movement keys. You can also take advantage of *speed highlighting:* When you type any character (letter, number, or symbol), WordPerfect highlights to the first occurrence of that character. To highlight to the end of a sentence, for example, press . (a period). If you highlight too much, use the arrow keys to remove the highlighting. To cancel the Block feature, press Alt+F4 again or press Esc.

To enhance a block, press the appropriate function key: for example, F6 to apply bold, or F8 to underline. You can also use the menu system to enhance a block.

Follow these steps at your computer:

1. Move the cursor under the *M* in *Midwestern,* under the heading *2. Regional Updates.*

2. Press **Alt+F4** to turn on the Block feature. The prompt

   ```
   Block on
   ```

   remains active on the status line until you either cancel the block (Alt+F4 or Esc) or enhance it in some way. Notice, also, that the Pos measurement is highlighted (or colored).

3. Press → several times to highlight *Midwestern Region.* As you press the arrow key, each character is highlighted, in the same way that the Pos measurement is highlighted (see Figure 5.2).

4. Press **F6** to apply bold to the highlighted text. *Midwestern Region* is now bold. The highlight defining the block disappears, as does the prompt.

PRACTICE YOUR SKILLS

1. Repeat the preceding steps to define a block, applying bold to the following region headings:

   ```
   Northeastern Region
   Southern Region
   ```

Figure 5.2   **The defined block**

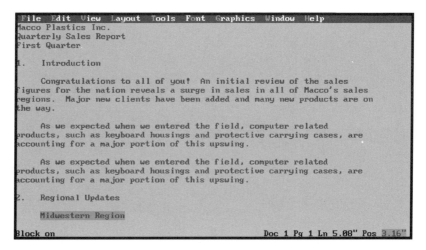

2. Block and then underline the following text in the numbered section headings:

```
Introduction
Regional Updates
Computer Study
Quarterly Meeting
Conclusion
```

CENTERING A BLOCK

To center a block of text, define it, and then press the Center keys, Shift+F6.

Let's center a block of text:

1. Move the cursor to the top of the document, before any codes, by pressing **Home, Home, Home,** ↑.

2. Press **Alt+F4** to turn on the Block feature.

3. Press ↓ three times to highlight the three-line heading.

4. Press **Shift+F6** to center the block. Notice that the heading is now centered (see Figure 5.3). The highlighting disappears, as does the prompt.

Figure 5.3　　　**The centered heading**

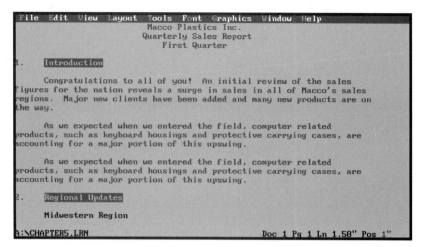

 CHANGING THE TYPE SIZE OF A BLOCK

To change the type size of a block of text, define the block, press the Font keys, Ctrl+F8, and select 4. Relative Size. Finally, select a size.

Let's change the size of a block of text:

1. In the heading on the top of page 1, move the cursor under the *M* in *Macco*.

2. Press **Alt+F4** to turn on the Block feature, and press ↓ three times to highlight the entire heading.

3. Press **Ctrl+F8** to open the Font dialog box.

4. Choose **4. Relative Size**, choose **6 Extra Large**, and press **Enter**. (If your printer does not support this particular size, select another size that is supported by your printer.) The heading now appears highlighted (or in a different color) to indicate the change in text size. In any case, the program has inserted the codes necessary to make your text print extra large, though there may be no apparent change on your screen. (Changes in the type size are visible in Graphics mode.)

5. Press **Shift+F7** to bring up the Print dialog box, and choose **7. Print Preview** to see how your document will look when printed.

6. Press **F7** to return to the typing area.

CONVERTING A BLOCK TO UPPERCASE CHARACTERS

To change text to uppercase, highlight it, open the Convert Case dialog box by pressing Shift+F3, and choose 1. Uppercase. To change a block to all lowercase, follow the same steps but choose 2. Lowercase. To capitalize the first letter of each selected word, choose 3. Initial Caps.

Let's convert our heading to all uppercase characters:

1. Move the cursor under the *M* in *Macco* in the heading on page 1.

2. Turn on the Block feature (press **Alt+F4**).

3. Press ↓ three times to select the three-line heading.

4. Press **Shift+F3** to open the Convert Case dialog box shown in Figure 5.4.

5. Choose **1. Uppercase**. The heading changes to all uppercase.

Figure 5.4   **Convert Case dialog box**

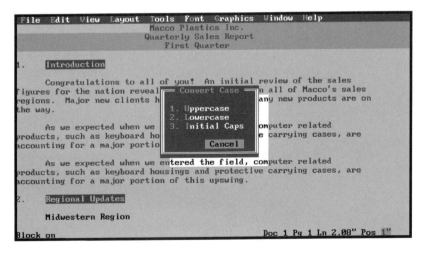

DELETING A BLOCK

To delete a block, highlight the text with the Block keys, and press Del or Backspace.

Note: If you accidentally delete something, use the Esc (Undelete) key to restore it, as you learned in Chapter 2.

Follow these steps at your computer:

1. Move to the *left margin* of the line beginning *As we...* in the second paragraph on page 1 (Pos 1"). (You'll notice that the second and third paragraphs are identical.)

2. Press **Alt+F4** to start a block.

3. Press ↓ four times to highlight the three-line paragraph *and* its trailing blank line.

4. Press **Del**. The paragraph has been deleted. If necessary, press **Del** to delete any extra blank lines *before* the block.

MOVING AND COPYING BLOCKS OF TEXT

WordPerfect provides you with two methods for moving and copying blocks of text: The first involves the Cut, Copy, and Paste commands; the second involves the Move Block and Copy Block commands. If you are a mouse user, or if you are a keyboard user who prefers working through the menu bar, we recommend using Cut, Copy, and Paste. If you are a keyboard user who prefers shortcut keys, and especially if you are familiar with an earlier version of WordPerfect, we recommend using Move Block and Copy Block.

Cut, Copy, and Paste

Three of the most useful commands available in the Edit menu are Cut, Copy, and Paste. Edit, Cut removes the selected text from the document you are working in and places it in computer memory. Edit, Copy *copies* the selected text into memory, leaving the original intact. Edit, Paste places a copy of the text stored in memory at the position of the cursor.

Note: Computer memory serves as a *temporary* storage area for the information you are copying or moving. Text placed in memory will remain there only until the next time you use Edit, Cut or Edit, Copy—or until you exit WordPerfect.

To cut or copy text to computer memory:

- Select the text that you wish to move or duplicate.

- Choose Edit, Cut to move the selection or Edit, Copy to duplicate it.

Once you have moved or copied text to computer memory, you can paste it to the desired destination. To do so,

- First, display the desired destination. If the desired destination is another WordPerfect document, you will need to open its file.

- Place the cursor where you want to place (paste) the text that has been stored in memory.

- Choose Edit, Paste.

When you paste the text that you've previously saved in memory, it is *not* removed from memory. Actually, only a copy of the cut or copied text is pasted to the destination. This means that you can continue pasting copies of these same contents to as many different locations as you desire. However, remember that the contents of memory are lost the next time you choose Edit, Cut or Edit, Copy, or when you exit WordPerfect.

The Cut and Paste and Copy and Paste options are simply menu versions of Move Block and Copy Block, which are covered in the next two sections.

Using Move Block

The Block and Move features (Alt+F4 and Ctrl+F4) make a powerful combination. To move a block of text using this combination, follow these steps:

- Use the Block keys, Alt+F4, to select the text you want to move.

- Press the Move Block keys, Ctrl+F4. This displays the Move Block dialog box.

- Choose 1. Cut and Paste.

- Position the cursor where you wish to move text, and press Enter.

Moving text removes it from the screen and stores it in memory; it can be recalled from memory and inserted anywhere in your document—or in several places or different documents. Even after you recall the block by pressing Enter, a copy of the block remains in memory. You can retrieve it by pressing Ctrl+V or by choosing Edit, Paste. It stays there until you move another block or until you exit WordPerfect; moving (or copying) another block deletes the first moved block.

Some helpful hints:

- Sometimes, you may wish to save a block of text in a separate file. To do this, highlight the text, press F10 to save, and then name the block when prompted. (The name you give the block will become its file name.)

- To copy a block of text to the end of another file, highlight the text with the Block keys and press the Move Block keys, Ctrl+F4. Then choose 4. Append, type the name of the file to which you want to append the text, and press Enter.

A keyboard shortcut: When you wish to move a selected block of text, you can bypass the Move Block dialog box by pressing Ctrl+Del (instead of Ctrl+F4), or by choosing Edit, Cut and Paste.

Let's select and move a block of text:

1. Move to the left margin (Position 1"), at the left of the heading *Midwestern Region* in the middle of page 1.

2. Turn on Block (press **Alt+F4**).

3. Press ↓ *seven* times to block the title, the blank line, the following paragraph, and the blank line below it (see Figure 5.5).

4. Press **Ctrl+F4** to move the block. The Move Block dialog box is displayed (see Figure 5.6).

5. Choose **1. Cut and Paste**. The block is removed from the screen and stored in memory. You are prompted (on the status line) to move the cursor to the place to which you want to move the text:

   ```
   Move cursor; press Enter to retrieve.
   ```

6. Move to Position 1" of the line reading *Southern Region* and press **Enter**. The block is inserted in the new location. If necessary, scroll to view the moved block of text.

Figure 5.5   **Selected block to be moved**

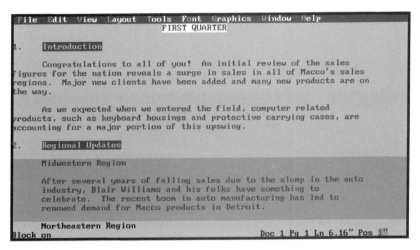

Figure 5.6   **Move Block dialog box**

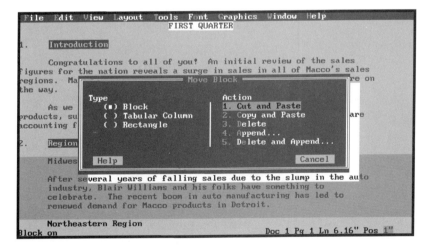

Copying a Block

Copying a block of text works much the same as moving it. The
Copy and Paste option in the Move Block dialog box places a copy
of the block in memory (like Move), while the original block remains
on the screen (unlike Move). Figure 5.7 shows the differences between moving and copying text. You can retrieve the copy from
memory anywhere in the document or in several places, including

different documents. The copy of the block remains in memory until you move or copy a different block, or until you exit WordPerfect. You can retrieve it by pressing Ctrl+V or by choosing Edit, Paste.

Figure 5.7　　　**Moving versus copying text**

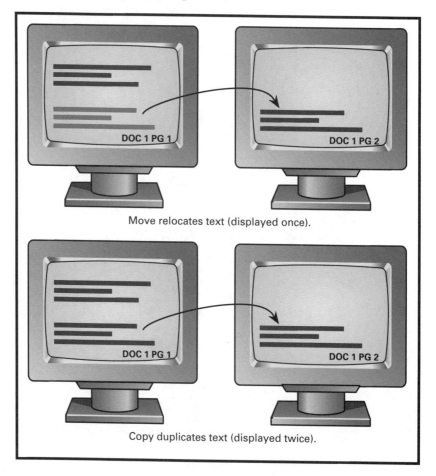

Move relocates text (displayed once).

Copy duplicates text (displayed twice).

To copy a block:

- Use the Block keys, Alt+F4, to select the text you want to copy.

- Press the Move keys, Ctrl+F4.

SWITCHING BETWEEN TWO DOCUMENTS • 109

- Choose 2. Copy and Paste from the Move Block dialog box.

- Position the cursor where you wish the copy to be inserted and press Enter.

Let's select and copy a block of text:

1. Move to the very top of the document by pressing **Home, Home, Home,** ↑. Using Home, Home, Home, ↑ positions the cursor before the Center Justification and other codes; selecting the heading to be copied selects these codes as well. You will copy the heading at the top of page 1 to the top of page 2.

2. Turn on Block (press **Alt+F4**).

3. Press ↓ three times, and then press → once to block the three lines of the title *and* the trailing blank line.

4. Press **Ctrl+F4** to open the Move Block dialog box.

5. Choose **2 Copy and Paste**. The reverse video highlight disappears. Text remains on the screen and a copy is stored in memory. WordPerfect prompts you to specify where you want to move the block:

   ```
   Move cursor; press Enter to retrieve.
   ```

6. Move to the top of page 2 by pressing **PgDn**, or **Ctrl+Home** and **2** to go to page 2.

7. Press **Enter**. The copied heading now appears at the top of page 2. Add or delete blank lines, if necessary.

A keyboard shortcut: When you wish to copy a selected block of text, you can bypass the Move Block dialog box by pressing Ctrl+Ins (instead of Ctrl+F4), or by choosing Edit, Copy and Paste.

SWITCHING BETWEEN TWO DOCUMENTS

WordPerfect offers you a way to toggle between two documents. The Switch feature allows you to edit two documents in the same work session without repeatedly closing one document and retrieving the other.

Earlier you learned that when you define a block and press the Switch keys, Shift+F3, you can make the block either all uppercase or all lowercase. If you press the Switch keys with *no block defined*, the result is entirely different: You switch between *documents,* with the status line reading Doc 1 or Doc 2. This feature allows you to edit two documents at virtually the same time; it is especially handy if you want to move or copy text between documents. (See Figure 5.8.) The menu equivalent of pressing Shift+F3 is choosing Window, Switch.

Figure 5.8   **The Switch feature**

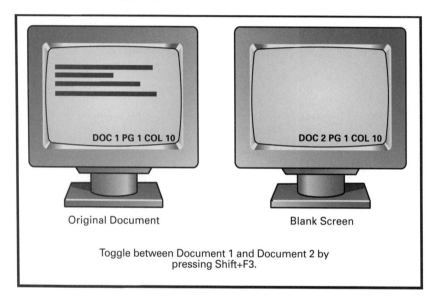

Original Document   Blank Screen

Toggle between Document 1 and Document 2 by
pressing Shift+F3.

Follow these steps at your computer:

1. Move the cursor to the top of the document by pressing **Home, Home,** ↑.

2. Press **Shift+F3** to switch documents. The status line reads:

   ```
   Doc 2 Pg 1 Ln 1" Pos 1"
   ```

   A second typing area is now available for your use. The Switch feature moves you between the two typing areas.

3. Insert the Data Disk in drive A (if necessary) and press **Shift+F10** to open a new document.

4. Type **a:\xletter.txt** and press **Enter**. The file comes up in the typing area of Document 2.

5. Press **Shift+F3** to switch documents. The status line informs you that you are in Doc 1, editing the file CHAPTER5.LRN.

6. Press **Shift+F3** to switch documents again. The status line informs you that you are now in Doc 2, editing the file XLETTER.TXT.

7. Press **F7** to exit. WordPerfect prompts

   ```
   Save A:\XLETTER.TXT?
   ```

8. Choose **No** to clear the typing area without saving. (Pressing any other key would save the document.) WordPerfect prompts again, because *two* files are active:

   ```
   Exit Document 2?
   ```

9. Choose **Yes** to exit document 2 and return to document 1. (Choosing No would clear the typing area and leave you in document 2.)

10. Press **F7** to exit. This time, you are prompted:

    ```
    Save A:\CHAPTER5.LRN?
    ```

11. Choose **Save As** (type **S**) to open the Save Document 1 dialog box. We'll save this document under a new name.

12. Type **mychap5.lrn** to save the document with a new name and press **Enter**. Finally, WordPerfect prompts

    ```
    Exit Document 1?
    ```

13. Choose **Yes** to remain in WordPerfect and clear the typing area.

Note: You've seen that WordPerfect automatically provides two typing areas—one for Doc 1 and the other for Doc 2. Actually, the program allows you to have up to nine documents open at a time. To open a new document (Doc 3), choose File, New from the menu. Each time you do so, another clear typing area will be created, up to Doc 9.

Unfortunately, once you have three or more documents opened, switching among them becomes a bit trickier. For example, suppose that, while you were in Doc 2, you chose File, New to open a new document, Doc 3. Now, let's say you wish to return to Doc 1. In this case, pressing Shift+F3 would only serve as a switch to toggle you between Doc 2 and Doc 3, because you were in Doc 2 when you created Doc 3. Instead, we recommend that, in such cases, you press Home, 0 (zero) or choose Window, Switch To to open the Switch To Document dialog box. This dialog box contains a list of all the open documents, along with their file names (if any). To choose the document you wish to go to, simply press its corresponding number, which is the same as its "Doc" number.

PRACTICE YOUR SKILLS

This section gives you the opportunity to practice the skills you just learned. You will edit a document on your Data Disk, shown in Figure 5.9, to produce the final document in Figure 5.10.

Follow these steps at your computer:

1. If necessary, clear the typing area (Chapter 1). Open the file PRACTICE.CH5.

2. Block the heading and switch to uppercase.

3. Block the heading and make it bold.

4. Block and delete the duplicate first paragraph.

5. Block the following headings and make them bold:

   ```
   Northeastern Region
   Southern Region
   Midwestern Region
   ```

6. Block the paragraph title *Midwestern Region*, the blank line beneath the title, and the paragraph following the blank line. Move the block *above* the paragraph titled *Northeastern Region*.

7. Block the paragraph beginning *Congratulations,* and then make it the first paragraph in the document.

8. Block and delete the duplicate paragraph beginning *If the recovery....*

9. Block and underline *banner* in the paragraph beginning with *If the recovery....*

10. Save the file as CORRECT.CH5 (Chapter 1).

11. Print the document (Chapter 1), and compare your printed version to the one shown in Figure 5.10.

Figure 5.9   **The incorrect document PRACTICE.CH5**

```
                    Macco Plastics Inc.
                   Quarterly Sales Report
                       First Quarter

      As we  expected when  we entered the field, computer related
products,   such  as  keyboard  housings  and  protective carrying
cases, are accounting for a major portion of this upswing.

      As we  expected when  we entered the field, computer related
products,   such  as  keyboard  housings  and  protective carrying
cases, are accounting for a major portion of this upswing.

   Northeastern Region

   John Martinson  and his  group are doing a great job in
   Nashua.  They have secured major  contracts for  a wide
   range  of  new  and  existing  products.   Much of this
   business is  coming from Computer Equipment Corporation
   (CEC), a major client of Macco's.

   Southern Region

   Mark Daley and his group have done a fine job of maintaining
   relations with XYZ's Product Development Division in London.
   They  have been working closely  with XYZ product  people to
   develop new products to be used in XYZ's existing line.

   Midwestern Region

   After several years of falling sales due to the slump in the
   auto industry, Blair Williams  and his  folks have something
   to celebrate.  The recent boom in auto manufacturing has led
   to renewed demand for Macco products in Detroit.

      Congratulations  to all of you!  An initial  review of the
sales figures  for the nation reveals a surge in sales  in all of
Macco's sales  regions.   Major new  clients have  been added and
many new products are on the way.

      A companywide study will begin in March, under the direction
of Cathy Donaldson  and  Bill  Schuster  in  data  processing, to
determine  how  to  most  effectively implement automation in our
firm.  We will be making a large commitment to productivity gains
via computerization sometime in the last quarter.

      If  the  recovery  continues  at the current pace, this year
should be a banner year for all of us at Macco.  We want to thank
all  of  you  for  the  outstanding  jobs  you've  done and, most
important, for standing by Macco in hard times.  Keep up the good
work!

      If  the  recovery  continues  at the current pace, this year
should be a banner year for all of us at Macco.  We want to thank
all  of  you  for  the  outstanding  jobs  you've  done and, most
```

Figure 5.9   **The incorrect document PRACTICE.CH5 (Continued)**

```
important, for standing by Macco in hard times. Keep up the good
work!


John Smith
Regional Coordinator
Macco Plastics, Inc.
```

If you have finished the activity, you might like to try a more challenging one requiring similar skills. Edit the document on the Data Disk, as shown in Figure 5.11, to again produce the document you just worked on, shown in Figure 5.10.

Follow these steps at your computer:

1. Clear the typing area (Chapter 1). Retrieve the file PRAC-OPT1.CH5 (Chapter 2).

2. Make the last sentence of the first paragraph the first sentence of the same paragraph.

3. Move your cursor to the left margin (Pos 1") of the paragraph beginning *A companywide....*

4. Switch to the second document's typing area.

5. Retrieve the file PRACCH5.BAK *into* the second document's typing area (Chapter 2).

6. Block all three sections about regions, along with their descriptive paragraphs, and prepare to copy them into document 1.

7. Switch to document 1.

8. Retrieve the sections about regions into the document, *above* the paragraph beginning *A companywide....*

9. Block and delete the duplicate paragraph beginning *The quarterly....*

10. Move your cursor to the top of the document.

Figure 5.10   **The corrected document**

MACCO PLASTICS INC.
QUARTERLY SALES REPORT
FIRST QUARTER

Congratulations to all of you! An initial review of the sales figures for the nation reveals a surge in sales in all of Macco's sales regions. Major new clients have been added and many new products are on the way.

As we expected when we entered the field, computer related products, such as keyboard housings and protective carrying cases, are accounting for a major portion of this upswing.

Midwestern Region

After several years of falling sales due to the slump in the auto industry, Blair Williams and his folks have something to celebrate. The recent boom in auto manufacturing has led to renewed demand for Macco products in Detroit.

Northeastern Region

John Martinson and his group are doing a great job in Nashua. They have secured major contracts for a wide range of new and existing products. Much of this business is coming from Computer Equipment Corporation (CEC), a major client of Macco's.

Southern Region

Mark Daley and his group have done a fine job of maintaining relations with XYZ's Product Development Division in London. They have been working closely with XYZ product people to develop new products to be used in XYZ's existing line.

A companywide study will begin in March, under the direction of Cathy Donaldson and Bill Schuster in data processing, to determine how to most effectively implement automation in our firm. We will be making a large commitment to productivity gains via computerization sometime in the last quarter.

If the recovery continues at the current pace, this year should be a _banner_ year for all of us at Macco. We want to thank all of you for the outstanding jobs you've done and, most important, for standing by Macco in hard times. Keep up the good work!

John Smith
Regional Coordinator
Macco Plastics, Inc.

Figure 5.11   **The incorrect document PRACOPT.CH5**

> An initial review of the sales figures for the nation reveals a surge in sales in all of Macco's sales regions. Major new clients have been added and many new products are on the way. Congratulations to all of you!
>
> As we expected when we entered the field, computer related products, such as keyboard housings and protective carrying cases, are accounting for a major portion of this upswing.
>
> A companywide study will begin in March, under the direction of Cathy Donaldson and Bill Schuster in data processing, to determine how to most effectively implement automation in our firm. We will be making a large commitment to productivity gains via computerization sometime in the last quarter.
>
> The quarterly meeting will take place in Memphis this time. You will find the agenda attached to this report.
>
> The quarterly meeting will take place in Memphis this time. You will find the agenda attached to this report.
>
> If the recovery continues at the current pace, this year should be a <u>banner</u> year for all of us at Macco. We want to thank all of you for the outstanding jobs you've done and, most important, for standing by Macco in hard times. Keep up the good work!
>
>
> John Smith
> Regional Coordinator
> Macco Plastics, Inc.

11. Switch to document 2.

12. Copy the heading. Make sure to use **Home, Home, Home,** ↑.

13. Switch to document 1.

14. Retrieve the heading from memory and place it at the top of the document.

15. Save the file as CORROPT1.CH5 (Chapter 1).

16. Print the document (Chapter 1), and compare it to the one shown in Figure 5.10.

17. Exit both documents.

CHAPTER SUMMARY

As you have seen, the ability to work with blocks of text can help you edit your documents quickly and efficiently. This chapter has only begun to touch on the many ways you can use this powerful feature in your own work. In this chapter you've learned how to create and enhance blocks, move and copy blocks, switch between two documents, and copy and move blocked text between documents.

The real mastery of WordPerfect comes with practice; the more you practice the skills you've learned in this and other chapters, the more they will become second nature. You might at this point want to review some of the topics presented before moving on.

Here's a quick technique reference for Chapter 5:

Feature or Action	How to Do It
Block text	Alt+F4
Delete blocked text	Del
Change the case of blocked text	Shift+F3
Save a text block as a file	F10, *block name*, Enter
Append a text block to a file	Ctrl+F4, 4. Append, *file name* to append to, Enter
Open a file	Shift+F10, *file name*, Enter
Switch between documents	Shift+F3

In the next two chapters you will learn about formatting lines and pages, respectively. Together with what you know already—how to edit and enhance text, get around in a document, work with codes, and use blocks—formatting skills will give you most of what you need to create your own documents.

If you need to break off here, please exit from WordPerfect. If you want to proceed directly to the next chapter, please do so now.

CHAPTER 6: LINE FORMATTING

Line Spacing

Relative Tabs

Left and Right Margins

Using the Menu System to Format Lines

When you finish typing and editing, it is helpful to ask yourself how you can make your document look so attractive and interesting that people will want to read it. You can enhance the appearance of your document in many ways. This chapter discusses enhancements known as *line formatting;* the next chapter looks at *page formatting*.

When done with this chapter, you will be able to:

- Adjust line spacing
- Work with various types of tabs
- Change margin settings
- Use the Layout menu to format lines

LINE SPACING

Line spacing defines the distance between lines. In WordPerfect, the default is single spacing: Every available line of the page contains text, unless a line is skipped. Text that is double-spaced wraps to every second line; triple-spaced text wraps to every third line. Naturally, the higher the line-spacing number, the fewer the lines of text on a page. For most purposes, single or double spacing suffices.

Before you adjust line spacing, position the cursor where you want the new line spacing to begin. In WordPerfect, a change in line spacing affects the document from the position of the cursor to the bottom of the document or until another line-spacing code is encountered. (You can view codes in the Reveal Codes area by pressing Alt+F3, which you learned about in Chapter 4.)

To set line spacing:

- Position the cursor at the point from which you want to set line spacing.
- Press the Format keys, Shift+F8.
- Choose 1. Line.
- Choose 3. Line Spacing.
- Type the line-spacing value (1 for single spacing, 2 for double spacing, and so on).
- Press Enter (or F7) three times to accept the change and return to the typing area.

You can also space in half-line increments (for example, 1.5). Because not all printers support all different line spacings, consult your printer manual before fine-tuning your spacing. To reset line spacing to single spacing (the default) after using the line-spacing option, follow the preceding steps, typing 1 for the line-spacing value.

If you are not currently running WordPerfect, please start the program now.

Let's open a new document and adjust its line spacing:

1. Open CHAP6A.LRN from your Data Disk, using either **F5** to list files or **Shift+F10** to retrieve the file by typing its name.

2. Move to page 4 of the document by pressing **Ctrl+Home** (Go To), typing **4**, and pressing **Enter**. Notice that all text is single-spaced.

3. Move to the left margin of the first paragraph on page 4, which begins *The annual meeting agenda....* Figure 6.1 shows how this page will look when you're done with this chapter.

4. Press **Shift+F8** to display the Format dialog box.

5. Choose **1. Line** to display the Line Format dialog box, as shown in Figure 6.2.

6. Choose **3. Line Spacing**, type **2** to double-space the text, and press **Enter** three times to return to the typing area. Notice that the text below the cursor is now double-spaced.

7. View the Reveal Codes area (press **Alt+F3**). Find the code that turns double spacing on:

   ```
   [Ln Spacing]
   ```

8. In the Reveal Codes area, place the cursor on the line-spacing code. Notice that the code expands to provide more information:

   ```
   [Ln Spacing:2.0]
   ```

9. Hide the Reveal Codes area (press **Alt+F3**).

10. Press **PgUp**, and examine the screen. The line spacing on page 3 is still set to single, because space codes affect the document until the end of the document or the next space code.

11. Press **PgDn** to move the cursor to page 4.

12. Move the cursor so that it is positioned on the blank line just below the first paragraph on page 4, at the left margin.

Figure 6.1 **Page 4 of the completed document**

```
                    ANNUAL MEETING AGENDA

      The annual meeting agenda of Macco Plastics, Inc.
will be held on the first Wednesday of the month in the
LLI Amphitheatre. The following items will be discussed:

      1)    The election of a corporate director
            for a two-year term to fill the
            vacancy created by the resignation
            of Charles E. Springon.

      2)    The approval or disapproval of a
            proposal to acquire a majority share
            of the stock of Creative Crafts,
            Inc.

      The Board would like to bring the following accounts
to the attention of the stockholders. The Board Members
feel that this information clarifies our significant
gains and supports a positive vote for the merger.

              CREATIVE CRAFTS, INC.

      Account       This year      Next Year

      Taxes         $4,397.10      $4,900.71
      Loans          7,120.88       6,334.90
      Payables       8,987.55       9,786.89
```

13. Press **Shift+F8** to display the Format dialog box.

14. Choose **1. Line** to display the Line Format dialog box.

15. Choose **3. Line Spacing**, type **1** for single spacing, and press **Enter** three times to return to the typing area. Notice that the text below the cursor is now single-spaced.

Figure 6.2

The Line Format dialog box

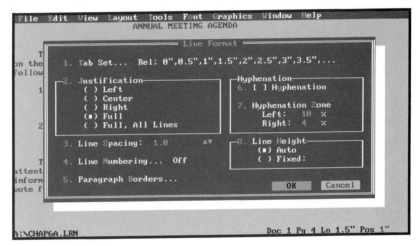

PRACTICE YOUR SKILLS

1. Position the cursor on the blank line above the last paragraph (beginning *The Board would like...*), and apply double spacing.

2. Move to the blank line below the last paragraph, and restore single spacing.

RELATIVE TABS

In WordPerfect, tab stops are set by default every half inch from 0", the left edge of the paper, so that the first tab is set at 0.5". The different tab types offered by WordPerfect are shown in Table 6.1. These tabs can be useful in aligning text in tables of contents, creating charts and reports, and displaying numeric data.

Table 6.1   **Tab Types**

Tab Type	Aligns Text at...
Left-aligned	First letter of word
Right-aligned	Last letter of word
Center-aligned	Center of word
Decimal	Columns of numbers aligned at common character, usually a decimal point (.)
Left-aligned, with dot leader	First letter of word, preceded by a series of dots, or leader
Right-aligned, with dot leader	Last letter of word, preceded by a series of dots, or leader
Decimal, with dot leader	Columns of numbers aligned at alignment character, preceded by series of dots, or leader

 ## EXAMINING THE DEFAULT TABS

You can view the default tab settings by displaying the Format dialog box (Shift+F8), choosing 1. Line, and 1. Tab Set. By default, WordPerfect uses *relative* tabs, which are set relative to the left margin setting.

Let's take a look at WordPerfect's default tab settings:

1. Move the cursor to the last blank line of the document.

2. Press **Caps Lock**, and then press **Shift+F6** to center text. Type **CREATIVE CRAFTS, INC.** to title the table shown in Figure 6.1, press **Caps Lock** again, and press **Enter** twice.

3. Press **Shift+F8** to display the Format dialog box.

4. Choose **1. Line** to display the Line Format dialog box.

5. Examine the menu choice

    ```
    1. Tab Set...
    ```

    followed by the message

    ```
    Rel; 0",0.5",1",1.5",2",2.5",3",3.5", . . . .
    ```

This is the default tab-stop setting: relative tab stops set every half inch beginning at 0".

6. Choose **1. Tab Set** to activate the Tab Set area, shown in Figure 6.3.

Figure 6.3   **The Tab Set area for relative tabs**

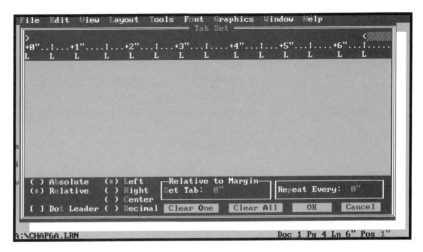

7. Press **Home**, **Home**, ← to move to the left edge of the paper. The tabs at 0" and 0.5" are now visible. Notice that the left edge of the paper is position 0". The left margin is 1". The top of the screen displays a line that lists the current tab settings. The numbers represent positions on the line. The *Ls* represent left-aligned tabs.

In the next section, you'll learn to reset the tab settings and use the new tabs to create a table.

CREATING CENTERED TABS FOR CENTERED COLUMN HEADINGS

Pressing the Center keys, Shift+F6, normally centers text on the line. However, if your cursor is at a center-aligned tab stop, pressing Shift+F6 centers text there. Forming columns for a table by tabbing from column to column allows you to center the column headings.

Take another look at the table shown in Figure 6.1. Before typing the table, you'll want to set tabs to center the column headings. To set centered tabs, display the Format dialog box by pressing Shift+F8. Choose 1. Line and 1. Tab Set. Find the position on the tab ruler (in the Tab Set area) where you want to set the tab, and type a lowercase or uppercase *c* (for center-aligned).

Follow these steps at your computer:

1. With the Tab Set area still displayed, press **Ctrl+End** to delete the default tab settings. Notice that all the *L*s have disappeared.

2. Position the cursor at 2.5" on the tab ruler (use ← and →), and type **c** (or **C**) to set a center-aligned tab there. Do the same at positions 4" and 5.5". Notice that as you set each center tab, the precise tab measurement is displayed in the Set Tab box, near the bottom of the Tab Set area. For example, the 2.5" tab might actually be 2.51", the 4" tab 4.01", and the 5.5" tab 5.52".

3. Press **F7** to leave the Tab Set area and return to the Line Format dialog box. Notice that the precise measurements of the three new tab settings are now listed at the top of the dialog box.

4. Press **Enter** twice to return to the typing area.

5. Display the Reveal Codes area, and position the cursor on the Tab Set code. The code expands to show the tab settings.

6. Hide the Reveal Codes area.

7. Tab to the first tab stop (the first column).

8. Type **Account** (the heading of the first column), and tab to the second column.

9. Type **This Year**, press **Tab**, type **Next Year**, and press **Enter** twice. Don't worry that the columns are too close together; you will fix this momentarily.

 SETTING TABS FOR A TABLE

Tabs for table entries are set in much the same way as centered tabs for column headings. From the Tab Set area, press Ctrl+End to delete the existing tab settings, move the cursor to the position at which you would like to set the tab, and type the letter representing the kind of tab you would like to set.

Follow these steps at your computer:

1. Press **Shift+F8** to display the Format dialog box.

2. Choose **1. Line** to display the Line Format dialog box.

3. Choose **1. Tab Set** to use the Tab Set area. Notice that the current tab settings show the last changes you made to those settings.

4. Press **Ctrl+End** to delete the tab settings.

5. Position the cursor at approximately 2.2", and type the letter **l** or **L** to set a left-aligned tab there.

6. Position the cursor at 4.2", and type **d** or **D** to set a decimal tab there. Do the same at position 5.7".

7. Press **F7**, and press **Enter** twice to return to the typing area.

TYPING A TABLE

Once you've made your settings, tab to each stop, and type the text.

Follow these steps at your computer:

1. Tab to the first stop (the first column of the table).

2. Type **Taxes**. The left-aligned relative tab aligns the *T* in *Taxes* at position 2.2".

3. Press **Tab**. WordPerfect prompts

        Align char = .

    until you type a decimal point.

4. Type **$4,397.10**. The prompt disappears when you type the decimal point (.) after the **7**.

5. Press **Tab**, type **$4,900.71** and press **Enter**.

PRACTICE YOUR SKILLS

Finish entering the table as shown in Figure 6.4.

Figure 6.4   **The completed table with relative tabs**

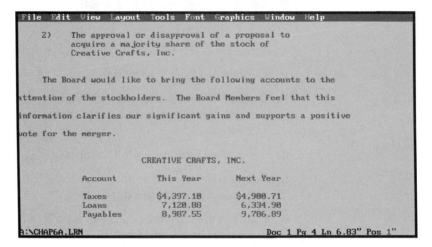

MOVING CENTER-ALIGNED TAB SETTINGS

If you don't like the position of a tab stop, move it to another location. From the Tab Set area, position the cursor under the tab you wish to move, and press Ctrl+→ or Ctrl+← to move it to the right or left.

Follow these steps at your computer:

1. Move to position 1" on the line that contains the column headings.

2. Display the Reveal Codes area. Position the cursor past the Tab Set code, if necessary, and hide the Reveal Codes area.

3. Press **Shift+F8** to display the Format dialog box.

4. Choose **1. Line** to display the Line Format dialog box.

5. Choose **1. Tab Set** to open the Tab Set area.

6. Position the cursor at the first centered tab (above the *Account* heading).

7. Press **Ctrl+→** several times. Notice that the *Account* heading moves to the right as it follows its centered tab.

8. Press **Ctrl+←** several times, until the centered tab returns to approximately the 2.5" position.

PRACTICE YOUR SKILLS

Experiment with moving the other two centered tabs, as you did in steps 7 and 8 above. When you're finished, press Esc three times to cancel any changes you've made and return to the typing area.

RESTORING DEFAULT TABS

Now that you are done typing the table, you should reset the tabs to the default settings. Otherwise, the tabs you set for the table will remain in effect for the rest of the document.

Follow these steps at your computer:

1. Move the cursor to a position just below the table, on a line by itself.

2. Press **Shift+F8** to display the Format dialog box.

3. Choose **1. Line** to display the Line menu.

4. Choose **1. Tab Set** to use the Tab Set area.

5. Move to the *L* at Position 2.2", and press **Del** to delete the tab stop at the cursor. Should you choose to, you can delete each tab individually.

6. Press **Home**, **Home**, ←, and press **Ctrl+End** to delete all the tab stops from the cursor to the right margin.

7. Choose **Repeat Every** (press **p**), type **.5** and press **Enter**. This places left-aligned tabs every half inch, starting from position 0", the left edge of the paper. This is the default tab setting for every document. (See Figure 6.5.)

8. Press **F7** to exit the Tab Set area and return to the Line Format dialog box. Notice that the tabs are set back to the default setting.

9. Return to the typing area (press **Enter** twice).

A helpful hint: The method you just used to reset tabs to the default setting can also be used to set them at regular intervals. Remember to delete existing tabs before setting new ones.

Figure 6.5   **The completed table with relative tabs**

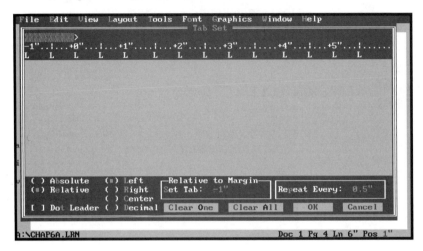

LEFT AND RIGHT MARGINS

Margins define the length of the line on which text appears on screen and in print. The left and right margins are measured in inches from the left and right edges of the paper, respectively. If you are using 8.5" x 11" paper and the margins are 1 inch each, 6.5 inches remain for text on each line.

New left and right margins are set from the cursor position forward (down) in your document. If you wish to change margin settings for the entire document, press Home, Home, ↑ to position the cursor at the top of the document (after any codes). To type half inches when setting margins, use a decimal. For example, for margins of an inch and a half, type 1.5.

Follow these steps at your computer:

1. Move to the top of page 4 using ↑ or Go To (**Ctrl+Home**).

2. Display the Format dialog box (press **Shift+F8**).

3. Choose **2. Margins** to open the Margin Format dialog box.

4. Under Document Margins, choose **1. Left Margin**; then type **1.5** and press **Enter**. The left margin is changed to 1.5".

5. Choose **2. Right Margin**, type **1.5**, and press **Enter**. The right margin is now also 1.5". Compare your screen to Figure 6.6.

Figure 6.6   **Changing left and right margins**

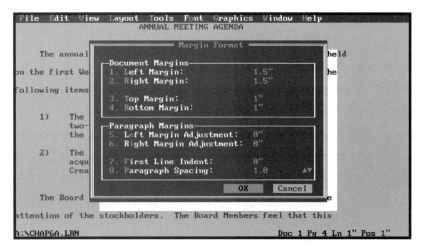

6. Press **Enter** twice to return to the typing area. Notice that the margins, as displayed on screen, have visibly widened.

7. Display the Reveal Codes area, and place the cursor on the [Lft Mar] and [Rgt Mar] codes. The codes expand to [Lft Mar:1.5"] and [Rgt Mar:1.5"], respectively.

8. Hide the Reveal Codes area.

9. Move to the word *enclosure* at the bottom of page 3.

10. Examine the new margins. Because the left margin of page 3 is 1", text appears farther to the left than the text on page 4, which now has a left margin of 1.5".

11. Save the document as MYCHAP6A.LRN, and clear the typing area.

USING THE MENU SYSTEM TO FORMAT LINES

You can also format lines with WordPerfect's menu system, which gives you another way to adjust margins and line spacing. This can be helpful if you forget keystrokes or if you use a mouse.

USING MENUS TO CHANGE MARGINS

To change left and right margin settings using the menu system, choose Layout, Margins to display the Margin Format dialog box, as shown in Figure 6.6.

Follow these steps at your computer:

1. Open the file CHAP6B.LRN (use **File, Open**). The document is similar to CHAP6A.LRN.

2. Choose **Layout** and **Margins** to display the Margin Format dialog box.

3. Use the method you learned in the previous exercise to set the left and right margins to 1.5".

4. Return to the typing area (press **Enter** twice). The text adjusts to the new margin settings.

USING MENUS TO CHANGE LINE SPACING

You can also use the menu system to change line spacing. Choose Layout and Line to display the Line Format dialog box, which is the same one you used earlier.

Follow these steps at your computer:

1. Move the cursor near the top of the document, under the *1* in *1. Introduction*.

2. Choose **Layout** and **Line** to display the Line Format dialog box.

3. Choose **3. Line Spacing**, type **1.5** to set line spacing at an inch and a half, and press **Enter**.

4. Return to the typing area. You can see that the line spacing of the document has increased.

5. Rename the document by saving it as MYCHAP6B.LRN, and clear the typing area.

PRACTICE YOUR SKILLS

In this chapter you have learned several ways to make your work look better. The next activity gives you the opportunity to practice formatting lines. The instructions guide you through the creation of the document shown in Figure 6.7.

1. If necessary, clear the typing area (Chapter 1).

2. Retrieve the file PRACTICE.CH6.

3. Complete the chart in Figure 6.7. Use the decimal tabs already set to align the numbers in the columns.

4. Change the line spacing of the last paragraph to 2.

5. Type the last paragraph, as shown in Figure 6.7, beginning with *Those stockholders* and ending with *meeting*.

6. Rename the document CORRECT.CH6 (Chapter 1).

7. Print your work (Chapter 1).

8. Compare your printout to Figure 6.7.

If you have finished this activity and want to try one that is a bit more challenging, follow the instructions below. Use the document in Figure 6.8 as a model.

1. Clear the typing area and retrieve the document PRACOPT1.CH6.

2. Move to the bottom of the document.

3. Change the line spacing to 1.

4. Erase all tabs. Set center-aligned tabs at positions 2.0", 3.5", and 5.0".

5. Type the column headings **1st Year**, **2nd Year**, and **3rd Year** at positions 2.0", 3.5", and 5.0", respectively.

6. Erase all tabs. Set a left-aligned tab at position .3". Set decimal tabs with dot leaders at positions 2.1", 3.6", and 5.1". (For dot-leader tabs, type the alignment letter and then a period.)

7. Complete the table on the second page of Figure 6.8.

8. Reset the tabs to every half inch, beginning at position 1.5".

9. Restore double spacing.

10. Type the remainder of the document, beginning with *The Board* and ending with *vote*.

11. Rename the document CORROPT1.CH6 (Chapter 1).

Figure 6.7   **Using decimal tabs**

ANNUAL MEETING AGENDA

The annual meeting of Macco Plastics, Inc. will be
held on the first Wednesday of the month, in the LLI
Amphitheater. The purpose of the meeting shall be:

The election of a corporate director for a
two-year term to fill the vacancy created by
the resignation of Charles E. Springon.

The approval or disapproval of a
proposal to acquire a majority
share of the stock of Creative
Crafts, Inc.

The Board would like to bring the following
accounts to the attention of the stockholders. The
Board Members feel that this information clarifies our
significant gains and supports a positive vote for the
merger.

Account	This Year	Next Year
Taxes.	.$3,296.09. . .	. $3,899.60
Loans Payable. . .	. 1,538.44. . .	. . .899.75
Accounts Payable .	. 4,140.54. . .	. .5,688.38
Benefits	. 3,600.00. . .	. .5,450.00
Deferred Income. .	. . 387.90. . .	. . .476.25

Those stockholders of record at the close of the
business day, are entitled to receive this notice and
to vote at the stated meeting.

Figure 6.8   **The completed document (CORROPT1.CH6)**

```
                        ANNUAL MEETING AGENDA


     The annual  meeting of Macco Plastics, Inc. will be

held on the first  Wednesday  of the month,  in  the LLI

Amphitheater. The purpose of the meeting shall be:

     The  election  of  a  corporate director for a
     two-year term to fill  the vacancy  created by
     the resignation of Charles E. Springon.

          The  approval  or  disapproval  of a
          proposal   to  acquire  a   majority
          share  of  the   stock  of  Creative
          Crafts, Inc.

     The  Board  would  like  to  bring  the  following

accounts  to  the  attention  of  the stockholders.  The

Board Members feel that  this information  clarifies our

significant gains  and supports  a positive vote for the

merger.

          Account      This Year        Next Year

     Taxes. . . . . . .$3,296.09. . . .$3,899.60
     Loans Payable. . . .1,538.44. . . . . 899.75
     Accounts Payable . 4,140.54. . . . 5,688.38
     Benefits . . . . . .3,600.00. . . . 5,450.00
     Deferred Income. . .387.90. . . . . 476.25

     Those stockholders  of record  at the  close of the

business  day,  are entitled to  receive this notice and

to vote at the stated meeting.
```

Figure 6.8   **The completed document (CORROPT1.CH6) (Continued)**

Additional information follows about the proposed merger company. Creative Crafts, Inc. was established in May, 1985, by two men: Joshua Miller and Peter Stevens. They shared a common interest in crafts, especially quilting. Over the years, their company has grown to 29 employees, and their sales revenues have steadily increased to $786,000 per year. The chart below reflects the growth in some of their major products.

```
                1st Year      2nd Year       3rd Year
   Yarn  . .$25,000.00. .$57,000.00. . . $93,000.00
   Cloth . . 10,000.00. . 15,000.00 . . . 23,900.00
   Quilting. 30,000.00. . 50,000.00 . . .102,000.00
```

The Board hopes that this information proves valuable as you consider the merger. For further information, or to answer any questions, please call Anna Scott, the Public Relations director at Creative Crafts, Inc.

Please be present at the annual meeting to cast your vote.

12. Print the document (Chapter 1).

13. Compare your printout to Figure 6.8.

CHAPTER SUMMARY

In this chapter, you've learned about line formatting with WordPerfect: how to set different kinds of tabs, adjust intervals, and create tables using tabs. You've also learned how to set left and right margins and change line formatting options using WordPerfect's menu system.

Here's a quick technique reference for Chapter 6:

Feature or Action	How to Do It
Change line spacing	**Shift+F8** (Format), **1. Line**, **3. Line Spacing**, type number, **Enter**
Change margin settings	**Shift+F8** (Format), **2. Margins**, **1. Left Margin**, type number, **Enter**, **2. Right Margin**, type number, **Enter**
Set tabs	**Shift+F8** (Format), **1. Line**, **1. Tab Set**
Clear tab in Tab Set Area	Place cursor under tab to be deleted, press **Del**
Clear all tabs in Tab Set area	Press **Ctrl+End**
Using the menu bar:	
Open the Line Format dialog box	Choose **Layout, Line**
Open the Margins Format dialog box	Choose **Layout, Margins**

The next chapter introduces techniques for gaining even more control over the look of your work. You'll learn about page formatting—page length, page breaks, and headers and footers. These and other techniques define the page as a whole. Effective use of line and page formatting techniques can make all your documents more attractive.

If you need to break off here, please exit from WordPerfect. If you want to proceed directly to the next chapter, please do so now.

CHAPTER 7:
PAGE FORMATTING

You face some new challenges as your documents get longer. Perhaps you want to keep related sections of text together on one page. Perhaps you want to center several lines of a title vertically on a page. Perhaps you want to number pages. These effects are all achieved by *page formatting*.

In Chapter 6, you learned techniques for controlling the appearance of lines. In this chapter, you'll learn to control the appearance of the overall page. When done with this chapter, you will be able to:

- Insert and delete manual page breaks

- Center text vertically on the page

- Create headers and footers

- Number pages

- Retrieve a file from disk using the Retrieve command

RETRIEVING VERSUS OPENING A FILE

You have already learned two ways to open a file from disk: through the File Manager and with the Open command. Both these methods *open* the file into a new document.

Retrieving a document, on the other hand, denotes placing a copy of the document on disk in the *current* typing area. If you have no document currently open in the typing area, it makes essentially no difference whether you use Open or Retrieve to place the document in the typing area. However, if a document *is* open, retrieving a document places it in the currently open document at the location of the cursor.

The typing area should be clear before you retrieve a document. If another document is present in the typing area, any document you retrieve is inserted into it. Consolidating documents can be useful (for example, in bringing together in one file the sections of a chapter). However, when you save a consolidated document, the file from which you retrieved text will *not* be saved with your changes, and you will have multiple versions of the same text.

As with the Open command, you can choose the Retrieve command from the File menu or from within the File Manager. In the File Manager, choose 2. Retrieve into Current Doc. Either way, the rest of the procedure is the same as opening a document.

There is no keyboard shortcut that *directly* issues the Retrieve command. For example, pressing Shift+F10 displays the Open Document dialog box; there is no analogous key combination that directly displays the Retrieve Document dialog box. However, you will see a way around this "shortcoming" in the exercise that follows.

If you are not currently running WordPerfect, please start the program now.

Let's examine a couple of different ways to retrieve a document into the current typing area:

1. First, insert your Data Disk in the drive you've been using.

2. Open the File Manager, displaying the contents of your Data Disk. Notice the 2. Retrieve into Current Doc option, but do *not* choose it. This is one way to retrieve a document from disk.

3. Press **Esc** to return to the typing area without issuing any commands.

4. Now, choose **File, Retrieve**. The Retrieve Document dialog box is displayed (see Figure 7.1). Notice that this dialog box is quite similar to the Open Document dialog box. There is, however, one important difference (other than that of the title): Under Method, Retrieve into Current Document is currently selected. Notice, too, that next to "Method," the message

   ```
   (Shift+F10 to change)
   ```

   is displayed.

Figure 7.1   **Retrieve Document dialog box**

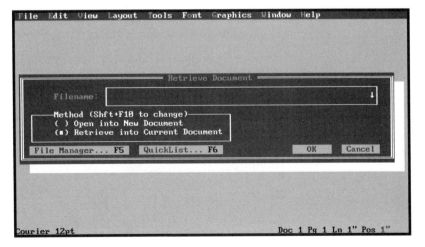

5. Press **Shift+F10**. Open into New Document is now selected. Notice that the name of the dialog box has changed to Open Document. Shift+F10—the same key combination used to display the Open Document dialog box from the typing area—acts as a toggle between the two commands while either dialog box is open.

6. Press **Shift+F10** again to select Retrieve into Current Document.

7. Retrieve the document A:\CHAPTER7.LRN. The document is displayed in the typing area. Notice that, because no document was displayed in the typing area, we could use either Open or Retrieve to the same effect.

PAGINATION

Pagination means dividing text into pages, separated by discrete page breaks and usually numbered sequentially. In WordPerfect, there are two kinds of page breaks, automatic and manual.

 AUTOMATIC (SOFT) PAGE BREAKS

When you type enough lines of text to fill a page, WordPerfect automatically inserts a page break. An *automatic* page break is inserted by the program itself, and is known as a *soft page break.* The soft page break shows up on the screen as a solid, horizontal line that extends from the left to the right margin.

With your Data Disk in drive A, follow these steps at your computer:

1. View the document in Print Preview (press **Shift+F7** and choose **7. Print Preview.**) The document is three pages long, with the second page containing only a few lines. (The actual number of lines will vary, depending on the printer you have selected.)

2. Choose **Pages, Next** to view more of the document.

3. Exit to the typing area by pressing **F7**.

4. Move to the top of the document.

5. Advance three screens of text (press the **+** key on the numeric keypad three times).

6. Move the cursor to the blank line under the *3* in *3. Computer Study*. Notice that an automatic page break separates the title from the paragraph, as shown in Figure 7.2. The automatic page break appears as a single solid line, and the manual page break between pages 2 and 3 as a double solid line.

Figure 7.2   **Automatic and manual page breaks**

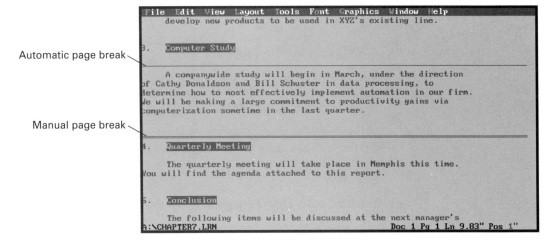

Automatic page break

Manual page break

7. Display the Reveal Codes area. The Soft Page code [HRt-SPg] cannot be deleted.

8. Hide the Reveal Codes area and return to the typing area.

MANUAL (HARD) PAGE BREAKS

By inserting automatic page breaks, WordPerfect saves you the trouble of deciding where to break each page. However, there are times when you must specify where you want a page to begin or end. For example, it's common practice to begin each section of a document (particularly if the section begins with a heading) on a new page, even if the program would not automatically break the page there.

A manual, or *hard,* page break is used to break a page where *you* wish; it is a way of overriding WordPerfect. A manual page break necessarily occurs before the page would break automatically; you cannot force WordPerfect to exceed a specific number of text lines per page. In the typing area, a manual page break appears as a double line. Figure 7.2 shows a manual page break.

Deleting a Manual Page Break

To delete a manual page break in the typing area, position your cursor directly above the page break and press Del. Alternatively, move your cursor immediately below the page break and press Backspace. To delete a manual page break from the Reveal Codes area, press Backspace with the cursor to the *right* of the code or Del with the cursor *on* the code.

Follow these steps at your computer:

1. Move your cursor above the *4* in *4. Quarterly*, at the top of page 3. The double solid line on your screen represents the manual, or hard, page break.

2. Display the Reveal Codes area by pressing **Alt+F3**. Notice the Hard Page Break code [HPg], as shown in Figure 7.3.

Figure 7.3   **Page breaks and Hard Page Break code**

Hard Page Break code ——

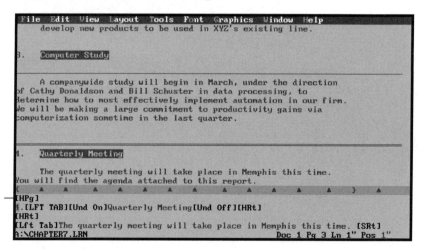

3. Position the cursor on [HPg].

4. Press **Del** to delete the code.

5. Hide the Reveal Codes area and return to the typing area. The manual page break is removed.

Inserting a Manual Page Break

To insert a manual page break as you are typing, press Ctrl+Enter at the point where you would like the page to break. The double line appears, the cursor advances to the new page, and the page number in the status line increases by one. If you'd like to insert a manual page break after typing text, position the cursor *under* the first character that you want to appear on the new page, and press Ctrl+Enter.

Follow these steps at your computer:

1. Move the cursor under the *3* in *3. Computer Study* (at the bottom of page 1).

2. Press **Ctrl+Enter** to insert a page break. Notice the double solid line marking the end of the page. The manual page break is placed above the cursor. The parts of the section beginning *3. Computer Study* appear together on one page, and the automatic page break has disappeared. Your manual page has fewer lines than WordPerfect's automatic page.

3. Move the cursor to the top of the document, and position it under the *1* in *1. Introduction*.

4. Press **Ctrl+Enter** to insert a page break, and examine the screen. The title is now on a separate page.

5. Display the document in Print Preview by pressing **Shift+F7** and choosing **7. Print Preview**. The document now has four pages, the title page plus three report pages. The title is at the top of page 1.

6. Exit to the typing area by pressing **F7**.

7. Save the document as MYCHAP7.LRN, and keep it in the typing area.

PAGE FORMATTING OPTIONS

WordPerfect's Page Format dialog box controls the appearance and amount of text on a page. In the upcoming sections, you will learn three very important page formatting techniques:

● Centering text vertically on the page

- Adding headers and footers
- Numbering pages

To display the Page Format dialog box, press the Format keys, Shift+F8, and choose 3. Page.

CENTERING TEXT VERTICALLY

Charts, tables, and brief letters are examples of short pages that may require special treatment. In such cases, you might want to center the text vertically, between the top and bottom margins.

To center text vertically on a page:

- Position the cursor at the top of the page.
- Open the Page Format dialog box (Shift+F8, 3. Page).
- Choose 2. Center Current Page to center the page vertically.
- Press Enter twice to return to the typing area.

Follow these steps at your computer:

1. Move the cursor to the top of the document.
2. Display the Format dialog box (press **Shift+F8**).
3. Choose **3. Page** to display the Page Format dialog box.
4. Choose **2. Center Current Page** (top to bottom). Compare your screen to Figure 7.4.
5. Press **Enter** twice to accept the change and return to the typing area.
6. Go to the Reveal Codes area, and find the code [Cntr Cur Pg].
7. Return to the typing area.
8. View the document in Print Preview (press **Shift+F7** and choose **7. Print Preview**). The title is now centered vertically on page 1.
9. Return to the typing area (press **F7**).

Figure 7.4   **Page Format dialog box**

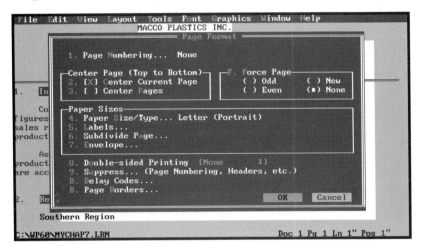

 CREATING A HEADER

In longer documents, you may wish to include a *header,* repeating text at the top of every page: a date, chapter title, section heading, department name, or some combination of these items, for example. You can create up to two different headers per document. You would use a second header if you were planning to print a two-sided bound document and wanted different (alternating) headers on left and right pages. A header is created in its own mini-document area, and it can be as long as one page. Of course, a header longer than a few lines begins to limit the space for regular text.

Most of WordPerfect's enhancement features work within headers. For example, you can create a header with text that is centered, flush right, bold, or underlined. You can also insert the date by using the Date function, Shift+F5.

To create a header:

- Position the cursor at the top of the first page on which you want the header to appear.

- Press the Format keys, Shift+F8.

- Choose 5. Header/Footer/Watermark.

- Choose 1. Headers; then choose 1. Header A. (Choose Header B only if you are creating the second of two headers for alternating pages.)

- Choose 1. All Pages, 2. Even Pages, or 3. Odd Pages to specify the pages on which to print the header you are creating.

- Press Enter or choose Create.

- Type the text that you want the header to contain.

- Press F7 to exit to the Header/Footer/Watermark dialog box.

- Press Enter twice to return to the typing area.

To discontinue a header, move your cursor to the beginning of the appropriate page; follow the steps above, but instead of typing in header text, choose Off from the Header A dialog box. To delete a header altogether, delete the header code in the Reveal Codes area.

Follow these steps at your computer:

1. Move the cursor to the top of page 2. (The title page of most documents does not contain a header.)

2. Display the Format menu (press **Shift+F8**).

3. Choose **5. Header/Footer/Watermark**. The Header/Footer/Watermark dialog box is displayed (see Figure 7.5).

Figure 7.5   **Header/Footer/Watermark dialog box**

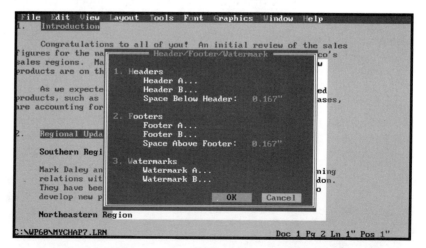

4. Choose **1. Headers**; then choose **1. Header A**. The Header A dialog box is opened.

5. Choose **1. All Pages** (the default setting) and press **Enter** or select **Create** to tell WordPerfect to display the header on every page of the document. The Header A typing area is displayed, and the prompt

       Press Exit (F7) when done

   appears in the status line.

6. Press **Shift+F5** to display the Date dialog box, and choose **1. Insert Date Text**.

7. Press **Enter** twice to end the current line and leave a blank line.

8. Press **F7** to leave the header typing area and return to the Header/Footer/Watermark dialog box. Next to Header A, notice the message:

       All Pages

9. Press **Enter** twice to return to the typing area.

Remember: When you add a header, change line spacing, or adjust margins, you limit the amount of text that can appear on a page. Because the header does not print in the top margin but in the *active* part of the page, it must share this area with regular text. WordPerfect automatically adjusts the pagination of the document, according to line spacing, margin settings, and any headers or footers.

 CREATING A FOOTER

WordPerfect also lets you create footers, repeated text at the bottom of every page. You can create up to two different footers per document. You would use a second footer if you were planning to print a two-sided bound document and wanted different (alternating) footers on left and right pages.

Like a header, a footer is created in its own mini-document area, and it can be as long as one page. Most of WordPerfect's enhancement features work within footers. For example, you can create a footer with text that is centered, flush right, bold, or underlined. You can also use the Date function (Shift+F5) within a footer.

To create a footer:

- Position the cursor at the top of the first page on which you want the footer to appear.

- Press the Format keys, Shift+F8.

- Choose 5. Header/Footer/Watermark.

- Choose 2. Footers.

- Choose 1. Footer A. (Choose Footer B only if you are creating the second of two footers for alternating pages.)

- Choose 1. All Pages, 2. Even Pages, or 3. Odd Pages to specify the pages on which to print the footer you are creating.

- Type the text that you want the footer to contain.

- Press F7 to exit to the Header/Footer/Watermark dialog box.

- Press Enter twice to return to the typing area.

To discontinue a footer from the current page forward, move your cursor to the beginning of the appropriate page, follow the steps above, but instead of typing in footer text, choose Off from the Footer dialog box. To delete a footer altogether, delete the footer code in the Reveal Codes area.

 INCLUDING PAGE NUMBERS IN A HEADER OR FOOTER

To automatically number pages in a header or footer, position your cursor where you want the page number to appear within the header or footer, and press Ctrl+P. The page number appears. Pages will be numbered sequentially. As you make changes that will affect spacing and margins, WordPerfect automatically updates page numbers. To make the page numbering appear as *Page #* with *#* representing the actual page number, create a footer, align the cursor (flush left, center, or flush right), type *Page,* press the Space-bar to add a space after *Page,* and press Ctrl+P. The footer now reads *Page* followed by the number.

Follow these steps at your computer:

1. Make sure the cursor is positioned at the top of page 2.

2. Display the Format dialog box.

3. Choose **5. Header/Footer/Watermark** to open the Header/Footer/Watermark dialog box.

4. Choose **2. Footers**, and choose **1. Footer A**. The Footer A dialog box is displayed.

5. Choose **1. All Pages** (if necessary) and press **Enter**. The Footer A typing area is displayed.

6. Press **Alt+F6** to right-align the text. The footer text will appear in the bottom-right corner of the page.

7. Type **Page** to create the footer text, and then press **Spacebar**, **Ctrl+P**, and **Enter** twice. The screen displays

       Page 2

8. Press **F7** to leave the footer area and return to the Header/Footer/Watermark dialog box. Next to Footer A, notice the message:

       All Pages

9. Press **Enter** twice to return to the typing area.

10. Display the Reveal Codes area to examine the header and footer codes:

       [Header A][Footer A]

11. Return to the typing area.

Remember that adding a footer reduces the amount of text that can appear on a page.

 VIEWING AND PRINTING THE FINAL DOCUMENT

Now that you've formatted the pages of your document in various ways, let's look at the results. In this procedure, you will open your document in the Print Preview area and—if you are satisfied with the way it looks—print it.

Follow these steps at your computer:

1. Display the Print Preview area, and examine the document. Headers, footers, page numbering, and text can all be seen at the same time, giving you an idea of what the printout will look like.

2. Return to the typing area.

3. Save the document using **F10**, press **Enter**, and type **Y** at the Replace prompt.

4. Press **Shift+F7** to open the Print dialog box.

5. Choose **1. Full Document** to print the entire document. Compare your printout to the one shown in Figure 7.6.

6. Save the document and clear the typing area.

CHAPTER SUMMARY

In this chapter, you have learned several important page formatting techniques, such as paginating manually, centering text vertically, and creating headers and footers.

Here's a quick technique reference for Chapter 7:

Feature or Action	How to Do It
Manual page break	**Ctrl+Enter**
Center page vertically	**Shift+F8** (Format), **3. Page, 2. Center Current Page**
Header	**Shift+F8** (Format), **5. Header/Footer/ Watermark, 1. Headers, 1. Header A** or **2. Header B, 1. All Pages**
Footer	**Shift+F8** (Format), **5. Header/Footer/ Watermark, 2. Footers, 1. Footer A** or **2. Footer B, 1. All Pages**
Insert page number	**Ctrl+P**

In the next chapter, you'll learn how you can use WordPerfect to correct spelling and improve the clarity and accuracy of your text.

If you need to break off here, please exit from WordPerfect. If you want to proceed directly to the next chapter, please do so now.

Figure 7.6   **The final document MYCHAP7.LRN**

```
              MACCO PLASTICS INC.
           QUARTERLY SALES REPORT
                FIRST QUARTER
```

Figure 7.6   The final document MYCHAP7.LRN (Continued)

April 12, 1993

1.   <u>Introduction</u>

Congratulations to all of you! An initial review of the sales figures for the nation reveals a surge in sales in all of Macco's sales regions. Major new clients have been added and many new products are on the way.

As we expected when we entered the field, computer related products, such as keyboard housings and protective carrying cases, are accounting for a major portion of this upswing.

2.   <u>Regional Updates</u>

Southern Region
Mark Daley and his group have done a fine job of maintaining relations with XYZ's Product Development Division in London. They have been working closely with XYZ product people to develop new products to be used in XYZ's existing line.

Northeastern Region

John Martinson and his group are doing a great job in Nashua. They have secured major contracts for a wide range of new and existing products. Much of this business is coming from Computer Equipment Corporation (CEC), a major client of Macco's.

Midwestern Region

After several years of falling sales due to the slump in the auto industry, Blair Williams and his folks have something to celebrate. The recent boom in auto manufacturing has led to renewed demand for Macco products in Detroit.

Southern Region
Mark Daley and his group have done a fine job of maintaining relations with XYZ's Product Development Division in London. They have been working closely with XYZ product people to develop new products to be used in XYZ's existing line.

Page 2

Figure 7.6   **The final document MYCHAP7.LRN (Continued)**

April 12, 1993

3.   Computer Study

    A companywide study will begin in March, under the direction of Cathy Donaldson and Bill Schuster in data processing, to determine how to most effectively implement automation in our firm. We will be making a large commitment to productivity gains via computerization sometime in the last quarter.

4.   Quarterly Meeting

    The quarterly meeting will take place in Memphis this time. You will find the agenda attached to this report.

5.   Conclusion

    The following items will be discussed at the next manager's meeting:

1.   Marketing and sales strategies for the introduction of the new System 400 product line.
2.   Current available positions resulting from the early retirement program.
3.   Development of the new expense form to facilitate the prompt payment of travel reimbursements.

    If the recovery continues at the current pace, this year should be a banner year for all of us at Macco. We want to thank all of you for the outstanding jobs you've done and, most important, for standing by Macco in hard times. Keep up the good work!

John Smith
Regional Coordinator
Macco Plastics, Inc.

Page 3

Figure 7.6   **The final document MYCHAP7.LRN (Continued)**

```
April 12, 1993


               ANNUAL MEETING AGENDA


    The annual meeting agenda of Macco Plastics, Inc.

will be held on the first Wednesday of the month in the

LLI Amphitheatre. The following items will be discussed:

    1)   The election of a corporate director
         for a two-year term to fill the
         vacancy created by the resignation of
         Charles E. Springon.

    2)   The approval or disapproval of a
         proposal to acquire a majority share
         of the stock of Creative Crafts,
         Inc.

    The Board would like to bring the following accounts

to the attention of the stockholders. The Board Members

feel that this information clarifies our significant

gains and supports a positive vote for the merger.


              CREATIVE CRAFTS, INC.

         Account       This year       Next Year

         Taxes         $4,397.10       $4,900.71
         Loans          7,120.88        6,334.90
         Payables       8,987.55        9,786.89




                                            Page 4
```

CHAPTER 8:
THE SPELLER,
HYPHENATION, AND
THE THESAURUS

The WordPerfect
Speller

Hyphenation

The WordPerfect
Thesaurus

In previous chapters, you've learned how to create, edit, and enhance a document. After you complete a draft, you probably want to review it carefully, checking for errors in spelling and grammar. You may also want to make sure that you've used words correctly and expressed yourself as clearly as possible. WordPerfect's Speller and Thesaurus enable you to do these tasks more efficiently and accurately.

In this chapter, you'll learn how to use these features to correct and clarify your writing. You'll also learn how to use hyphenation to improve the spacing of fully justified text and to make left-aligned and right-aligned text less ragged. When done with this chapter, you will be able to:

- Use the Speller
- Hyphenate text
- Use the Thesaurus

THE WORDPERFECT SPELLER

The Speller helps you proofread a document by searching for each word in a list of correctly spelled words—a 100,000-word dictionary! Any misspelled word can be either replaced with a word from a list of possible corrections or edited to alter its spelling. You can spell-check a word, a block, a page, or your entire document. After every spell-check, the Speller tells you the number of words checked.

The Speller also features *pattern lookup* and *phonetic lookup*. Using pattern lookup, you type those letters of a word that you know, substituting *wildcards* for the letters you don't know. Word-Perfect then lists possible matching words from which you can select a word to place in your document. In *phonetic lookup*, the Speller looks up homonyms: words that sound like the incorrectly spelled word. These homonyms are listed on the screen, and you can select one to replace the incorrect word.

Many documents contain properly spelled words that are not in the Speller dictionary, such as proper names and acronyms. You can instruct the Speller to continue the spell-check without correcting these words. You can even add words that the Speller dictionary does not have (for example, company names) to a *supplemental dictionary*. When you use those words in future documents, they will be considered correct. WordPerfect also checks for the occurrence of repeated words (*the the*, for example) and words containing both letters and numbers.

CHECKING AN ENTIRE DOCUMENT FOR SPELLING

To use the Speller to check spelling for an entire document:

- Save the document.

- Position the cursor at the top of the document.

- Press the Spell keys, Ctrl+F2.

- Choose 3. Document.

- When the Speller highlights a misspelled word, use the options on the right side of the Word Not Found dialog box to make any corrections, and continue. If the correct replacement word is listed in the Suggestions list box, press the highlighted letter that appears to the left of that word to replace the misspelled word instantly.

- When the spell-check is complete, press Enter to return to the typing area.

- Save the document.

If you are not currently running WordPerfect, please start the program now.

Let's open a new document; then we'll check it for spelling errors:

1. Open CHAPTER8.LRN from your Data Disk.

2. Press the Spell keys, **Ctrl+F2**, to bring up the Speller dialog box (see Figure 8.1). Notice that the 3. Document option is selected by default.

3. Choose **3. Document**. WordPerfect spell-checks the document, stopping at the first word it cannot find in its dictionary, *MACCO*—a company name. The typing area is displayed in the upper portion of the screen, with *MACCO* highlighted. The Word Not Found dialog box is displayed in the lower portion of the screen (see Figure 8.2). At the top of the dialog box, the prompt

   ```
   Word Not Found: MACCO
   ```

   is displayed. On the left side of the dialog box is a list of suggested replacement words; directly above the list, the program tells you how many suggested replacement words are in the list. On the right side of the of the dialog box is a list of menu options.

Figure 8.1   **Speller dialog box**

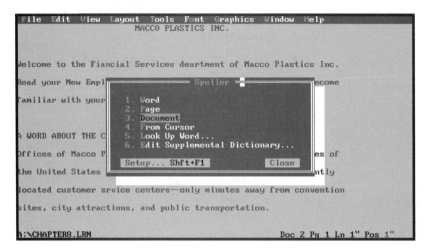

Figure 8.2   **Word Not Found dialog box**

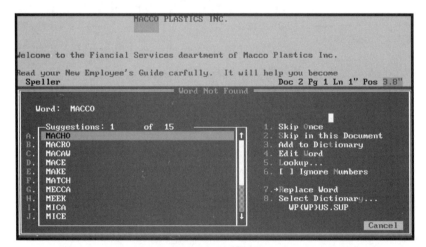

4. Choose **2. Skip in this Document**. Because *MACCO* is a
proper name and is correctly spelled, you are instructing
WordPerfect to skip this and every occurrence of the name
for the rest of the document. (To skip *MACCO* in this document *and* add it to the supplemental dictionary used to spell-
check other documents, you would press 3. Add to Dictionary.) The Speller then moves on to the next word not found,

Fiancial. A list of alternatives appears on the screen. (In this case, WordPerfect provided only one possible correction.)

5. Type **A** to insert *Financial* into the text.

PRACTICE YOUR SKILLS

1. Continue hunting for and correcting misspelled words. When the Capitalization Difference dialog box is displayed, highlighting *Macco*, choose **5. Disable Case Checking**, which tells the Speller to ignore differences in case (during the current spell-checking session only).

2. When the Speller finds the misspelled word *faclities*, no replacement words will be suggested. Choose **4. Edit Word**, correct the spelling of the word in the typing area, and then press **Enter** (or **F7**) to continue spell-checking.

3. Stop when *clinete* is found; you'll correct this misspelling in the next exercise.

 LOOKING UP THE SPELLING OF A WORD

You can also use the Speller to check the spelling of an individual word while you are typing.

- Position the cursor anywhere within the word you want to check.

- Press the Spell keys, Ctrl+F2.

- Choose 1. Word.

- Make the correction, if necessary.

The misspelled word *clinete* should be highlighted (from the last "Practice Your Skills" section). The intended word was *clientele*, but *clientele* is not on the list of suggested words in the Speller area. To find the correct word, you must use a wildcard.

Follow these steps at your computer:

1. Choose **5. Look Up Word**. The Look Up Word dialog box is displayed. At the bottom of the dialog box is the prompt

```
Word or Word Pattern:
```

followed by the highlighted misspelling *clinete*.

2. Type **client*** and press **Enter**. The asterisk (*) is the wildcard character, which tells WordPerfect to list all words beginning with *client* and ending with any number of letters (for example, *clients* and *clientele*). The new word list in the Speller area includes *clientele*, choice C (see Figure 8.3).

Figure 8.3   **Look Up Word dialog box**

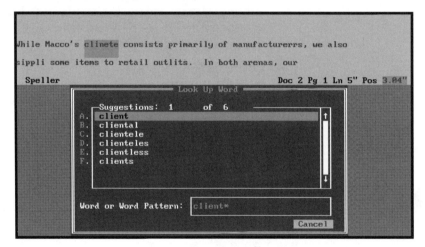

3. Type **C** to replace *clinete* with the correctly spelled word *clientele*.

PRACTICE YOUR SKILLS

1. Continue correcting the misspelled words.

2. When the prompt

```
Spell Check Completed
```

is displayed, press **Enter** to return to the typing area.

HYPHENATION

Text that is left-justified has a ragged-right margin, and text that is right-justified has a ragged-left margin. To maintain the ragged margin but reduce raggedness, you can hyphenate the text. Fully justified text has smooth margins but gappy spacing between words. To fill in the gaps and improve the text fit, you can, again, hyphenate the text.

To hyphenate a document:

- Position the cursor at the top of the document.

- Display the Line Format dialog box by pressing Shift+F8, choosing 1. Line, and then choosing 6. Hyphenation.

- Press Enter twice to return to the document.

WordPerfect uses special dictionary files when hyphenating your documents. The program asks you to hyphenate a word manually only when the hyphenation program cannot find a word in its dictionary files: for example, a company name, proper name, or foreign expression. Look at the hyphenated document shown in Figure 8.4.

Figure 8.4   **A hyphenated document**

```
the United States and Canada.  All facilities include convenient-

ly located customer service centers--only minutes away from

convention sites, city attractions, and public transportation.


While Macco's clientele consists primarily of manufacturers, we

also supply some items to retail outlets.  In both arenas, our

reputation is for providing high quality products and reliable

services.  We are prod to have you join this tradition.


Read the organization chart on the facing page.  It will show you

just where your department lies in the chain of command.  It will

also help you become acquainted with the names and responsibili-
```

To cancel hyphenation for a particular word, position the cursor on the first character of the hyphenated word and press the Home key together with a forward slash (Home, /). Then, delete the hyphen character. The whole word wraps to the next line. If you turn hyphenation on or off, a code is automatically inserted in the document. Like a line-spacing or margin code, a hyphenation code affects the document from its position forward. If you want to hyphenate the entire document, simply move to the top of the document before turning on hyphenation.

To turn off hyphenation from the position of the cursor forward, display the Line Format dialog box by pressing Shift+F8, selecting 1. Line, and choosing 6. Hyphenation.

If you edit your text or change paragraph indents, type, type size, or printer drivers, the text shifts. If hyphenation has been turned on for a document, it is automatically rehyphenated; if a long word is no longer hyphenated, the hyphen is no longer visible on the screen.

WordPerfect has several hyphenation characters that allow you to control the division of words, especially long words or words that need to be kept together.

- Use a normal hyphen (-) to break the word at the end of a line.

- Use a *nonbreaking* or *hard* hyphen (Home, -) for hyphenated words, such as *Mrs. Jayne Smith-Howe*, that should not be broken at the end of a line.

- The *soft hyphen* appears automatically when words are broken into syllables at the end of a line.

- Press Home, -, - to keep two hyphens together, forming a dash.

Follow these steps at your computer:

1. Move the cursor to the top of the document.

2. Display the Line Format dialog box (press **Shift+F8**, and choose **1. Line**).

3. Choose **6. Hyphenation** to turn on hyphenation.

4. Press **Enter** twice to accept the change and return to the document.

5. Observe your document, scrolling down to look at the result of turning on hyphenation. Note: Hyphenation might not have affected your document, depending on the type of printer you are using. If hyphenation is not visible, you might try typing a few additional sentences (or even paragraphs) at the end of the document, until the program actually hyphenates one or more words.

6. Display the Reveal Codes area, and look for the code [Hyph]. Then close the Reveal Codes area.

THE WORDPERFECT THESAURUS

If you can't find the exact word you would like to use and want to look up a group of words with similar meanings, you can use Word-Perfect's on-line Thesaurus to find *synonyms* (words or phrases with similar meanings). The Thesaurus also provides you with *antonyms* (words or phrases with opposite meanings).

When you press the Writing Tools keys, Alt+F1, the Writing Tools list appears on the screen. (You'll notice that you can also activate the Speller by first displaying the Writing Tools list.) To activate the Thesaurus, choose 2. Thesaurus.

The Thesaurus area, shown in Figure 8.5, consists of three columns. The *headword*, the word you are looking up, appears at the top of the first column. Word *references* appear underneath the headword. References are divided into as many as four *subgroups* underneath the headword: nouns, verbs, adjectives, and antonyms. Not all headwords have all four subgroups.

Figure 8.5 **The WordPerfect Thesaurus**

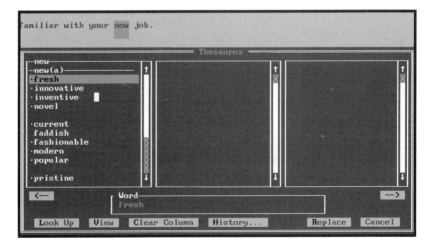

To replace the headword, highlight the replacement word in the Thesaurus list, and choose Replace. To highlight a word appearing in the second or third column, press → to go to the column.

To look up synonyms and antonyms for a word in your document:

- Position the cursor on the word you want to look up.

- Press the Writing Tools keys, Alt+F1.

- Choose 2. Thesaurus.

- Press ← or → to position the cursor in the column that contains the word you want.

- Highlight the desired word.

- Choose Replace.

Follow these steps at your computer:

1. Position your cursor anywhere under the word *new*, on the last line of the first paragraph.

2. Press **Alt+F1** to display the Writing Tools list.

3. Choose **2. Thesaurus**, and compare your screen to Figure 8.5. Notice that the Thesaurus column that contains words is divided into two sections. The upper section contains synonyms of *new*.

4. Scroll to view the lower section of the Thesaurus column. The lower section contains antonyms of *new*. Notice that the list of antonyms concludes with the word *used*.

5. Scroll to highlight *current*, and choose Replace (type **R**) to replace *new* with *current*.

6. Save the document as MYCHAP8.LRN and clear the typing area.

CHAPTER SUMMARY

In this chapter, you learned how to use WordPerfect's Speller and Thesaurus to help you write more efficiently and accurately. You also learned how to use hyphenation to improve the appearance of justified documents.

Here's a quick technique reference for Chapter 8:

Feature or Action	How to Do It
Speller	**Ctrl+F2** (Speller)
Check spelling for entire document	**Ctrl+F2** (Speller), **3. Document**
Check spelling of a single word	**Ctrl+F2** (Speller), **1. Word**
Look up the spelling of a word	**Ctrl+F2** (Speller), **5. Look Up Word**
Turn hyphenation on or off	**Shift+F8**, **1. Line**, **6. Hyphenation**
Hard hyphen	- (Hyphen)
Hyphen	**Home,-** (Home, hyphen)
Dash	**Home, -, -** (Home, hyphen, hyphen)
Cancel hyphenation for a single word	Position cursor on first letter of word, and then press **Home,/** (Home, forward slash)
Thesaurus	Position cursor on word, press **Alt+F1**, choose **2. Thesaurus**, ← or → (to move between word-choice columns), highlight desired word, and choose **Replace**

A final reminder: Always remember to save your document before you use the Speller or Thesaurus. That way, if anything goes wrong, you can retrieve the original. You should also save the final corrected document.

If you need to break off here, please exit from WordPerfect. If you want to proceed directly to the next chapter, please do so now.

CHAPTER 9: TABLES

If you want to arrange information in a table, you could do so by setting tabs. Setting tabs, however, is a slow and tricky process; you must figure out exactly how the table should look, measure the width of each column, and then set tabs that correspond to each measurement. You could also run into problems if your text does not fit within your tabs. WordPerfect's Table feature allows you to create rows and columns of information without having to set tabs. You can use this feature to present data effectively, create forms such as invoices, and even do calculations in a table.

When you are finished with this chapter, you will be able to:

- Create a table
- Edit and format a table
- Apply simple formulas to numbers in tables

AN OVERVIEW OF THE TABLE FEATURE

Tables consist of horizontal *rows* and vertical *columns*, as shown in Figure 9.1. In WordPerfect, the intersection of a row and a column is a *cell*. Cells are labeled with a letter followed by a number. The letter refers to the column, from left to right, and the number refers to the row, from top to bottom. For example, cell A4 in Figure 9.1 is at the intersection of the first column (A) and the fourth row (4).

Figure 9.1   **Table elements**

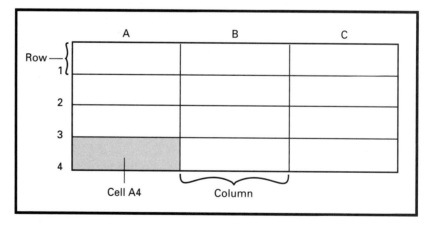

WordPerfect creates a table according to default settings. By default, the "skeleton" of rows and columns, the table's *structure*, is displayed as solid horizontal and vertical lines; these lines print with the table. The outside borders of the table are double lines, and any text you add is aligned flush left in a cell. You can change these and other defaults according to your needs. (Changing these defaults is discussed in "Editing the Table.")

WordPerfect has two modes for working with tables. In the normal editing mode, you can enter, delete, insert, and block text in a cell just as you would in the typing area. In the *Table Edit mode*, you can change the structure of the table but not enter or edit text. You can enhance text (center, underline, apply bold, and so on) in either mode.

MOVING THE CURSOR IN A TABLE IN NORMAL EDITING MODE

The cursor occupies one character position in the normal editing mode and works as it does in the normal typing area, with the following exceptions:

- Press Tab to move one cell to the right. Tabbing at the end of one row moves you to the beginning of the next.

- Press Shift+Tab to move one cell to the left. Shift+tabbing at the beginning of one row moves you to the end of the previous one.

If you are not currently running WordPerfect, please start the program now.

Let's open a new document; then we'll experiment with moving within a table:

1. Retrieve CHAP9A.LRN from your Data Disk.

2. Move to the top of page 3.

3. Look closely at the table (Figure 9.2). It contains columns and rows, intersecting in cells. Observe the solid lines that separate rows and columns. The solid lines print with the table by default but can be changed to another pattern or removed.

4. Move to the cell labeled *POSITION*, the first cell in the table.

5. Tab one cell to the right.

6. Examine the status line. The cursor is in cell B1, the intersection of the second column and the first row.

7. Press **Tab** several times until you reach cell B2.

8. Press **Shift+Tab** to move the cursor to the left, to cell A2.

Figure 9.2   **Sample table (from CHAP9A.LRN)**

```
 File  Edit  View  Layout  Tools  Font  Graphics  Window  Help
       C.     Available Positions

The following is a list of available positions and offices, and the

dates by which they must be filled:

 ┌─────────────────────┬─────────────────────┬─────────────────┐
 │      POSITION       │       OFFICE        │  CLOSING DATE   │
 ├─────────────────────┼─────────────────────┼─────────────────┤
 │Regional Office      │Atlanta Office       │September 6      │
 │Manager              │367 Randwich Rd.     │                 │
 │                     │Atlanta, GA  36301   │                 │
 ├─────────────────────┼─────────────────────┼─────────────────┤
 │Statewide Sales      │Chicago Office       │July 10          │
 │                     │1135 College Ave.    │                 │
 │                     │Chicago, IL  66604   │                 │
 ├─────────────────────┼─────────────────────┼─────────────────┤
 │District Production  │La Jolla Office      │June 30          │
 │Manager              │46 Lindell Blvd.     │                 │
 │                     │La Jolla, CA  93108  │                 │
 └─────────────────────┴─────────────────────┴─────────────────┘

Contact Marlene Marques for more information.

A:\CHAP9A.LRN                              Doc 1 Pg 3 Ln 1" Pos 1"
```

9. Press **Shift+Tab** again to move up one row, to cell C1.

10. Press ↓ to move down one cell, to cell C2.

11. Move to the *R* in *Regional* in cell A2 by pressing **Shift+Tab** twice.

 MOVING THE CURSOR WITHIN A CELL

To move the cursor within a cell in the normal editing mode:

- Press Home, ← to move to the beginning of a line of text.

- Press Home, → to move to the end of a line of text.

- Press Ctrl+Home, ↑ to move to the beginning of text in a cell.

- Press Ctrl+Home, ↓ to move to the last line of text in a cell.

With your cursor in cell A2, follow these steps at your computer:

1. Press **Home**, → to move to the end of the line of text.

2. Press **Home**, ← to move to the beginning of the line of text.

3. Press ↓ to move to the next line of text.

ADDITIONAL CURSOR-MOVEMENT TECHNIQUES

Other techniques allow you to move quickly in one direction in a table:

- Press Ctrl+Home (Go To), Home, ↑ to move to the first cell in a column.

- Press Ctrl+Home (Go To), Home, ↓ to move to the last cell in a column.

- Press Ctrl+Home (Go To), Home, ← to move to the first cell in a row.

- Press Ctrl+Home (Go To), Home, → to move to the last cell in a row.

- Press Ctrl+Home (Go To), Home, Home, ↑ to move to the first cell in the table.

- Press Ctrl+Home (Go To), Home, Home, ↓ to move to the last cell in the table.

INSERTING AND DELETING TEXT IN A CELL

Just as WordPerfect is normally in Insert mode when you're in the typing area, it is also in Insert mode when you're in the normal editing mode. This means that if you want to insert text in your table, simply position your cursor, and type. Keystrokes you would normally use to delete text work the same way. For example, press Del to delete the character positioned at the cursor.

Follow these steps at your computer:

1. Press ↓ to position the cursor in the *Statewide Sales* cell (if necessary).

2. Press **Home**, → to move to the end of the text line after the word *Sales*.

3. Press **Spacebar**, and type **Coordinator**. The text wraps to the next line of the same cell.

4. Press ↓ to move down one cell to *District Production* and position the cursor on *Production* (if necessary).

5. Press **Ctrl+Backspace** to delete the word *Production*. *Manager* now appears on the first line of the cell.

CREATING A TABLE

You can create a table in the typing area, whether you're starting from a blank screen or an existing document, by following these general steps:

- Position the cursor where you want the table to begin.

- Press the Columns/Tables keys, Alt+F7, to open the Columns/ Tables dialog box; then choose 2. Tables and 1. Create. Or, choose Layout, Tables, Create.

- Enter the number of columns that you want the table to contain; the maximum is 32.

- Enter the number of rows that you want the table to contain; the maximum is 32,765.

When you create a table, you are automatically placed in Table Edit mode.

Let's create another table in our document:

1. Move to the blank line directly above *III. PERSONNEL CHANGES* on page 2.

2. Press **Alt+F7** to open the Columns/Tables dialog box (see Figure 9.3).

Figure 9.3   **Columns/Tables dialog box**

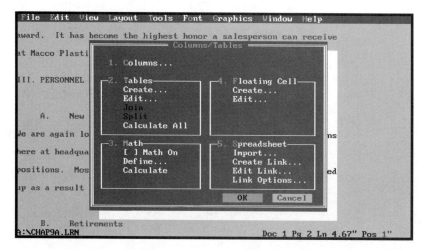

3. Choose **2. Tables**, then choose **1. Create** to open the Create Table dialog box. WordPerfect suggests *3* as the default number of columns.

4. Type **2** to create two columns, and press **Enter**. WordPerfect suggests *1* as the default number of rows.

5. Type **3** to create three rows, and press **Enter**. Compare your screen to Figure 9.4.

Figure 9.4   **Specifying the number of columns and rows in the Create Table dialog box**

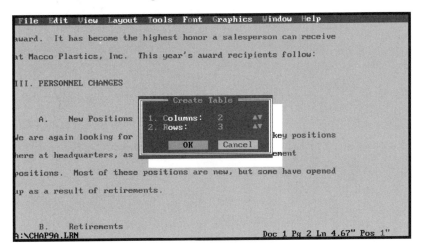

6. Press **Enter** to create the table. The table and the Table Edit menu appear. Compare your screen to the one shown in Figure 9.5.

MOVING THE CURSOR IN TABLE EDIT MODE

In Table Edit mode, the cursor occupies (highlights) an entire cell. To move the cursor in Table Edit mode:

- Press ↑, ↓, ←, or → to move one cell up, down, left, or right, respectively.

- Press Home, ↑ to move to the first cell in a column.

- Press Home, ↓ to move to the last cell in a column.

Figure 9.5   **A newly created table**

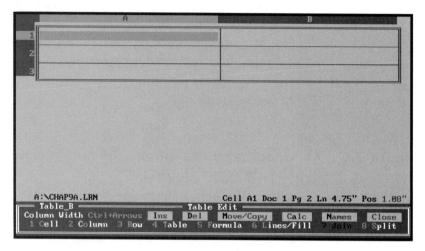

- Press Home, ← to move to the first cell in a row.

- Press Home, → to move to the last cell in a row.

- Press Home, Home, ↑ to move to the first cell in the table.

- Press Home, Home, ↓ to move to the last cell in the table.

- Press Ctrl+Home (Go To), and type a cell location (for example, a2 or A2) to move to a specific location. In specifying a cell, you can type either lowercase or uppercase letter (column) designations.

With the cursor positioned in the table, follow these steps at your computer:

1. Observe that an entire cell is selected. Examine the status line. The selected cell is A1.

2. Press ↓ twice to move down two cells to the last row. Confirm that this is cell A3.

3. Press → to move one cell to the right. Confirm that this is cell B3.

4. Press **Home**, ↑ to move to the first cell in the column, B1.

5. Press **Home**, ↓ to move to the last cell in the column, B3.

6. Press **Ctrl+Home** (Go To). WordPerfect prompts:

   Go To

7. Type **a1** and press **Enter**. The cursor moves to cell A1.

PRACTICE YOUR SKILLS

1. Press **Home**, **Home**, ↓ and observe where the cursor moves.

2. Press **Home**, **Home**, ↑ and observe where the cursor moves.

TYPING TEXT FOR THE TABLE

Before you enter text into the table, you need to leave the Table Edit menu by pressing the Exit key, F7. With your cursor positioned in the correct cell, begin typing.

Follow these steps at your computer:

1. Move to cell A1 (if necessary).

2. Press **F7** to leave the Table Edit menu.

3. Type **RECIPIENT** and tab to the blank cell to the right, B1.

4. Type **LOCATION**, and tab to the first cell of the next row, A2.

5. Type **George Schwartz**, and tab to the next cell.

PRACTICE YOUR SKILLS

1. Complete the table as shown in Figure 9.6.

2. Save the document as MYCHAP9A.LRN, and remain in the typing area.

EDITING THE TABLE

When working with a table, you will often want to insert or delete columns or rows. These structural changes are made using the Table Edit menu. To display that menu in normal editing mode, position the cursor anywhere in the table and press the Columns/Tables keys, Alt+F7.

Figure 9.6   **Table with text**

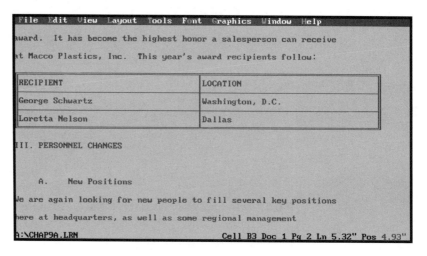

 INSERTING ROWS AND COLUMNS

To insert a row or a column:

- Press Alt+F7, choose 2. Tables, and choose 2. Edit to display the Table Edit menu and thereby enter Table Edit mode.

- Place the cursor in the row or column just past where you want to insert the new row or column.

- Press Ins.

- Choose 1. Column or 2. Row from the Table Edit menu.

- Type the number of rows or columns you need, and press Enter. The new row or column is inserted *before* the row or column containing the cursor.

The new row or column has the same settings, such as row height or column width, as the row or column containing the cursor. However, if the table already extends to the right margin, the last column is split to make room for the new one.

With your cursor positioned inside the table, follow these steps at your computer:

1. Press **Alt+F7** to open the Columns/Tables dialog box.

2. Choose **2. Tables**, and choose **2. Edit** to display the Table Edit menu.

3. Move to the column labeled *LOCATION*.

4. Press **Ins**. The Insert dialog box is displayed (see Figure 9.7). Notice that, by default, 1. Columns is selected, and that the number *1* is displayed next to the 3. How Many? option. The number *1* refers to the number of columns that WordPerfect will insert by default. Notice, too, that 4. Before Cursor Position is selected; by default, new columns are inserted before (to the left of) the column containing the cursor.

Figure 9.7   **Insert (columns and rows) dialog box**

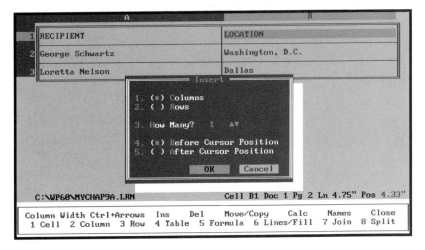

5. Press **Enter** to accept the default and insert one column. Observe that the column was inserted to the left of the column where the cursor was positioned.

6. Press **F7** to leave the Table Edit menu.

7. In cell B3, type **President's Award**. Depending on your setup, the word *Award* may wrap to the next line.

8. In cell B2, again type **President's Award**.

9. In cell B1, type **AWARD**, the column heading.

10. Move to cell A2, the cell that contains the name *George Schwartz*.

11. Display the Table Edit menu (press Alt+F7, choose **2. Tables**, and choose **2. Edit**).

12. Press **Ins** to open the Insert dialog box, and choose **2. Rows**.

13. Choose 3. **How Many?**, type **3** and press **Enter** twice to insert three blank rows. Observe that the rows were inserted above the *George Schwartz* row.

14. Press **F7** to leave the Table Edit menu.

15. Move to cell A3, type **Alice Johnson**, and tab to the next cell.

16. Type **Harvey Mudd Award**, and tab to the next cell.

17. Type **Chicago**, and tab to the next row.

PRACTICE YOUR SKILLS

Enter the following text in the new row: **Leslie Wu**, **Harvey Mudd Award**, **San Francisco**.

DELETING A ROW OR COLUMN

To delete a row or a column:

- Display the Table Edit menu.

- Position the cursor in the column or row you wish to delete, and press Del.

- Choose 1. Columns or 2. Rows from the Table Edit menu.

- Counting downward for rows or to the right for columns (including the row or column containing the cursor), choose 4. How Many, type the number of rows or columns you wish to delete, and press Enter. Any text within the column or row will also be deleted.

Follow these steps at your computer:

1. Move the cursor to cell A2 of the blank row.

2. Display the Table Edit menu.

3. Press **Del** to open the Delete dialog box, and choose **2. Rows**. WordPerfect displays the default:

> 4. How Many? 1

4. Press **Enter** to accept the default and delete the row. Compare your screen to Figure 9.8.

Figure 9.8 **Table after the blank row has been deleted**

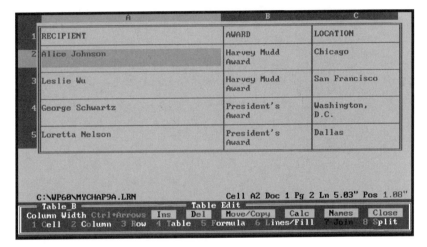

ADDING A ROW OR COLUMN TO THE END OF A TABLE

To add a row or a column at the end of a table:

- Place the cursor in the last row (to add a row) or column (to add a column) of the table.

- Display the Table Edit menu, and press Ins.

- Choose either 1. Columns or 2. Rows.

- Choose 3. How Many, and type the number of rows or columns that you want to add to the table.

- Choose 5. After Cursor Position, and press Enter.

With the Table Edit menu displayed, follow these steps at your computer:

1. Move to the column with the heading *LOCATION*.

2. Press **Ins** to open the Insert dialog box.

3. Choose **3. How Many?**, type **1**, and press **Enter**. We'll add one column to our table.

4. Choose **5. After Cursor Position** to tell the program to add the column to the right of the column containing the cursor (the default setting would insert a column to the left).

5. Press **Enter**. The table now has four columns; one blank column was added to the right side of the table. Observe the text in the third column. The column width was split in half to accommodate the fourth column, as shown in Figure 9.9.

Figure 9.9   **Column added to table**

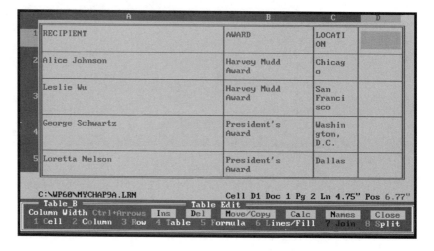

PRACTICE YOUR SKILLS

Delete the column that was just inserted. Notice that the third column does not expand to its original width; you will widen it in the next activity.

FORMATTING CELLS AND COLUMNS

WordPerfect provides you with many ways of formatting cells and columns in a table. If, for example, a column heading is too wide for the column, you can widen the column. You can also center the heading, change its type size and style, and so on. In Table Edit mode, you can both modify the structure of a table and enhance the text it contains. Remember, however, that you cannot enter or edit text in this mode.

- To apply a particular format (such as centering, justifying, or underlining text), to a single cell, position the cursor within the cell, and choose 1 Cell from the Table Edit menu.

- To format a group of cells, first block the cells using Alt+F4, and then choose 1 Cell.

- To format a column, position the cursor in one cell of that column, and choose 2 Column.

- To format a row, position the cursor in that row, and choose 3 Row.

- To format the entire table, choose 4 Table.

Each of the above actions will open the Format dialog box that pertains to that action. For example, choosing 1 Cell opens the Cell Format dialog box, choosing 2 Column opens the Column Format dialog box, and so on.

 COLUMN WIDTH

When you create a table, WordPerfect bases the default column widths on the current margins and the number of columns selected. Column widths can be changed in two ways, by menu and by special keystrokes. When you *increase* the width of a column, WordPerfect widens the entire table until the right margin is reached, then decreases the widest column to the right of the increased column. When you *decrease* the width of a column, the table width decreases from the right.

Changing Column Widths with the Table Edit Menu
To change the column width by using the Table Edit menu:

- Position the cursor within the column that you want to change.

- Display the Table Edit menu.

- Choose 2 Column.

- Choose 8. Width.

- Enter the desired measurement, and press Enter.

With the Table Edit menu displayed, follow these steps at your computer:

1. Move to the column labeled *RECIPIENT*.

2. Choose **2 Column** to display the Column Format dialog box (see Figure 9.10).

Figure 9.10   **Column Format dialog box**

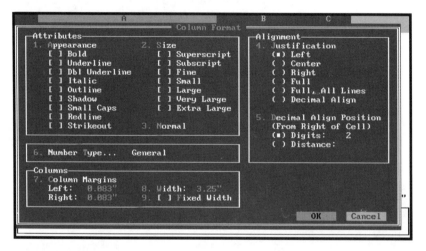

3. Choose **8. Width**. WordPerfect displays the current setting, 3.25".

4. Type **2.25**, and press **Enter** twice. The column width is decreased by an inch. The size of the table decreases accordingly.

Changing Column Widths with Key Combinations

You can change the column width one character at a time by using key combinations. This is useful if you want to refine your table structure but don't know what fraction of an inch to use.

• Press Ctrl+→ to increase the column width by one character.

• Press Ctrl+← to decrease the column width by one character.

With the Table Edit menu displayed, follow these steps at your computer:

1. Move to any cell in the column labeled *AWARD*.

2. Press **Ctrl+→**. The column increases by one character.

3. Continue pressing **Ctrl+→** until all text fits on one line within each cell of the column.

PRACTICE YOUR SKILLS

1. Move to the cell labeled *LOCATION*.

2. Increase the cell width until all text fits on one line.

COLUMN AND CELL FORMATTING

In normal editing mode, you can enhance text in columns and cells in your table just as you would regular text. You can also do this in Table Edit mode, through the Table Edit menu. To format table text in Table Edit mode, you must use the formats found in the Table Edit menu; you cannot, for example, use Shift+F6 to center text while you're in a table.

Centering Cell Text

To center text within a cell:

• Position your cursor in the cell containing the text.

• Choose 1 Cell.

• Choose 4. Justification.

• Choose 2. Center.

With the Table Edit menu displayed, follow these steps at your computer:

1. Move to cell A1 by pressing **Ctrl+Home**, typing **a1**, and pressing **Enter**.

2. Choose **1 Cell** to display the Cell Format dialog box (see Figure 9.11).

3. Choose **4. Justification**, choose **2. Center**, and press **Enter**. The heading *RECIPIENT* is centered.

Centering Text in More Than One Cell

To center text in several adjacent cells, follow these steps:

• Position your cursor in a cell containing text you want to center.

Figure 9.11   **Cell Format dialog box**

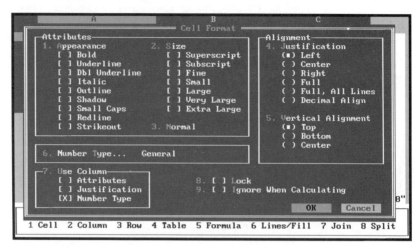

- Use the Block feature (Alt+F4 or F12) to highlight the text.
- Choose 1 Cell.
- Choose 4. Justification.
- Choose 2. Center.

With the Table Edit menu displayed, follow these steps at your computer:

1. Press → to move to cell B1.
2. Highlight cells B1 and C1 by turning on the Block feature and pressing → . Both cells are now selected.
3. Choose **1 Cell** to display the Cell Format dialog box.
4. Choose **4. Justification**, choose **2. Center**, and press **Enter** to center the blocked headings. Now all three column headings appear centered.

Justifying Text within a Column

To format text in a column, position the cursor in *any* cell in that column before selecting a formatting command. To justify text within a column using the Table Edit menu, follow these steps:

- Position the cursor in any cell of the column you wish to justify.
- Choose 2 Column.
- Choose 4. Justification.

- Choose one of the justification options.

With the Table Edit menu displayed, follow these steps at your computer:

1. Move your cursor anywhere within the column labeled *LOCATION*.

2. Choose **2 Column** to display the Column Format dialog box.

3. Choose **4. Justification**, choose **3. Right**, and press **Enter**. The text in the entire column is right-aligned, except for the heading *LOCATION*, which retains its earlier, centered, formatting.

To override any previous formatting for a cell, position the cursor within the cell, choose 1 Cell, and select new formatting. Note: Formatting a single *cell* overrides any previous *column* formatting that was applied to that cell. For example, you could center all the text in a column, and then format the text within one cell of that column to be left-aligned, which would override the earlier column formatting.

Enhancing Cell Text

You can apply formatting such as underline and bold to text in a cell by following these general steps:

- Position your cursor in the cell containing the text you wish to format.
- Choose 1 Cell.
- Choose 1. Appearance.
- Choose an Appearance option, such as 1. Bold or 4. Italic.

With the Table Edit menu displayed, follow these steps at your computer:

1. Move your cursor to the column heading *RECIPIENT*.

2. Choose **1 Cell** to display the Cell Format dialog box, and choose **1. Appearance**.

3. Choose **2. Underline** and press **Enter**. The heading is underlined.

Note: In Table Edit mode, the underlining applied to the cell's text will not be visible until you move the cursor to another cell. However, the Pos measurement shows that underlining has been activated. If your computer has graphics capability, you can switch to Graphics mode to view formatting changes.

PRACTICE YOUR SKILLS

1. Underline the remaining column headings.

2. Exit Table Edit mode, and compare your screen to Figure 9.12.

Figure 9.12 **Enhanced and justified cell text**

```
 File  Edit  View  Layout  Tools  Font  Graphics  Window  Help
award.  It has become the highest honor a salesperson can receive
at Macco Plastics, Inc.  This year's award recipients follow:

      ┌──────────────────┬──────────────────┬──────────────────┐
      │     RECIPIENT    │      AWARD       │     LOCATION     │
      ├──────────────────┼──────────────────┼──────────────────┤
      │ Alice Johnson    │ Harvey Mudd Award │          Chicago │
      ├──────────────────┼──────────────────┼──────────────────┤
      │ Leslie Wu        │ Harvey Mudd Award │    San Francisco │
      ├──────────────────┼──────────────────┼──────────────────┤
      │ George Schwartz  │ President's Award │ Washington, D.C. │
      ├──────────────────┼──────────────────┼──────────────────┤
      │ Loretta Nelson   │ President's Award │           Dallas │
      └──────────────────┴──────────────────┴──────────────────┘

III.  PERSONNEL CHANGES


   A.    New Positions

C:\WP60\MYCHAP9A.LRN            Cell C1  Doc 1  Pg 2  Ln 4.75"  Pos 5.68"
```

LINES

The option 6 Lines/Fill in the Table Edit menu enables you to change the appearance of cell borders in a table. You can use the Block feature to block the cells whose borders you wish to change in the same way; otherwise, only the cell containing the cursor will be affected.

The Table Lines dialog box displays the following choices to control which cell borders are changed.

Left   Left border of the cell or blocked cells

Right   Right border of the cell or blocked cells

Top   Top border of the cell or blocked cells

Bottom   Bottom border of the cell or blocked cells

Inside   Inside borders of the cell or blocked cells

Outside	Outside borders of the cell or blocked cells
Line color	Border color of the cell or blocked cells
Fill	The percentage of shading (100% = black) within the cell or blocked cells

Inside lines separate cells from one another. *Outside* lines separate the block from the rest of the table. To see what the borders look like before you print, leave the Table Edit menu, and use Print Preview.

In addition, two choices provide you with control over the border of the entire table:

- Default Line allows you to choose the style and color of the line used in the table border.

- Border/Fill allows you to choose the style of border and the degree of fill (shading) within the table border.

Removing the Table Lines

To remove the inside lines from a group of cells in a table:

- Position your cursor at one corner of the range of cells you wish to define.

- Highlight the range of cells whose lines you wish to remove.

- Choose 6 Lines/Fill.

- Choose 7 Inside.

- Make sure [None] is selected, choose 1. Select, and press Enter.

Follow these steps at your computer:

1. Display the Table Edit menu; then move your cursor to cell A1.

2. Select the text from cell A1 through cell C5 (all the cells in the table).

3. Choose **6 Lines/Fill**. The Table Lines dialog box is displayed (see Figure 9.13).

4. Under Current Cell or Block, choose **7. Inside** to affect the lines inside the table. The Line Styles dialog box is displayed (see Figure 9.14).

5. Highlight [None], if necessary, choose **1. Select**, and press **Enter**. All the lines on the inside of the table are removed.

Figure 9.13   **Table Lines dialog box**

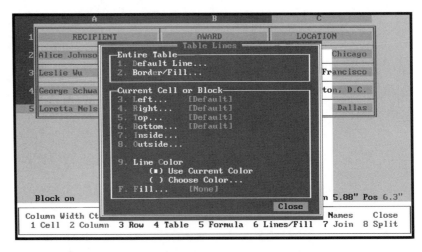

Figure 9.14   **Line Styles dialog box**

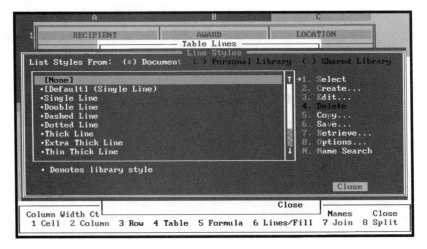

 CENTERING THE TABLE BETWEEN THE LEFT AND RIGHT MARGINS

Selecting 4 Table in the Table Edit menu enables you to (among other things) position a table in relation to the right and left margins. The default justification setting, *Full*, causes the table to fill the space between the left and right margins. *Left* aligns the table with

the left margin; *Right* aligns the table with the right margin; and *Center* centers the table between the left and right margins.

To center the table on the page:

- Choose 4 Table.

- Choose P. Position.

- Choose Center.

- Press Enter to return to the Table Edit menu.

With the Table Edit menu displayed, follow these steps at your computer:

1. Return to the typing area.

2. Print Preview the document. Notice that the table is now flush with the left margin.

3. Return to the typing area.

4. Display the Table Edit menu.

5. Choose **4 Table** to display the Table Format dialog box.

6. Choose **P. Position** to display the Position options (see Figure 9.15).

Figure 9.15   **Position options displayed in Table Format dialog box**

7. Choose **Center** to center the table between the margins.

8. Press **Enter** to return to the Table Edit menu, and press **F7** to exit Table Edit mode. The table is now centered between the left and right margins. Compare your screen to Figure 9.16.

Figure 9.16 **Completed table**

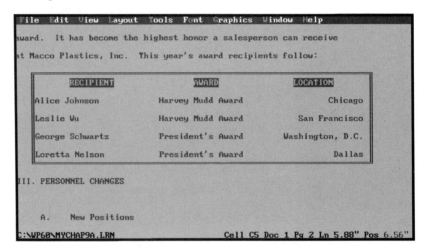

9. Save the document (under the same name), and clear the typing area.

MATH IN TABLES

Until now, you've been entering only text into your table. WordPerfect is especially powerful if you work with numbers. The Math feature enables you to enter numbers, apply formulas to your data, and do simple calculations, such as subtotals. All math operations are done through the Table Edit menu.

ENTERING NUMBERS IN A TABLE

To enter numbers into your table, position the cursor on the cell in which you wish to enter a number, and type. Follow these steps at your computer:

1. Retrieve CHAP9B.LRN.

2. Scroll to the bottom of page 1, using ↓ to display a second table. Notice that the table is not formatted.

3. Move to the cell in which the *ADVANCES* column and the *Los Angeles* row intersect (cell B5).

4. Type **400.00**, and tab to cell C5.

5. Type **700.00**, and tab three times to cell B6. Compare your screen to the one shown in Figure 9.17.

Figure 9.17   **Table with numbers**

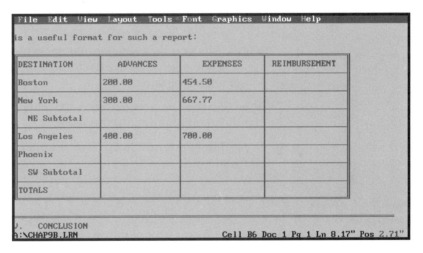

SETTING A COLUMN WITH DECIMAL ALIGNMENT AND INSERTING NUMBERS

The numbers you've entered appear to be aligned at the decimal point, but only because they contain the same number of digits. If you were to enter the amount 4,000.00 in one of the cells, the decimal point would not be aligned with the decimal points of the other numbers.

Let's format numbers so that their decimal points are aligned:

1. With your cursor in the column labeled *ADVANCES,* display the Table Edit menu.

2. Choose **2 Column** to display the Column Format dialog box.

3. Choose **4. Justification**, and choose **6. Decimal Align**. Then press **Enter**. The numbers for the entire column are aligned at their decimal points, and are right-aligned within the column.

4. Move the cursor to the column labeled *EXPENSES,* and repeat Steps 2 and 3 to align the decimals in the column. (The *REIMBURSEMENT* column, though empty, is already set for decimal alignment.)

5. Tab to cell B6.

6. Leave the Table Edit menu. You must leave the menu and return to normal editing mode before you can type text or numbers into a table. Notice the status line message

    ```
    align char = .
    ```

    which tells you that when you enter a number with a decimal point, it will align with the decimal point of the other numbers in the same column.

7. Type **350.00**. The number automatically aligns at the decimal point as you enter it into the table.

8. Press **Tab** and type **396.60**. This number, too, is aligned at its decimal point.

 FORMULAS

A formula performs an operation (such as addition) on numbers in cells you specify, and places the results of the operation in the cell where you put the formula. For example, placing the formula *A1+B1* in cell C1 adds any number in cell A1 to any number in cell B1 and displays the result in cell C1.

Entering a Formula

To enter a formula in a table:

*   Position your cursor in the cell where you wish to enter the formula.

*   In the Table Edit menu, choose 5 Formula.

*   Type the formula. For example, entering *a1+a2* (or *A1+A2*) in cell A3 calculates the sum of any numbers in cells A1 and A2 and displays the results in A3.

*   Press Enter.

Calculating Subtotals

Suppose that you need to add the Boston and New York figures to obtain subtotals for the northeast region.

Let's use a formula to calculate the subtotal for the northeast region:

1. Move your cursor to cell B4, the first NE Subtotal cell.

2. Display the Table Edit menu.

3. Choose **5 Formula**. The Table Formula dialog box is displayed.

4. Type **b2+b3** (case is not significant). Compare your screen to Figure 9.18.

Figure 9.18   **Entering a formula in a table**

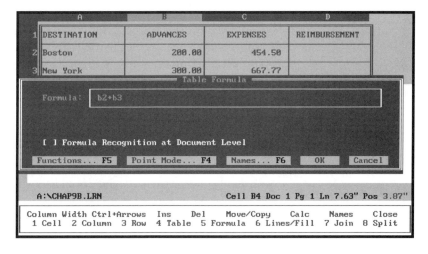

5. Press **Enter** twice. The subtotal, *500.00*, for Boston and New York is calculated and appears in cell B4. The cell formula

    =B2+B3

is displayed in the status line.

PRACTICE YOUR SKILLS

Find the remaining NE Subtotals and all the SW Subtotals in the rest of the table.

Now, let's create a formula that uses subtraction to calculate the value for the first blank cell in the *REIMBURSEMENT* column:

1. Move your cursor to cell D2, the first blank cell in the *REIM-BURSEMENT* column.

2. Choose **5 Formula** to open the Table Formula dialog box.

3. Type **c2-b2** and press **Enter** twice. The result of the calculation appears in cell D2. The cell formula

   =C2-B2

   is displayed in the status line.

Copying a Formula

To repeat a formula already used in one cell in another cell, you could retype the formula. But to save time and avoid the possibility of typing errors, you can copy a formula from one cell to another. This can be useful if a subtotal, for example, must be calculated for many columns.

To copy a formula:

- Position the cursor in the cell with the formula you wish to copy.

- Choose Move/Copy from the Table Edit menu.

- Choose Copy.

- Specify whether to copy Down or to the Right, and specify the number of times the formula should be copied. For example, if you choose *Down* and enter *3*, the formula is copied down to the next three cells.

With your cursor positioned in cell D2 and the Table Edit menu displayed, follow these steps at your computer:

1. Choose **Move/Copy** (type **m**) to open the Move dialog box, and choose **Copy** (type **p**) to open the Copy Cell dialog box (see Figure 9.19).

Figure 9.19   **Copy Cell dialog box**

```
          A              B              C              D
1 DESTINATION      ADVANCES       EXPENSES       REIMBURSEMENT

2 Boston             200.00         454.50            254.50

3 New York           300.00         667.77
                              ═══ Copy Cell ═══
4   NE Subtotal    ┌─────────────────────────────┐
                   │  1. (■) To Cell             │
5 Los Angeles  1.  │  2. ( ) Down                │
               2.  │  3. ( ) Right               │
6 Phoenix      3.  │                             │
               4.  │  4. How Many?  1            │
7   SW Subtotal    │                             │
               M   │      ┌────┐  ┌────────┐  1  │
8 TOTALS           │      │ OK │  │ Cancel │     │
                   └─────────────────────────────┘

  =C2-B2                        Cell D2 Doc 1 Pg 1 Ln 7.1" Pos 6.82"
```

```
Column Width Ctrl+Arrows   Ins     Del     Move/Copy    Calc     Names    Close
1 Cell   2 Column  3 Row   4 Table  5 Formula  6 Lines/Fill  7 Join  8 Split
```

2. Choose **2. Down** to copy the formula to the cells below it, and type **5** to copy the formula to five cells. Then press **Enter** twice. The formula is copied down the column (down five rows), and the reimbursements are calculated. Cell references within the formula are relative; they automatically adjust to the row into which they are copied. For example, if you were to copy the formula *A1+A2* from cell A3 to cell B3, WordPerfect's Math feature would automatically adjust the formula in cell B3 to read *B1+B2*.

CALCULATING TOTALS

WordPerfect's Math feature provides you with the following mathematical operators:

+	Addition
–	Subtraction
*	Multiplication
/	Division

With the Table Edit menu displayed, let's calculate the totals in our table:

1. Move your cursor to cell B8.

2. Choose **5 Formula** to open the Table Formula dialog box.

3. Type **b4+b7** and press **Enter** twice. The total, *1250.00,* is displayed in cell B8.

PRACTICE YOUR SKILLS

1. Find the totals of the remaining two columns. (Copy the formula.) Leave Table Edit mode, and compare your screen to the one shown in Figure 9.20. At this point, you may wish to print your document. Figure 9.21 shows how the printout should look.

2. Close the Table Edit menu, leave the document and save it as MYCHAP9B.LRN.

Figure 9.20   **Table with calculated totals**

File Edit View Layout Tools Font Graphics Window Help

is a useful format for such a report:

DESTINATION	ADVANCES	EXPENSES	REIMBURSEMENT
Boston	200.00	454.50	254.50
New York	300.00	667.77	367.77
NE Subtotal	500.00	1,122.27	622.27
Los Angeles	400.00	700.00	300.00
Phoenix	350.00	396.60	46.60
SW Subtotal	750.00	1,096.60	346.60
TOTALS	1,250.00	2,218.87	968.87

J.   CONCLUSION

=D4+D7   Cell D8 Doc 1 Pg 1 Ln 8.7" Pos 7.42"

Figure 9.21   **The completed document MYCHAP9B.LRN**

C. Available Positions

The following is a list of available positions and offices, and the dates by which they must be filled:

POSITION	OFFICE	CLOSING DATE
Regional Office Manager	Atlanta Office 367 Randwich Rd. Atlanta, GA 36301	September 6
Statewide Sales Coordinator	Chicago Office 1135 College Ave. Chicago, IL 66604	July 10
District Manager	La Jolla Office 46 Lindell Blvd. La Jolla, CA 93108	June 30

Contact Marlene Marques for more information.

IV. NEW EXPENSE REPORT FORMATS

A short note on procedures. Due to the large increase in travel by Macco employees, we are requesting that you and your staff submit a travel expense report on a quarterly basis. It should detail where, when, how much, and what advances were made. The following is a useful format for such a report:

DESTINATION	ADVANCES	EXPENSES	REIMBURSEMENT
Boston	200.00	454.50	254.50
New York	300.00	667.77	367.77
NE Subtotal	500.00	1,122.27	622.27
Los Angeles	400.00	700.00	300.00
Phoenix	350.00	396.60	46.60
SW Subtotal	750.00	1,096.60	346.60
TOTALS	1,250.00	2,218.87	968.87

Figure 9.21   The completed document MYCHAP9B.LRN (Continued)

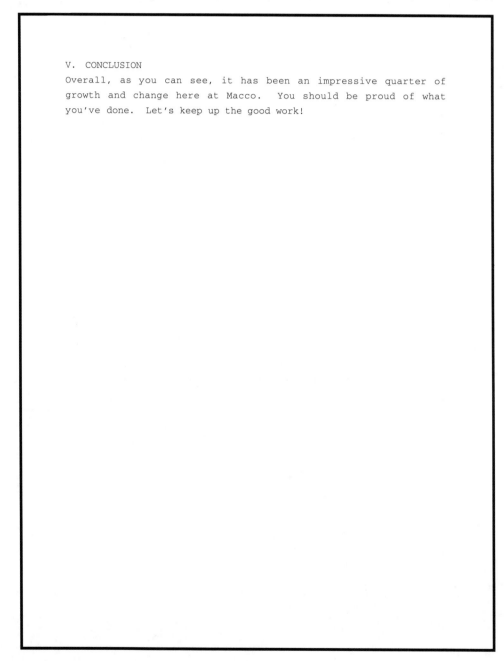

```
V.  CONCLUSION
Overall,  as  you  can  see,  it  has  been  an  impressive  quarter  of
growth  and  change  here  at  Macco.   You  should  be  proud  of  what
you've  done.   Let's  keep  up  the  good  work!
```

PRACTICE YOUR SKILLS

In this chapter, you have learned how to create and edit tables. The following activity gives you the opportunity to practice these techniques while producing the document shown in Figure 9.22 from the original document, PRAC9.LRN.

Follow these steps at your computer:

1. Clear the typing area, and retrieve the file PRAC9.LRN.

2. Move your cursor to the table at the bottom of page 1, and type the following information (in bold) into the table:

	Column A	Column B	Column C
Row 3	**Trader Tom's**	**2,300**	**1.49**
Row 4	**Aunt Emily's Market**	**4,900**	**1.29**
Row 5	**Hamlet Farms**	**6,500**	**1.09**

3. Delete the information for Price Farms Co.

4. Center the column headings *Vendors and Brokers*, *Boxes Sold*, and *Profit-Each*.

5. Change the column width for the *Boxes Sold* column to 1.43". Change the column width for *Profit-Each* to 1.63".

6. Decimal-align the *Boxes Sold* and *Profit-Each* columns.

7. Move to the row containing *Totals* and find the subtotal for *Boxes Sold*.

8. Save the document as MYPRAC9.LRN.

9. Print the document, and compare it to the one shown in Figure 9.22.

If you have finished the preceding activity and would like to try another one that requires similar skills but provides less guidance, follow the steps below, editing the file OPT9.LRN to match the document shown in Figure 9.23.

1. Retrieve the file OPT9.LRN.

2. Add a column to the end of the table.

3. Increase the width of the last column (the column you added in Step 2) to 1.61".

Figure 9.22   **The completed document MYPRAC9.LRN**

MOOSIE'S GARDEN PATCH

Organic and Pure

Product Line Announcement

Introduction

Moosie's Garden Patch is pleased to announce the unveiling of a new fruit line in the Garden Patch series: the Fruit Patch. The Fruit Patch product line was developed through the cooperation and dedication of Dr.'s Eugene Alfa and Vera Betta and their staffs after two years of intense work. The FDA recently approved the food and it will be released for public sale in three weeks.

The Fruit Patch includes a variety of organically grown fruit: the berries (cherries, strawberries, raspberries, blackberries, and blueberries), apricots, peaches, grapes, and plums.

Projected Quarterly Sales

Our finance department has been hard at work, determining sales projections for the next quarter. Those results are shown below in the table.

Projected Quarterly Sales Table

Vendors and Brokers	Boxes Sold	Profit-Each
Trader Tom's	2,300	1.49
Aunt Emily's Market	4,900	1.29
Hamlet Farms	6,500	1.09
B & J's	10,000	.79
Hout, Black, & Wallace Inc	11,500	.79
Totals	35,200.00	

Figure 9.23   **The completed document MYOPT9.LRN**

MOOSIE'S GARDEN PATCH

Organic and Pure

Product Line Announcement

<u>Introduction</u>

Moosie's Garden Patch is pleased to announce the unveiling of a new fruit line in the Garden Patch series: the Fruit Patch. The Fruit Patch product line was developed through the cooperation and dedication of Dr.'s Eugenie Alfa and Vera Betta and their staffs after two years of intense work. The FDA recently approved the food and it will be released for public sale in three weeks.

The Fruit Patch includes a variety of organically grown fruit: the berries (cherries, strawberries, raspberries, blackberries, and blueberries), apricots, peaches, grapes, and plums.

<u>Projected Quarterly Sales</u>

Our finance department has been hard at work, determining sales projections for the next quarter. Those results are shown below in the table.

Projected Quarterly Sales Table

Vendors and Brokers	Boxes Sold	Profit-Each	Total Profit
Trader Tom's	2,300	1.49	3,427.00
Aunt Emily's Market	4,900	1.29	6,321.00
Hamlet Farms	6,500	1.09	7,085.00
B & J's	10,000	.79	7,900.00
Hout, Black, & Wallace Inc	11,500	.79	9,085.00
Totals	35,200.00		33,818.00

4. Increase the width of the third column until *Profit-Each* fits on one line.

5. Move to the first cell in the last column, and type the heading **Total Profit**. Remember to leave Table Edit mode before typing.

6. Find the total profit for *Trader Tom's* by entering a formula. Use the operator *** in your formula to calculate the grand total.

7. Copy the formula down the column to find the total profit for the remaining vendors.

8. Find the subtotal of the *Total Profit* column.

9. Center the table on the page.

10. Save the document as MYOPT9.LRN

11. Print the document, and compare it to the one shown in Figure 9.23.

CHAPTER SUMMARY

In this chapter, you've learned much useful information about creating and editing a table. You've explored how to edit and enhance text in a table and to refine a table's structure. You've also learned to enter numbers and perform math calculations in a table.

Here's a quick technique reference for Chapter 9:

Feature or Action	How to Do It
Normal Editing Mode	
Move one cell to the right	**Tab**
Move one cell to the left	**Shift+Tab**
Move to the beginning of a line	**Home,** ←
Move to the end of a line	**Home,** →
Move to the beginning of text in a cell	**Ctrl+Home,** ↑
Move to the last line of text in a cell	**Ctrl+Home,** ↓

Feature or Action	How to Do It
Move to the first cell in a column	**Ctrl+Home, Home,** ↑
Move to the last cell in a column	**Ctrl+Home, Home,** ↓
Move to the first cell in a row	**Ctrl+Home, Home,** ←
Move to the last cell in a row	**Ctrl+Home, Home,** →
Move to the first cell in the table	**Ctrl+Home, Home, Home,** ↑
Move to the last cell in the table	**Ctrl+Home, Home, Home,** ↓
Table Edit Mode	
Move one cell up, down, left, or right	↑, ↓, ←, or →
Move to the first cell in a column	**Home,** ↑
Move to the last cell in a column	**Home,** ↓
Move to the first cell in a row	**Home,** ←
Move to the last cell in a row	**Home,** →
Move to the first cell in the table	**Home, Home,** ↑
Move to the last cell in the table	**Home, Home,** ↓
Move to a specific cell	**Ctrl+Home** (Go To), *cell identifier (for example, A2)*
Create a table	**Alt+F7** (Columns/Tables), **2. Tables, 1. Create,** *number of columns,* **Enter,** *number of rows,* **Enter** twice
Insert rows and columns (in Table Edit mode)	**Ins, 1. Columns** or **2. Rows,** *number of rows or columns to be inserted,* **Enter**

Feature or Action	How to Do It
Delete rows and columns (in Table Edit mode)	**Del**, **1. Columns** or **2. Rows**, *number of rows or columns to be deleted*, **Enter**
Insert rows or columns at the end of a table	**Ins**, **1. Columns** or **2. Rows**, choose **3. How Many?**, *total number of rows or columns that you want in the table*, choose **5. After Cursor Position, Enter**
Change column width	**2 Column**, **8. Width**, *measurement in inches*; **Ctrl+→** (increase a character at a time); **Ctrl+←** (decrease a character at a time)
Center text in a cell	**1 Cell, 4. Justification, 2. Center**
Right-align text in a cell	**1 Cell, 4. Justification, 3. Right**
Underline cell text	**1 Cell, 1. Appearance, 2. Underline**
Remove inside table lines	**6 Lines/Fill, 7. Inside**, highlight [None], choose **1. Select, Enter**
Center the table between the left and right margins	**4 Table, P. Position, Center**
Enter a math formula	**5 Formula**, *formula*, **Enter**
Copy a formula	**Move/Copy, Copy, Down** or **Right**, *number of cells*, **Enter** twice
Decimal-align numbers	**2 Column, 4. Justification, 6. Decimal Align**

In the next chapter, you'll learn how to use WordPerfect's Merge feature to make mailing labels and personalized form letters.

If you need to break off here, please exit from WordPerfect. If you want to proceed directly to the next chapter, please do so now.

CHAPTER 10: MERGING DOCUMENTS

In word processing, *merging* or *mail-merge* is the process of transferring selected information from one document to another document. For example, you can write a form letter and instantly merge it with your mailing list to produce a customized letter for everyone on the mailing list. Other common mail-merge documents include mailing labels and interoffice memos.

Before using WordPerfect's Merge feature, you should be familiar with two important terms. The *form file* is the document containing all the information that remains the same. In the case of a form letter, the form file contains the content of the letter, without the names and addresses that vary from letter to letter. The *data file* contains the variable information that is placed selectively in the form file. In a form letter, the data file is the mailing list.

To instruct WordPerfect how to merge files, you must place *merge codes* in the form and data files. In the form file, merge codes mark the places where the variable information from the data file is to be inserted; think of the merge code as the *X* in *Dear X*. In the data file, merge codes show WordPerfect how your information is organized so that it can pull in the exact kind and amount of information (Dear *Mr. Rodriguez,* for example).

In this chapter, first you'll learn how to merge documents to create the form letter shown in Figure 10.1. Later in the chapter, you'll learn how to create mailing labels. When you are finished with this chapter, you will be able to:

- Create a form file
- Create a data file
- Merge form and data files
- Merge from the keyboard
- Create mailing labels

Figure 10.1   Completed merge document

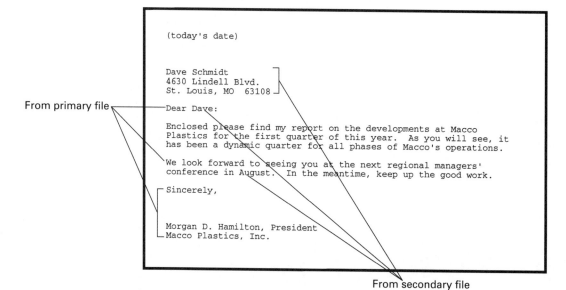

```
(today's date)


Dave Schmidt
4630 Lindell Blvd.
St. Louis, MO  63108

Dear Dave:

Enclosed please find my report on the developments at Macco
Plastics for the first quarter of this year.  As you will see, it
has been a dynamic quarter for all phases of Macco's operations.

We look forward to seeing you at the next regional managers'
conference in August.  In the meantime, keep up the good work.

Sincerely,


Morgan D. Hamilton, President
Macco Plastics, Inc.
```

From primary file

From secondary file

CREATING A FORM FILE AND ENTERING MERGE CODES

To merge files, begin by creating a form file containing the standard, non-varying text you want to include in each letter. Include special merge codes to identify where variable text—such as name and address, which vary from letter to letter—will be inserted from the data file. When the form and data files are merged, one letter is produced for each set of data in the data file.

The merge code FIELD marks the place in the form file where variable information from the data file is inserted. *Fields* are numbered data items from the list of names and addresses in the data file. For example, Field 1 may contain the first name, Field 2 the last name, and so on, as shown in Figure 10.2. To insert the same first name more than once in the form file—for example, in the address and the salutation—simply repeat the Field 1 code.

In this section you will create a form file containing several FIELD codes. In the next section, you will create the data file—a mailing list—organized according to the field numbers you placed in the form file. For example, in the form file you will put FIELD(2) where you expect to insert the recipient's last name. Later, in the data file, you'll need to enter the last name as the second item in each address.

In your own work, you will often create a form file from an existing data file, such as a mailing list. In such cases, you must base FIELD codes in the form file on the field organization of the data file. For example, you'll look at the data file to see where the last name appears in each address; if it is the second field, insert the FIELD(2) code in the form file wherever you want the recipient's last name to appear.

What if some addresses on your mailing list do not have an office designation? You don't want WordPerfect to leave a blank line in your letter when this occurs. To avoid spaces or blank lines in the merged document, type a question mark (*?*) after the field number in any field that might be empty for some letters, such as title or company name. Notice in Figure 10.2 that a line is left in the form file for an office designation, FIELD(3), and that this field is defined using a question mark. When the form and data files are merged, WordPerfect ignores fields without corresponding information in the data file. Merging blank fields that have not used the question mark after the field number produces spaces or blank lines in the final merged document. You will learn how to use the question mark in the upcoming exercise.

Figure 10.2   **Structure of the form file**

> **First Name Last Name**
> **Office Designation**
> **Street Address**
> **City, State Zip Code**
>
> Dear **First Name**:
>
> Enclosed please find my report on developments at Macco Plastics for the first quarter of this year. As you will see, it has been a dynamic quarter for all phases of Macco's operations.
>
> We look forward to seeing you at the next regional managers' conference in **Month**. In the meantime, keep up the good work.
>
> Sincerely,
>
> Morgan D. Hamilton, President
> Macco Plastics Inc.

> **FIELD(1) = First Name**
>
> **FIELD(2) = Last Name**
>
> **FIELD(3?) = Office Designation**
>
> **FIELD(4) = Street Address**
>
> **FIELD(5) = City**
>
> **FIELD(6) = State**
>
> **FIELD(7) = Zip Code**
>
> **FIELD(8) = Month**

Let's add merge codes to a form file:

1. Open or retrieve the document PRIMLT.LRN from your Data Disk. Position the cursor at the top of the document if it is not already there.

2. Press the Merge Codes keys, **Shift+F9** (or choose **Tools, Merge, Define**). The Merge Codes dialog box is displayed (see Figure 10.3).

3. Choose **1. Form**. The Merge Codes (Form File) dialog box is displayed (see Figure 10.4).

4. Choose **1. Field**. In the Parameter Entry dialog box (see Figure 10.5), you are prompted to assign a number to the first field in your form file.

Figure 10.3　　.**Merge Codes dialog box**

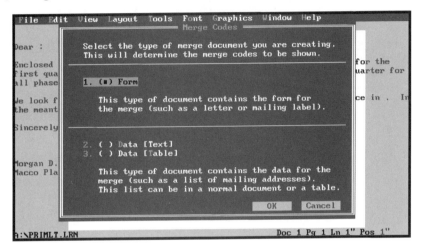

Figure 10.4　　**Merge Codes (Form File) dialog box**

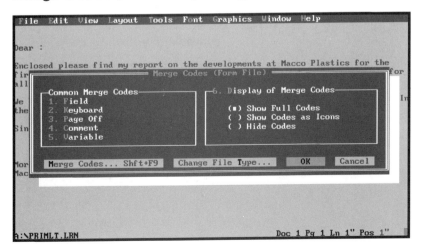

Figure 10.5   **Parameter Entry dialog box**

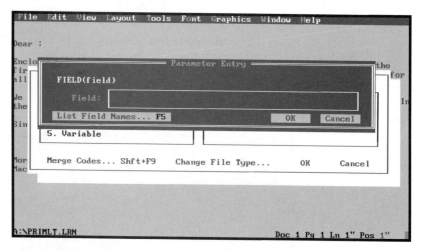

5. Type **1** and press **Enter**. The merge code FIELD(1) is inserted in the document.

6. Press the **Spacebar** to insert a space.

7. Press **Shift+F9** to insert another field. This time, the Merge Codes (Form File) dialog box opens directly.

8. Choose **1. Field**.

9. Type **2** and press **Enter**. FIELD(2) (which will contain the recipient's last name) is inserted in the document.

10. Press **Enter** to begin a new line, and then press **Shift+F9** to insert the third field, and choose **1. Field**.

11. Type **3?** and press **Enter**. This represents the information for Field 3 (office designation), which may be blank. The *?* instructs WordPerfect to determine whether the field is blank in the data file. If it is blank, this line is skipped in the form file.

12. Press **Enter** to begin a new line.

PRACTICE YOUR SKILLS

1. Insert the remaining field codes, as shown in Figure 10.6, to complete the form file. Don't forget the FIELD(8) code in the second paragraph.

2. Exit the document, renaming it MYPRIMLT.LRN, and remain in WordPerfect.

Figure 10.6

Form file with inserted merge codes

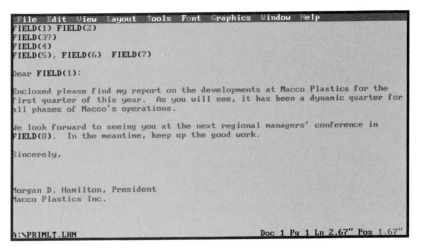

CREATING A DATA FILE

The data file contains *records*, each of which consists of fields. A record describes in detail a person or thing—for example, a person on a mailing list. Each field of a record contains information about a different facet of the person or thing. The number of records and sizes of fields are limited only by disk space, and each record can contain as much information—as many fields—as you need. Records are separated by an ENDRECORD code and a Hard Page code, [HPg].

To avoid confusion, all records in the data file must have the same field structure. For example, if Field 3 of the first record contains title information, then Field 3 of every record must either contain title information or be empty. If a record does not contain information for a certain field—you might be missing a zip code, for example—you should define it in the data document as an empty field by inserting an ENDFIELD code.

Let's create a data file:

1. From a clear screen, type **Mark** and press **F9** to insert the End Field code. The ENDFIELD code automatically advances the cursor to the next line. This field corresponds to FIELD(1) in the form file.

2. Type **Short** and press **F9**. This field corresponds to FIELD(2) in the primary file.

3. Press **F9**. This *empty* field corresponds to FIELD(3?) in the form file, and is ignored during the Merge because of the *?* in the form file.

4. Type **367 Randwich Road** and press **F9**. This field corresponds to FIELD(4) in the primary file.

5. Type **Savannah** and press **F9**. This field corresponds to FIELD(5) in the form file.

6. Type **GA** and press **F9**. This field corresponds to FIELD(6) in the form file.

7. Type **36301** and press **F9**. This field corresponds to FIELD(7) in the form file.

8. Type **July** and press **F9**. This field corresponds to FIELD(8) in the form file.

9. Press **Shift+F9** (Merge Codes), to open the Merge Codes dialog box, and choose **2. Data [Text]**. The Merge Codes (Text Data File) dialog box is displayed (see Figure 10.7).

10. Choose **2. End Record** to end the record and insert a hard page break (and its corresponding code). Notice the *ENDRECORD* code above the hard page break. Each record is considered a separate page by the program. There is only one record currently displayed, so only one page break is shown.

Here are some points to remember:

- Do not separate fields or records with an extra hard return.

- Do not insert spaces between the last word in a field and an ENDRECORD or ENDFIELD code.

Figure 10.7   **Merge Codes (Text Data File) dialog box**

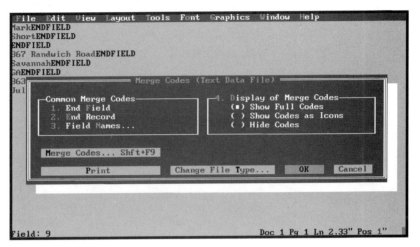

- Maintain the same field structure for each record. For example, in the data file you are now creating, Field 6 must always be a state, Field 8 must always be a month, and so on.

- Do not add any extra spaces before the ENDFIELD and ENDRECORD codes. These extra spaces will show up as extra spaces in the merged letter.

PRACTICE YOUR SKILLS

1. Complete record 2, for *Marlene Albert*, as shown in Figure 10.8.

2. Save the document as MYLIST.LRN and leave the document, but do not exit WordPerfect.

MERGING FORM AND DATA FILES

After you create the form and data files, you can merge them to create a customized letter for each record in the data file. The results of the merge are displayed on the screen, and you can edit and print them like any other document. The final step is for you to merge the files and create the two personalized letters.

Figure 10.8   **Data file with two records**

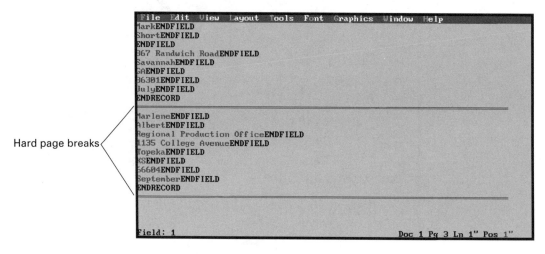

Hard page breaks

Let's merge our form and data files:

1. Press **Ctrl+F9** (Merge/Sort), and choose **1. Merge**. The Run Merge dialog box is displayed.

2. In the Form File box, type **myprimlt.lrn** and press **Enter**.

3. In the Data File box, type **mylist.lrn** and press **Enter**. Compare your screen to Figure 10.9.

4. Press **Enter** to begin the merge. After a moment, the merged files appear as a single document in the typing area. The cursor is positioned at the end of the second letter.

5. Move to the top of the first letter.

6. Choose **1. Full Document** from the Print dialog box (Shift+F7) to print both letters created by the merge. Compare your printout to Figure 10.10.

7. Exit the document and clear the typing area without saving the file. There is no need to save the file, because the merge can easily be re-created.

Figure 10.9   **Specifying merge documents in the Run Merge dialog box**

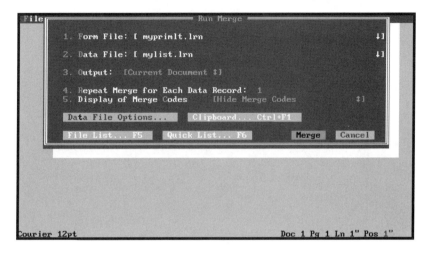

MERGING FROM THE KEYBOARD

Although you always need a form file for a merge, you do not always need a data file; instead, you can merge directly from the keyboard. In other words, you can type the variable information during the merge. This kind of merge is helpful when you need to create only one form letter from a form file or when you want to include variable information not found in a data file. To allow information to be typed from the keyboard rather than retrieved from a file, insert the KEYBOARD code in the form file. Here's how to do it:

- Press Shift+F9 (Merge Codes).

- Choose 2. Keyboard.

- Press Enter to insert the command into the document.

Using the KEYBOARD code in your form file, you can tell the program to display a message or prompt on the status line during the merge. This message, which you write, serves as a reminder or provides direction to you or the person doing the merge.

To merge from the keyboard:

- Press the Merge/Sort keys, Ctrl+F9.

- Type the name of the form file, and press Enter.

Figure 10.10   Merged documents

```
Mark Short
367 Randwich Road
Savannah, GA 36301

Dear Mark:

Enclosed please find my report on the developments at Macco
Plastics for the first quarter of this year. As you will see, it
has been a dynamic quarter for all phases of Macco's operations.

We look forward to seeing you at the next regional managers'
conference in July. In the meantime, keep up the good work.

Sincerely,


Morgan D. Hamilton, President
Macco Plastics,Inc.
```

```
Marlene Albert
Regional Production Office
1135 College Avenue
Topeka, KS 66604

Dear Marlene:

Enclosed please find my report on the developments at Macco
Plastics for the first quarter of this year. As you will see, it
has been a dynamic quarter for all phases of Macco's operations.

We look forward to seeing you at the next regional managers'
conference in July. In the meantime, keep up the good work.

Sincerely,


Morgan D. Hamilton, President
Macco Plastics,Inc.
```

- Press Enter again to bypass the prompt for the data file name. Then press Enter again to begin the merge. The form file's text is displayed on the screen, and the cursor is placed at the first KEYBOARD code. If you included a prompt or message, it now appears.

- Type the information.

- Press the ENDFIELD key, F9, to continue to the next KEYBOARD code.

This type of merge creates one customized letter. To create another letter, simply repeat the procedure.

Perform the following steps at your computer to update a memo using the special merge codes, and create the document shown in Figure 10.11.

Figure 10.11   **Form file MYKMERGE.LRN with merge codes**

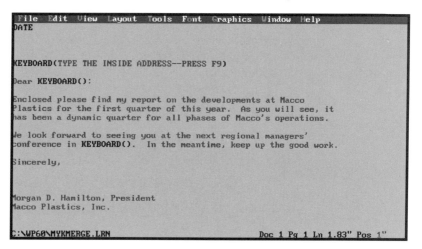

1. Retrieve the document KMERGE.LRN.

2. Examine the DATE code. This code inserts your computer's system date.

3. Examine the KEYBOARD codes. The merge stops at each one to allow for typing.

4. Move to the blank line directly above the *D* in *Dear* in the salutation.

5. Press **Shift+F9** to open the Merge Codes (Form File) dialog box, and press **2. Keyboard**. The Parameter Entry dialog box is displayed.

6. Enter the following message:

   ```
   TYPE THE INSIDE ADDRESS--PRESS F9
   ```

7. Press **Enter** to insert the prompt in the typing area, and press **Enter** again to insert a blank line.

8. Save the file as MYKMERGE.LRN. Then compare your screen to Figure 10.11.

9. Exit the document, but remain in WordPerfect.

10. Press **Ctrl+F9** (Merge/Sort), and choose **1. Merge** to merge information from the keyboard into the completed form file.

11. Choose **1. Form File**, type **mykmerge.lrn**, and press **Enter**.

12. Press **Del** to make sure the Data File box is cleared, and press **Enter** twice to bypass the data-file prompt and perform the merge from the keyboard. When WordPerfect gets to the first KEYBOARD merge code, it displays the message you entered in Step 6 in the status line:

    ```
    TYPE THE INSIDE ADDRESS- PRESS F9
    ```

13. Type **Dave Schmidt** and press **Enter**.

14. Type **4630 Lindell Blvd.** and press **Enter**.

15. Type **St. Louis, MO 63108**. Do *not* press Enter.

16. Press **F9** to end the field and advance the cursor to the next KEYBOARD code.

17. Type **Dave** and press **F9** to advance to the next KEYBOARD code.

18. Type **August** and press **F9** to complete the letter.

19. Save the document as MYMRGLTR.LRN.

20. Print the document and compare your printout to Figure 10.1 (near the beginning of this chapter).

21. Clear the typing area without saving the file again.

Here's a helpful hint: When merging from the keyboard, press F9 instead of Enter after typing information. However, don't use this technique if the information appears on more than one line, as do some addresses.

CREATING LABELS

Besides creating customized letters, you can also use WordPerfect's Merge feature to create mailing labels, by extracting names and addresses contained in a data file and printing them on mailing labels. There are several important steps in creating mailing labels:

- Create a *label definition,* which is a fancy way of saying that you must first tell the program that you want to produce labels. The program, in turn, gives the printer this information and automatically tells it what size and type of paper it should use. (Of course, you supply the paper.)

- Create a form file. The mailing-label form file should contain the basic information that you want to appear on each label. This information is provided in fields.

- Create a data file. The data file takes the exact same form as the one you created earlier for the form letter. (You can create the data file first, and it is often desirable to do so. For this exercise, you'll use an existing data file, which we have provided for you.)

- Perform the merge, using the method you learned earlier in the chapter.

CREATING A LABEL DEFINITION

As you learned in the previous section, the label definition ultimately provides the printer with the information it needs to print information onto labels. The program stores this information in codes. We recommend that you create these codes as *initial codes*—codes that are placed at the very beginning of a document. Placing these codes at the very top of the document ensures that no other such codes will be placed before them, and keeps the Reveal Codes area relatively uncluttered.

When you tell the program that you want to create labels, it automatically selects the appropriate paper size. If you wish to use a paper size other than the default, you must include this information in the label definition.

To create a label definition:

- Clear the typing area.

- Press Shift+F8 and choose 4. Document to display the Document Format dialog box.

- Choose 1. Document Initial Codes.

- Open the Page Format dialog box (press Shift+F8, and choose 3. Page).

- Choose 5. Labels.

- Highlight Predefined Labels (if necessary), and press Enter. (This step is only necessary the first time you create labels.)

- In the Labels dialog box, highlight the desired label type, and press Enter three times.

- Press F7 to exit the Document Initial Codes box.

- Press Enter twice to return to the typing area.

Let's create a label definition for use in our form file:

1. With the typing area cleared, press **Shift+F8** (Format) and choose **4. Document**. The Document Format dialog box is displayed (see Figure 10.12).

2. Choose **1. Document Initial Codes**. The Document Initial Codes box is displayed (see Figure 10.13). Notice that this box is currently empty.

3. Display the Page Format dialog box (press **Shift+F8** and choose **3. Page**).

4. Choose **5. Labels** to display the Label Files dialog box. This dialog box is displayed only the first time you create a label definition. If the Labels dialog box is displayed, skip to step 6.

5. In the Label Files dialog box, highlight Predefined Labels, and press **Enter**.

6. In the Labels dialog box, highlight 3M 7730 (see Figure 10.14), and then press **Enter** to return to the Page Format dialog box. (If the Labels Printer Information dialog box is displayed, press Enter to close it.) Notice that the 3M 7730 label is now listed to the right of options 4 and 5.

Figure 10.12   **Document Format dialog box**

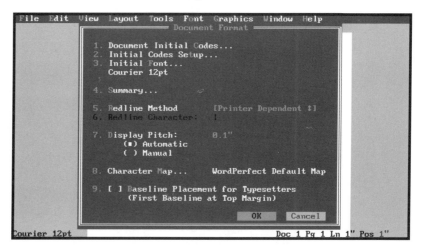

Figure 10.13   **Document Initial Codes box**

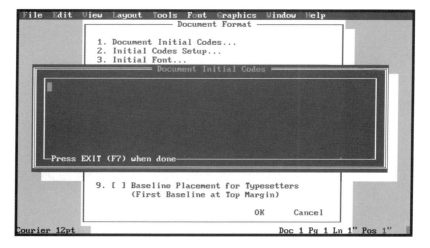

7. Press **Enter** twice to return to the Document Initial Codes dialog box. Notice that two codes are now inserted in the box: one specifying labels, the other providing information about paper size and type (see Figure 10.15).

Figure 10.14   **Specifying a label type in the Labels dialog box**

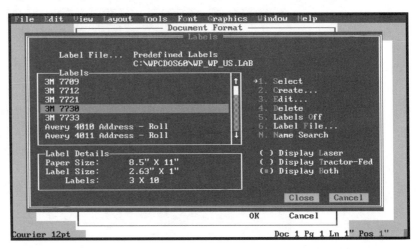

Figure 10.15   **Label definition codes in the Document Initial Codes box**

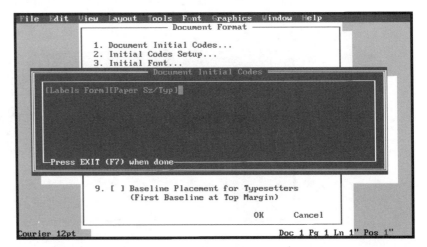

8. Place the cursor on each of the codes. Notice that each code expands to provide information specific to the type of label you have chosen.

9. Press **F7** (do *not* press Enter) to exit the Document Initial Codes box and return to the Document Format dialog box.

10. Press **Enter** twice to return to the typing area.

11. Display Reveal Codes, and place the cursor on the code that is present. Notice that all the label definition information is contained in this one code. In the next section, we'll use this label definition to create our form file.

CREATING THE FORM FILE

The next step in creating labels is to decide which fields you want printed from the data file and then to create the form file. Our form file uses six fields: first name, last name, street address, city, state, and zip code.

To insert numbered fields, use the same method you learned earlier:

- Position the cursor where you want to insert the field.

- Press Shift+F9.

- Choose 1. Form (necessary only when you first create the form file).

- Choose 1. Field, type the field number, and press Enter.

In the following exercise, we'll insert our fields to create the form file shown in Figure 10.16.

Figure 10.16   **Completed form file**

```
FIELD(1) FIELD(2)

FIELD(4)

FIELD(5), FIELD(6)  FIELD(7)
```

Let's create the form file for our mailing labels:

1. With the typing area that contains the label definition still displayed, turn off Reveal Codes, press **Shift+F9**, and choose

1. Form (if necessary) to open the Merge Codes (Form File) dialog box.

2. Choose **1. Field** to open the Parameter Entry dialog box.

3. Type **1** and press **Enter** to insert the FIELD(1) code at the top of the document.

4. Press the **Spacebar** to insert a space.

5. Press **Shift+F9**, choose **1. Field**, type **2**, and press **Enter**. The second field is inserted.

6. Press **Enter** to move to the next line, and insert the fourth field in the document.

PRACTICE YOUR SKILLS

1. Insert the remaining fields as shown in Figure 10.16. (Field 7 may wrap to the next line.)

2. Save the file as MYLABEL.LRN, and clear the typing area without exiting WordPerfect.

MERGING THE LABELS

The last step in creating labels is to merge the form and data files to create the final mailing labels. The data file that we'll be using is (appropriately enough) on your Data Disk. Normally, you would create the data file before performing the merge. In this case, however, we have already provided you with the data file.

Let's merge our form file with the data file to create our mailing labels:

1. Press **Ctrl+F9** and choose **1. Merge**.

2. Insert the Data Disk in drive A.

3. Enter **mylabel.lrn** as the form file name and **a:adlist.lrn** as the data file name. Then press **Enter** to begin the merge.

4. Move to the top of the merged document, if necessary, and compare your screen to Figure 10.17. Notice that, because the mailing labels are set to print three across, the hard page break after each record is shortened.

Figure 10.17   **Merged mailing labels**

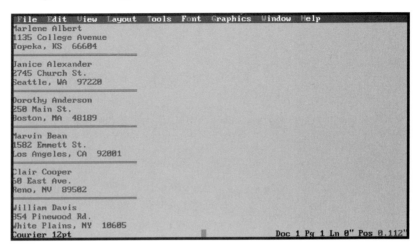

5. View the document in Print Preview. Notice that the labels are displayed three across.

6. Return to the typing area, and exit the document without saving it.

CHAPTER SUMMARY

In this chapter, you have learned to use WordPerfect's Merge feature to create and print form and data files and to merge them into one complete form letter or set of mailing labels.

Here's a quick technique reference for Chapter 10:

Feature or Action	How to Do It
Enter a Field code	**Shift+F9** (Merge), **1. Field**, *field number*, **Enter**
Insert an ENDFIELD code	**F9** (after typing each field)
End the record	**Shift+F9** (Merge), **2. Data [Text]**, **2. End Record**

Feature or Action	How to Do It
Merge documents	**Ctrl+F9** (Merge/Sort), **1. Merge**, *name of form file*, **Enter**, *name of data file*, **Enter** twice
Insert a KEYBOARD code in a form file	**Shift+F9** (Merge), **2. Keyboard**, *message*, **Enter**
Create a label definition	Clear the typing area, press **Shift+F8**, choose **4. Document**, choose **1. Document Initial Codes**, press **Shift+8**, choose **3. Page**, Choose **5. Labels**, highlight Predefined Labels (if necessary), press **Enter**, highlight the desired label type, press **Enter** three times, press **F7**, and press **Enter** twice

In the next chapter, you will learn how to import and edit graphics in your document. You'll also learn some additional printing techniques.

If you need to break off here, please exit from WordPerfect. If you want to proceed directly to the next chapter, please do so now.

CHAPTER 11: GRAPHICS AND PRINTING TECHNIQUES

Importing a Graphic

Editing a Graphic

Adding Borders To Enhance Text Appearance

Creating a Watermark

Additional Printing Techniques

You've seen many of the ways that WordPerfect enables you to create and manipulate text in your document. The program also provides you with a powerful tool for incorporating graphic images, or *graphics*, into your documents. In this chapter, you will learn how to incorporate and edit graphics in your document. You'll also learn some advanced printing techniques that give you better control over the printing process.

There are a couple of important reasons for adding graphics to a document:

- To illustrate material covered in the text. For example, suppose you have written a detailed analysis of the rise in world population in the twentieth century. Illustrating your findings with bar charts or graphs might help your readers grasp the information at a glance.

- To enhance the appearance of the document, since a document with graphics looks more professional. Figure 11.1 shows a newsletter containing an illustration that adds much to the overall look of the document.

When done with this chapter, you will be able to:

- Incorporate a graphic into your document
- Move, size, and rotate a graphic
- Add a caption to your graphic
- Add graphic borders to enhance text
- Create a watermark
- Print selected pages of a document
- Cancel, rush, and display print jobs

IMPORTING A GRAPHIC

You can place graphics in any WordPerfect document, as well as in headers and footers. Images can be *imported* into a WordPerfect document from many draw or paint software programs or from sources of digitized images (clip art). (For a list of the graphic programs WordPerfect supports, see the Graphic Images section in the appendix of the WordPerfect manual.) WordPerfect 6.0 also comes with a number of graphics files (denoted by the .WPG extension in the file name), which you can both use in your documents and edit.

WordPerfect cannot create graphics; however, once you load an image into WordPerfect, you can size it, move it, and rotate it. There is no limit to the number of graphics in a document. However, adding graphics is like adding text—the document's pagination adjusts automatically. The more graphics you add to the document, the more you must adjust the rest of the document. And the more graphics a document contains, the larger the file becomes; it can even fill an entire floppy disk and, therefore, require that you divide the file into smaller files. Even small files with graphics can take a long time to print.

Figure 11.1   **Sample document with graphic**

Figure 11.1   **Sample document with graphic (Continued)**

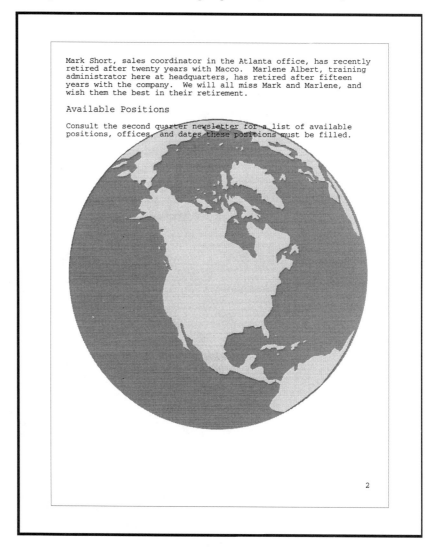

It's important to remember that you will only be able to print graphics if your printer has graphics capabilities. Also, to view graphics on your screen, your computer must be equipped with a graphics display card.

To import a WordPerfect graphic into a document:

- Press Alt+F9, and then press Shift+F10; or choose Graphics, Retrieve Image.

- Type the file name of the graphic you wish to import, and then press Enter; or press F5 and Enter to view a list of the graphic files contained in the WP60 directory, highlight the name of the desired file, and choose 1. Select or press Enter.

When you import a WordPerfect graphic, it is automatically placed inside a graphic box. The graphic box is itself visible in the typing area; however, the graphic is not. You can view the graphic in Print Preview (or in Graphics mode).

If you are not currently running WordPerfect, please start the program now.

Let's open a new document; then we'll import a graphic:

1. Open NEWS.LRN.

2. Press **Alt+F9**. The Graphics dialog box is displayed (see Figure 11.2).

3. Press **Shift+F10** to open the Retrieve Image File dialog box (see Figure 11.3).

Figure 11.2   **Graphics dialog box**

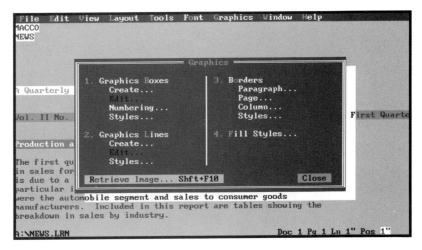

4. Type **factory.wpg** and press **Enter**. The graphic is placed in the upper-right corner of the document. A graphic box, labeled *BOX 1,* represents its position (see Figure 11.4). If you imported any additional graphics into this document, their graphic boxes would be labeled BOX 2, BOX 3, and so on.

Figure 11.3 **Retrieve Image File dialog box**

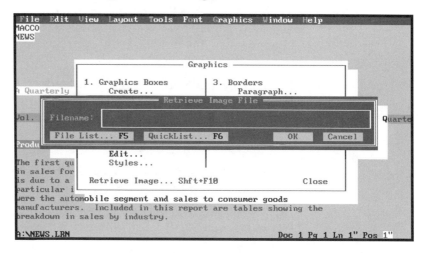

Figure 11.4 **The graphic box representing the imported figure**

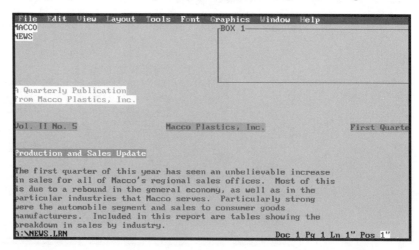

5. View the document in Print Preview. Notice that the graphic becomes visible. Then close Print Preview.

EDITING A GRAPHIC

To change the content of the image, you must edit it in the program in which it was created. In WordPerfect you can change its location, size, scale, and rotation. You can also add a caption to explain an image or to tie it into your text.

 MOVING AND SCALING THE GRAPHIC

In WordPerfect, there are two ways to change the position or size of a graphic: One method affects the entire graphic—the box *and* the image it contains—the other affects only the image inside the box, not the box itself. In this section, you'll learn the first method. In the section that follows, you'll learn the second one. Both these features are accessible from the Edit Graphics Box dialog box.

To open the Edit Graphics Box dialog box:

- Press Alt+F9.
- Choose 1. Graphics Boxes.
- Choose 2. Edit.
- Press Enter.

To move the graphic (including its box):

- Choose 8. Edit Position from the Edit Graphics Box dialog box.
- Choose 1. Horizontal Position or 2. Vertical Position, enter the desired placement, and press Enter.

To scale the graphic (including its box):

- Choose 9. Edit Size from the Edit Graphics Box dialog box.
- Choose 1. Set Width or 3. Set Height, type the desired value, and press Enter.
- Press Enter to return to the Edit Graphics Box dialog box.

Let's begin by changing the position of our graphic:

1. Press **Alt+F9** to open the Graphics dialog box.

2. Choose **1. Graphics Boxes** and **2. Edit**. The Select Box To Edit dialog box is displayed (see Figure 11.5). Notice that 1. Document Box Number is currently selected; the numeral *1* following this option represents BOX 1.

Figure 11.5   **The Select Box To Edit dialog box**

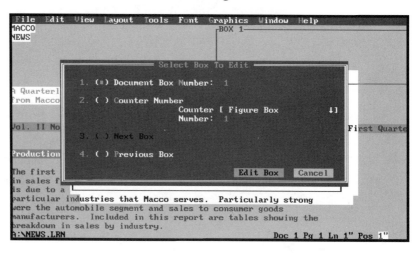

3. Press **Enter** to accept the selection and choose Edit Box. The Edit Graphics Box dialog box is displayed (see Figure 11.6).

4. Choose **8. Edit Position** to open the Paragraph Box Position dialog box (see Figure 11.7). From this dialog box, you can change the horizontal and/or vertical position of the dialog box on the page.

5. Choose **1. Horizontal Position**, and choose **Left** to place the box (and its graphic) at the left margin; then press **Enter** to return to the Edit Graphics Box dialog box. Notice that under the 8. Edit Position option, the horizontal position is now set at the left margin.

6. Press **Enter** to accept the change. BOX 1 is now displayed in the upper-left corner of the document (see Figure 11.8). Notice that the text now wraps down the right side of and below the graphic.

7. Block the text MACCO NEWS, and align it flush right.

Figure 11.6   **The Edit Graphics Box dialog box**

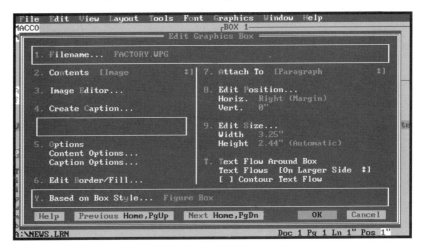

Figure 11.7   **The Paragraph Box Position dialog box**

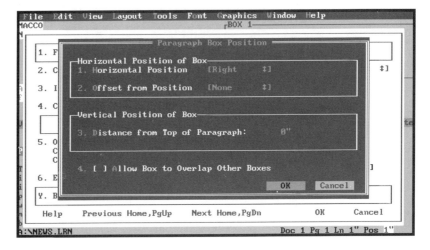

Now, let's adjust the scale of our graphic to make it smaller:

1. Press **Alt+F9** to open the Graphics dialog box.

2. Choose **1. Graphics Boxes** and **2. Edit**. The Select Box To Edit dialog box is displayed. Again, notice that 1. Document Box Number is currently selected.

Figure 11.8   **The moved graphic box**

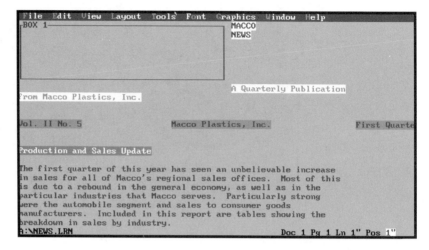

3. Press **Enter** to accept the selection and choose Edit Box. The Edit Graphics Box dialog box is displayed. Notice the current width and height measurements under the 9. Edit Size option.

4. Choose **9. Edit Size**. The Graphics Box Size dialog box is displayed (see Figure 11.9).

5. Under Width of Box, choose **1. Set Width**, type **2.5**, and press **Enter** to change the width.

6. Under Height of Box, choose **3. Set Height**, type **1.75**, and press **Enter** to change the height.

7. Press **Enter** to accept the changes and return to the Edit Graphics Box dialog box. Notice the new width and height measurements listed under the 9. Edit Size option.

8. Press **Enter** to close the dialog box and return to the typing area. Notice that BOX 1 is reduced in size. Compare your screen to Figure 11.10.

EDITING THE GRAPHIC WITHIN ITS BOX

To edit the graphic image without affecting the box that encloses it, you must first display the *Image Editor*. To display the Image Editor, choose 3. Image Editor in the Edit Graphics Box dialog box.

Figure 11.9   **The Graphics Box Size dialog box**

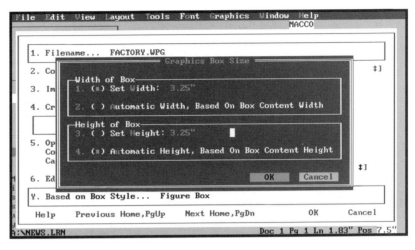

Figure 11.10   **The scaled graphic box**

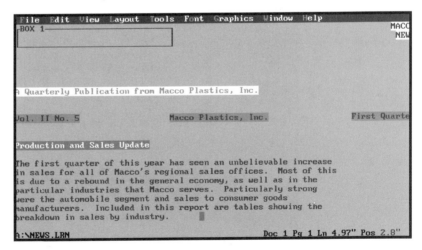

The Image Editor is quite similar in appearance to the Print Preview area. However, the Image Editor also provides a number of options at the bottom of the screen. To select one of these options, type its underlined letter. Then type the desired value and press Enter.

Let's rotate the image within its box:

1. Press **Alt+F9** to open the Graphics dialog box.

2. Choose **1. Graphics Boxes** and **2. Edit**. The Select Box To Edit dialog box is displayed. Again, notice that 1. Document Box Number is currently selected.

3. Press **Enter** to accept the selection and choose Edit Box. The Edit Graphics Box dialog box is displayed.

4. Choose **3. Image Editor.** The graphic is now displayed in the Image Editor area (see Figure 11.11). You'll notice that this area is somewhat similar in appearance to the Print Preview area. There is also an area at the bottom of the screen that provides many options for editing the image.

Figure 11.11   The Image Editor

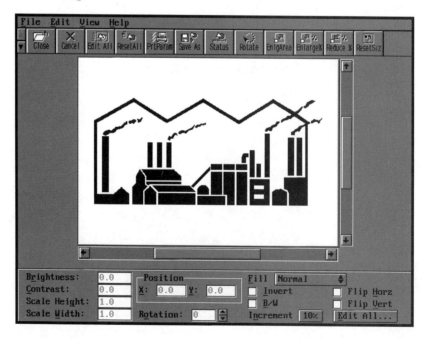

5. Choose **Rotation** (press **O**). The value in the Rotation box becomes highlighted.

6. Type **15** and press **Enter**. Notice that the image now appears skewed in its window. The angle of its display has changed, though that of its box (not currently visible) has not.

PRACTICE YOUR SKILLS

1. Try experimenting with some of the different options in the Image Editor.

2. Press **Ctrl+Home** (or choose **Edit, Reset All**) to revert the image to the settings it had before you displayed the Image Editor.

3. Press **F7** to return to the Edit Graphics Box dialog box.

CREATING A GRAPHIC BORDER

In the previous section, you learned how to edit only the image. WordPerfect also provides you with a number of options for editing the box, or *border*, that encloses it. These options are available in the Edit Graphics Box Border/Fill dialog box, which you can display by choosing 6. Edit Border/Fill from the Edit Graphics Box dialog box.

Some of the options available in the Edit Graphics Box Border/Fill dialog box are

- The border style; for example, single or double lines

- The color of the border

- The border shadow, which allows you to create a drop shadow effect

- The border corners; for example, square or rounded

- The Fill option, which allows you to shade the background within the border

Let's add a drop shadow border to our graphic:

1. With the Edit Graphics Box dialog box displayed, choose **6. Edit Border/Fill**. The Edit Graphics Box Border/Fill dialog box is displayed (see Figure 11.12).

2. Choose **5. Shadow** to open the Shadow dialog box (see Figure 11.13).

3. Choose **1. Shadow Type**, choose **5. Lower Right**, and press **Enter** to return to the Edit Graphics Box Border/Fill dialog box. Notice that Lower Right is now listed next to the 5. Shadow option.

Figure 11.12   The Edit Graphics Box Border/Fill dialog box

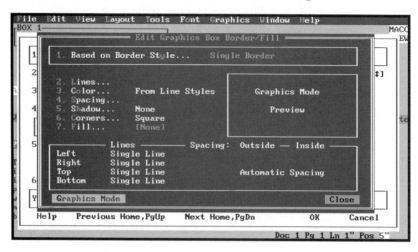

Figure 11.13   The Shadow dialog box

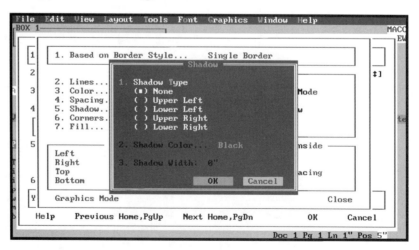

4. Press **Enter** twice to return to the typing area. Notice that the shadow border is not visible.

5. View the document in Print Preview. The shadow border is now visible. Then close Print Preview.

ADDING A CAPTION TO A GRAPHIC

You might want to add a caption to an illustration to help the reader understand it. In WordPerfect, not only can you create the text for the caption, but you can also format it in any way.

The caption can be as long as you want; it will wrap according to the width of the graphics box.

To add a caption to a graphic:

- Choose 4. Create Caption from the Edit Graphics Box dialog box.

- If you wish, edit or erase the default caption (for example, Figure 1) and type the new caption.

- Press F7 to return to the Edit Graphics Box dialog box.

Let's create a caption for our graphic:

1. With the Edit Graphics Box dialog box displayed, choose **4. Create Caption**. The Box Caption typing area is displayed, along with the default caption, Figure 1 (see Figure 11.14).

2. Press **Backspace** once. The entire caption is deleted.

Figure 11.14   **The Box Caption typing area**

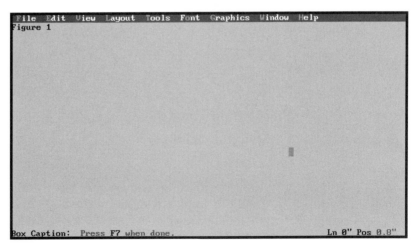

3. Type **All the News Worth Printing**. Notice how the text automatically wraps to the second line.

4. Press **F7** (as instructed at the bottom of the screen) to return to the Edit Graphics Box dialog box. Notice that option 4 has now become Edit Caption, and the caption is displayed directly below it.

5. Press **Enter** to return to the typing area. Notice that the height of the box has enlarged slightly to accommodate the caption; however, the caption itself is not visible.

6. View the document in Print Preview to see the caption, and change the view to 100%. Then return to the typing area.

ADDING BORDERS TO ENHANCE TEXT APPEARANCE

In WordPerfect, you can add graphic borders to your document, which can enhance the appearance of your text. Two of the more commonly used types of borders are paragraph borders and page borders. In addition, you can reverse the display of selected text so that it appears light on dark instead of the usual dark on light. Keep in mind, however, that these enhancements are not visible in the typing area; to view them, use Print Preview.

CREATING A PARAGRAPH BORDER

To create a paragraph border:

- Select (block) the desired paragraph.

- Press Alt+F9 and then Choose 3. Borders from the Graphics dialog box.

- Choose 1. Paragraph.

- Select the desired type of border, and press Enter.

Let's create a paragraph border in our document:

1. Near the top of the document, block the line of publication data that begins with *Vol. II No. 5.* It's important to remember that, although this is a single line of text, it is considered a paragraph by the program because it ends with a hard return.

2. Press **Alt+F9** to open the Graphics dialog box.

3. Choose **3. Borders**, and then choose **1. Paragraph**. The Create Paragraph Border dialog box is displayed (see Figure 11.15). Notice that the border style is currently set to Single Border.

Figure 11.15   **The Create Paragraph Border dialog box**

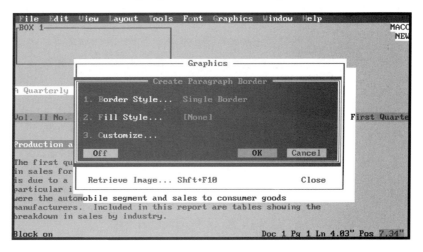

4. Press **Enter** to accept the change and return to the typing area.

5. Display Print Preview, view the paragraph border, and return to the typing area.

CREATING A REVERSED TEXT IMAGE

To create reversed text, you must change the appearance of both the background and the text itself.

To select the desired background shading:

- Select the desired paragraph.

- Press Alt+F9 and then choose 3. Border from the Graphics dialog box.

- Choose 1. Paragraph.

- Choose 2. Fill Style.

- Highlight the desired percentage of background shading (100% Shaded Fill produces a black background), and press Enter.

To change the color of the text:

- Select the text again.

- Open the Font dialog box (Ctrl+F8).

- Choose Color.

- Highlight the desired color (White to create a reverse image), and press Enter twice.

Let's reverse the appearance of text in a paragraph:

1. Block the line of text that begins *A Quarterly Publication*.

2. Press **Alt+F9** to open the Graphics dialog box.

3. Choose **3. Borders**, and then choose **1. Paragraph** to open the Create Paragraph Border dialog box.

4. Choose **2. Fill Style**. The Fill Styles dialog box is displayed (see Figure 11.16).

Figure 11.16   The Fill Styles dialog box

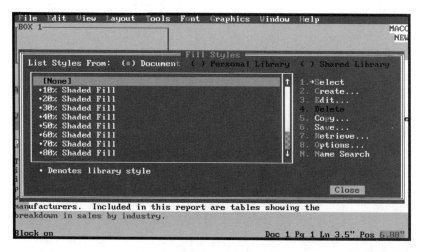

5. Highlight the 100% Shaded Fill option, and press **Enter** (or choose **1. Select**). Notice that the selected fill style is now listed in the Create Paragraph Border dialog box.

6. Press **Enter** to accept the change and return to the typing area.

7. Display Print Preview, and view the shaded text. Notice that because the text prints black, it is now invisible because of the 100% shading. (Keep in mind that, in this case, 100% shading means black.) To complete the process, we need to change the color of the text so that it stands out against the shaded background.

8. Close Print Preview, block the text again, and then open the Font dialog box (Ctrl+F8).

9. Choose **Color** (type **C**) to open the Color Selection dialog box (see Figure 11.17).

Figure 11.17   **The Color Selection dialog box**

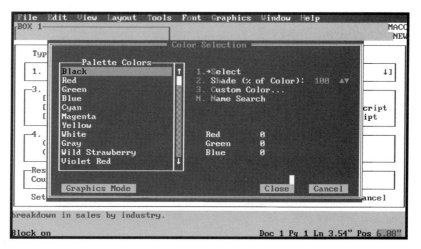

10. In the Palette Colors list, highlight White, and press **Enter** twice to return to the typing area.

11. Display Print Preview, view the reversed text, and return to the typing area.

CREATING A PAGE BORDER

To create a border around each page of a document:

● Press Alt+F9 and then choose 3. Borders from the Graphics dialog box.

- Choose 2. Page.

- Choose the desired border style, and press Enter.

Let's create a page border around the page:

1. Press **Alt+F9** to open the Graphics dialog box.

2. Choose 3. **Borders**, and then choose 2. **Page** to open the Create Page Border dialog box (see Figure 11.18). Notice that the default border style is a single border.

Figure 11.18   The Create Page Border dialog box

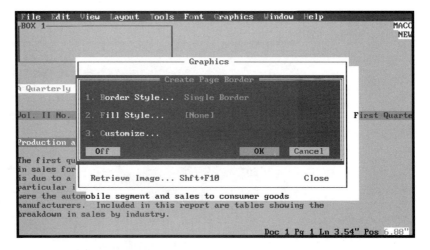

3. Press **Enter** to accept the default border and return to the typing area.

4. Display Print Preview, view the border on each page, and return to the typing area.

CREATING A WATERMARK

A *watermark* is a kind of "ghost" image that is usually meant to appear on every page of a document. It is a way of providing the reader with a "signature"—either text or a graphic that helps to identify the creator of the document. For example, a company might use its motto or logo as a watermark.

To create a watermark in a document:

- Choose Layout, Header/Footer/Watermark.

- Choose 3. Watermarks.

- Choose 1. Watermark A or 2. Watermark B (to create a second watermark).

- Select the desired frequency of the watermark's appearance (All Pages prints the watermark on every page), and press Enter.

- Type the desired watermark text, or import the desired graphic.

- Press F7.

- Press Enter.

Let's create a watermark in our document:

1. Choose **Layout, Header/Footer/Watermark** to open the Header/Footer/Watermark dialog box.

2. Choose **3. Watermarks,** and choose **1. Watermark A** to open the Watermark A dialog box (see Figure 11.19).

3. Verify that All Pages is selected, and then press **Enter** (to choose **Create**). The Watermark A typing area is displayed.

Figure 11.19   **The Watermark A dialog box**

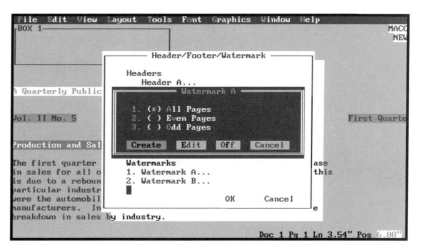

4. Press **Alt+F9** to open the Graphics dialog box, and then press **Shift+F10** to open the Retrieve Image File dialog box.

5. Type **globe.wpg** and press **Enter** to return to the Watermark A typing area. Notice that the watermark graphic is not displayed.

6. Press **F7** to return to the typing area. The watermark graphic is still not displayed.

7. Display Print Preview, and view the watermark on both pages. Compare your document to the printout in Figure 11.1.

8. Close Print Preview.

9. Save the file as MYNEWS.LRN

10. If you wish to print your document, do so now, and compare your printout to the one shown in Figure 11.1.

ADDITIONAL PRINTING TECHNIQUES

Now that you are creating longer and more complex documents that take advantage of many different WordPerfect features, you are probably printing your documents more often just to make sure they look right. You may find that you're wasting a lot of paper by printing draft copies. You may also find that printing pages with graphics can take a long time. WordPerfect offers you printing options to help you take better control of the printing process while saving you time and paper.

In Chapter 1, you learned how to print a full document. You also learned that WordPerfect allows you to print in the background, so that while printing you can continue to edit the same or another document or even create a new one. No doubt you will often want to print a full document. Sometimes, however, you will want to print only a page or selected pages. And at times you will want to control the flow of information to your printer—to rush or cancel a print job, for example.

 ### PRINTING SELECTED PAGES OF A DOCUMENT

When a document is in the typing area, you can choose 1. Full Document from the Print dialog box, shown in Figure 11.6, to print the entire document or 2. Page to print the page on which you have positioned the cursor.

To print selected pages of the document that is in the typing area, choose 4. Multiple Pages from the Print dialog box, choose 1. Page/ Label/Range from the Print Multiple Pages dialog box, and then type the numbers of the pages that you wish to print. Table 11.1 shows you how to enter numbers of selected pages or a range of pages.

Table 11.1   **Multiple Page Options**

Type	To Print...
#, Enter	Only page #
#-, Enter	From page # to the end of the document (for example, *2-, Enter* to print from page 2 to the end)
#-#, Enter	A range, from the first # to the second # (for example, *2-5* to print pages 2 through 5)
-#, Enter	From the beginning of the document to page # (for example, *-5* to print pages 1 through 5)
#,#, Enter	Only the two pages specified (for example, *2,5* to print pages 2 and 5)

Note: The symbol # represents any single page number that you type; for example, page *2*.

CANCELING, RUSHING, AND DISPLAYING PRINT JOBS

Whenever you tell WordPerfect to print a file, it copies it to a new location on disk to create a temporary file, and then prints from that temporary file. This allows you to continue working on the same document that is being printed. Each file or part of a file that you send to the printer is considered a *print job*. Because of the way WordPerfect prints, you can send multiple print jobs to the printer. WordPerfect then uses the print jobs to create a *Job List*, a list of files or parts of files waiting to be printed.

Once you have sent the file to the printer, the Print dialog box option 6. Control Printer enables you to cancel a print job or rush a job by placing it at the top of the list. You can also stop the printer temporarily to fix a paper jam and restart it. Figure 11.20 shows the Control Printer dialog box. The available Control Printer options are described in Table 11.2.

Figure 11.20   **Control Printer dialog box**

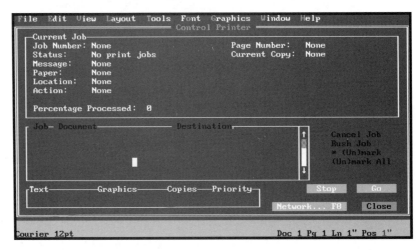

Table 11.2   **Control Printer Options**

Option	Purpose
Cancel Job	To remove any of the documents from the Job List. Enter the job number.
Rush Job	To change the priority of a document in the Job List. Enter the job number.
Go (start printer)	To restart the printer after you use the Stop option.
Stop	To stop the printer *without* canceling a job. Use stop when you need to change a ribbon or fix a paper jam; use Go to restart the printer.

CHAPTER SUMMARY

In this chapter, you have learned how to incorporate a graphic image into a document and to edit the graphic by moving it, changing its scale, and rotating it. You learned how to enhance text with graphic borders, how to create a reversed text image, and how to create a watermark. You also learned how to specify pages of a document to print and how to control the flow of data to your printer by canceling and rushing print jobs.

Here's a quick technique reference for graphics:

Feature or Action	How to Do It
Retrieve an image	**Alt+F9** (Graphics), **Shift+F10**, type the name of the graphics file or press **F5** to list the graphics files, **Enter**, **F7** (Exit)
Open the Edit Graphics Box dialog box	Press **Alt+F9**, choose **1. Graphics Boxes**, choose **2. Edit**, and press **Enter**
Change the graphic's position	Open the Edit Graphics Box dialog box, choose **8. Edit Position**, choose **1. Horizontal Position** or **2. Vertical Position**, enter the desired placement, and press **Enter**
Scale the graphic and its box	Open the Edit Graphics Box dialog box, choose **9. Edit Size**, choose **1. Set Width** or **3. Set Height**, type the desired value, and press **Enter** twice
Rotate the image within its box	Open the Edit Graphics Box dialog box, choose **3. Image Editor**, choose **Rotation** (type **O**), type the desired rotation value (in degrees), and press **Enter**
Reset Image Editor settings	Press **Ctrl+Home**
Create a shadow border	Open the Edit Graphics Box dialog box, choose **6. Edit Border/Fill**, choose **5. Shadow**, choose **1. Shadow Type**, choose the desired shadow position, and press **Enter** three times

Feature or Action	How to Do It
Create a caption for a graphic	Open the Edit Graphics Box dialog box, choose **4. Create Caption**, enter the desired caption, press **F7**, and press **Enter**
Create a paragraph border	Select (block) the desired paragraph, choose **3. Borders**, choose **1. Paragraph**, choose the desired type of border, and press **Enter**
Create background shading	Select the desired paragraph, choose **3. Borders** from the Graphics dialog box, choose **1. Paragraph**, choose **2. Fill Style**, highlight the desired percentage of background shading, and press **Enter**
Change text color	Select the text, open the Font dialog box, choose **Color**, highlight the desired color, and press **Enter** twice
Create a page border	Choose **3. Borders** from the Graphics dialog box, choose **2. Page**, choose the desired border style, and press **Enter**
Create a watermark	Choose **Layout, Header/Footer/Watermark**, choose **3. Watermarks**, choose **1. Watermark A** or **2. Watermark B**, select the desired frequency of the watermark's appearance and press **Enter**, type the desired watermark text or import the desired graphic, press **F7**, and press **Enter**

For a quick technique reference for printing, see Tables 11.1 and 11.2.

In the final chapter of this book, you will learn how to save time and keystrokes for repetitive tasks by creating and using macros.

If you need to break off here, please exit from WordPerfect. If you want to proceed directly to the next chapter, please do so now.

CHAPTER 12: MACROS

T hus far, you have learned how to use a broad range of Word-Perfect features, from the simple to the sophisticated. The simplest ones, such as applying bold, require a single keystroke; the sophisticated ones, such as formatting a document, can require a long series of keystrokes. If you often repeat the same series of keystrokes, then you'll want to learn how to use WordPerfect's Macro feature. It will enable you to assign any series of keystrokes to one or two keys.

A *macro* is a file that stores keystrokes that you must often repeat. By running the macro, you repeat those keystrokes automatically. You can create a macro to display a menu or series of menus; to access any WordPerfect feature; and even to type text automatically, saving you the time of retyping it yourself. When the macro is replayed, every recorded keystroke is repeated in sequence on the screen, just as if you had pressed all the keys yourself.

Macros can lessen the burden of tedious procedures, aid inexperienced users in doing complicated tasks, and automate and standardize procedures. Common macros do such things as closing letters, formatting and printing documents, and setting up headers and footers.

When done with this chapter, you will be able to:

- Create a macro

- Name a macro

- Replay macro keystrokes

- Edit a macro

CREATING A MACRO TO FORMAT A LETTER

Creating a macro is almost as easy as typing the keystrokes you want to record. To create a macro:

- Press the Record Macro keys, Ctrl+F10.

- Type a one- to eight-character name for the macro and press Enter. A keystroke recorder is turned on; it records every key you press until you turn the recorder off again.

- Type the keystrokes you want to record, exactly as you'd type them while working on a document. If you make a mistake, correct it the same way you normally do.

- Press Ctrl+F10 again to turn the macro recorder off.

Each macro is stored in its own file in the WP60 directory. WordPerfect appends .WPM, the three-character extension, to macro file names. However, macro files *cannot* be retrieved into the typing area through the Open, Retrieve, or File Manager features; you will learn how to use your macros later in this chapter.

With the typing area cleared, let's create a macro that will format a letter:

1. Press **Ctrl+F10** (Record Macro). The Record Macro dialog box is displayed (see Figure 12.1).

Figure 12.1   **The Record Macro dialog box**

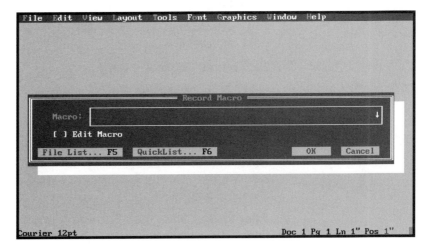

2. Type **myformat** to name your macro file, and press **Enter**. The following status-line message tells you that the keystroke recorder has been turned on:

   ```
   Recording Macro
   ```

   This message remains on the screen and the recorder records every keystroke you enter until you turn the recorder off.

3. Display the Margin Format dialog box (press **Shift+F8**, and choose **2. Margins**).

4. Set both the left and right margins to **1.5"**.

5. Press **Enter** or choose **OK** to return to the Format dialog box, and then display the Page Format dialog box (choose **3. Page**).

6. Choose **2. Center Current Page** to center the text vertically on the page; then press **Enter** until you return to the typing area.

 TYPING A HEADING FOR THE LETTER MACRO

You can now start typing the information that you want all of your letters to contain. Let's start with the return address. Follow these steps at your computer:

1. Turn on **Caps Lock**.

2. Position the cursor at the center of the line by pressing **Shift+F6**.

3. Turn on **bold**, and type **MACCO PLASTICS, INC.** The heading is bold and centered.

4. Turn off both **bold** and **Caps Lock**.

5. Press **Enter** to end the line.

PRACTICE YOUR SKILLS

1. Using Figure 12.2 as a guide, type and center the rest of the inside address. Do not insert today's date yet; you will do so in the next activity.

2. After the last line, press **Enter** four times to leave three blank lines.

Figure 12.2   **The macro for the letter opening**

```
                    MACCO PLASTICS, INC.
                  2345 Industrial Parkway
                  Nashua, NH   03060



(Today's Date)
```

INSERTING A DATE CODE

Macros automate a fixed sequence of keystrokes. By inserting the date or a pause, you can incorporate information that changes from letter to letter. A date code automatically inserts the current date in your letters any time you run the macro.

Follow these steps at your computer:

1. Press the Date keys (**Shift+F5**), and choose **2. Insert Date Code**. The current system date is inserted at the cursor position.

2. Press **Enter** four times to end the line and skip three blank lines.

3. Press **Ctrl+F10** to turn off the macro recorder. The "Recording Macro" message disappears from the status line, signaling the end of the macro recording session.

4. Move the cursor to the top of the document.

5. From the Reveal Codes area, examine the codes

   ```
   [Lft Mar][Rgt Mar][Cntr Cur Pg][Ctr on
   Mar][Bold On]
   ```

   When you create a macro, the keystokes you type actually take effect on the current document. You now have a document containing nothing but the keystrokes you just recorded.

6. Hide the Reveal Codes area and return to the typing area.

7. Exit the document *without* saving. Your macro is still saved as MYFORMAT.WPM. (You'll be playing back this macro later in this chapter.)

CREATING A MACRO WITH A PAUSE

A pause inserted in a macro allows you to enter information from the keyboard when you run the macro. For example, you might create a macro to generate the standard parts of a memo, such as the *TO:* and *FROM:* entries. Inserting a pause after *TO:* signals the macro to stop at that point so you can type the name of the person to whom the memo is addressed. Pressing Enter after typing the information signals the macro to continue where it left off.

To insert a pause in a macro:

• As you are recording keystrokes in the macro, press Ctrl+PgUp.

• Choose Macro Commands (press C).

• Highlight the PAUSE command in the list of macro commands that appears (you'll have to scroll to find it), and press Enter to insert the command, which will temporarily stop the macro. The cursor returns to the typing area.

• Press Enter to break the pause and continue creating the macro.

With the typing area cleared, follow these steps at your computer:

1. Press **Ctrl+F10** (Record Macro) to open the Record Macro dialog box.

2. Type **myclose** (the macro file name) and press **Enter**. WordPerfect automatically appends the .WPM extension. The "Recording Macro" message is displayed in the status line.

3. Press **Enter** to skip a blank line, type **Sincerely**, and press **Enter** four times to leave ample space for a signature.

4. Press **Ctrl+PgUp** to display the Macro Control dialog box (see Figure 12.3).

Figure 12.3   **The Macro Control dialog box**

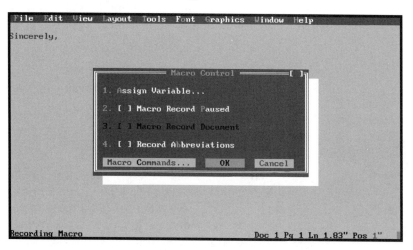

5. Choose **Macro Commands** (press **C**). The Macro Commands dialog box is displayed (see Figure 12.4). This dialog box contains a list of all the macro commands used in WordPerfect.

6. Type **P** to highlight the PAUSE command in the list, and press **Enter** to insert the pause in the typing area.

7. Press **Enter** to end the line.

8. Type **Macco Plastics, Inc.** and press **Enter** twice.

9. Type **Enclosure** and press **Enter** twice.

10. Type **cc:** and press **Tab** so that the macro will automatically tab to where the person using the macro should enter the list of *cc* names.

Figure 12.4   **The Macro Commands dialog box**

1. Using Figure 12.5 as a guide, type the names in the *cc* list. Press **Enter** after the last name in the list.

2. Press **Ctrl+F10** to end the macro recording session.

Figure 12.5   **The macro for the letter closing**

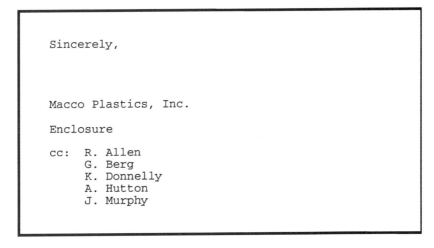

3. Exit the document without saving. The macro remains saved on disk.

A helpful hint: Macros can be deleted or renamed in WordPerfect's File Manager or in DOS. If you should ever decide to rename a macro file, be sure to include the .WPM extension; otherwise, WordPerfect will no longer recognize the file as a macro.

RUNNING A MACRO

When you run (play back) a macro, the keystrokes you stored in the macro are repeated. To run a macro:

- Position the cursor at the place where you want the macro to run.

- Press the Play Macro keys, Alt+F10.

- Type the macro name. Do not type the .WPM extension when prompted for the macro name.

- Press Enter to run the macro. There is no message that tells you when the macro has finished running. To stop a macro while it is running, press the Cancel key, Esc.

With the typing area cleared, follow these steps at your computer:

1. Press **Alt+F10** (Play Macro). The Play Macro dialog box is displayed (see Figure 12.6).

Figure 12.6   **The Play Macro dialog box**

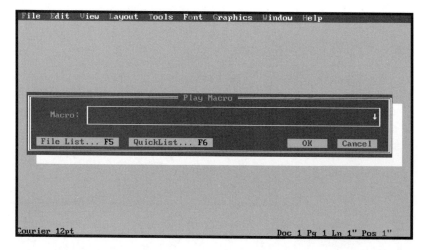

2. Type **myformat** (the name you assigned to the macro), and press **Enter**. (If that file is unavailable, insert the Data Disk in drive A, press **Enter**, and type **a:xmyforma**.) The stored keystrokes are played back.

3. Type **Frank Williams** and press **Enter** to move to the next line.

4. Type **80 Wellington Street** and press **Enter**.

5. Type **Toronto, Ontario M5K 1A2** and press **Enter** twice to end the line and skip a blank line.

6. Type **Dear Frank:** and press **Enter** twice.

7. Retrieve the file BODYTEXT.LRN from the Data Disk into the current document (press **Shift+F10** twice). The stored text is placed at the cursor position.

 RUNNING A MACRO WITH A PAUSE

The letter is not quite complete; it still needs a closing. You can quickly add the closing by running the MYCLOSE macro, following these steps at your computer:

1. Position the cursor at the bottom of the document.

2. Press **Alt+F10** (Play Macro), and type **myclose**. If that file is unavailable, type **a:xmyclose**.

3. Press **Enter** to run the closing macro. Although there is no prompt or message, the macro pauses to allow you to type the name of the person sending the letter.

4. Type your name and press **Enter**. The rest of the macro plays itself out.

5. Examine the completed letter. Compare it to the one shown in Figure 12.7.

6. Save the document as MYMACRO.LRN, and keep the document in the typing area.

USING THE ALT KEY TO NAME A MACRO

You know that macro file names can contain up to eight characters. You can also name a macro by pressing the Alt key followed by a single letter when prompted for the macro name. The advantage of

Figure 12.7   **The letter completed by combining macros and stored text**

MACCO PLASTICS, INC.
2345 Industrial Parkway
Nashua, NH 03060

May 11, 1993

Frank Williams
80 Wellington Street
Toronto, Ontario M5K 1A2

Dear Frank:

Welcome to our growing list of satisfied clients. You
have indeed made a wise buying decision. You can
depend on us for fast, reliable, and efficient service.
As a vendor for more than eight years, we can offer you
a wide range of experience in the field.

Enclosed are two copies of your maintenance contract
covering the system you recently purchased from us. If
you experience any problems with your system, contact
Bob Taylor, Customer Service. He will have one of our
service representatives call on you.

Sincerely,

Robert N. Kulik
Macco Plastics, Inc.

Enclosure

cc: R. Allen
     G. Berg
     K. Donnelly
     A. Hutton
     J. Murphy

naming a macro using the Alt+letter combination is that you run the macro by pressing only those two keys: You simply hold down the Alt key and type the single letter. In contrast, to start a macro without this shortcut, you must press the Play Macro keys (Alt+F10), type the full file name, and press Enter.

The disadvantage of naming macros using the Alt+letter combination is that the names are not very descriptive. When using these single-letter names, try to make them as obvious as possible. For example, use *C* for a letter-closing macro, *P* for a print macro, and so on. WordPerfect allows you to create up to 26 of these macros.

In the following activity, you will create a macro that prints a letter in draft mode. Before you begin the activity, the letter shown in Figure 12.7 should be in the typing area. (If it is not available, retrieve the file XMYMACRO.LRN from the Data Disk.)

1. Press **Ctrl+F10** (Record Macro).

2. Press **Alt+P** to name the macro and press **Enter**. The "Recording Macro" message is displayed in the status line.

3. Press **Shift+F7** to display the Print menu, choose **Text Quality** to display the Text Quality menu, choose **Draft**, and choose **1. Full Document** (if necessary) to tell the macro how you want to print the letter.

4. Return to the typing area, and press **Ctrl+F10** to stop recording.

When you use the Alt+letter combination to name a macro, the macro file is saved to the disk just as if you had typed *alt* plus the letter. The file you just created by pressing Alt+P is saved by Word-Perfect as *ALTP.WPM*.

EDITING A MACRO

What if you have made some mistakes in recording your macro, or you would simply like to change it? WordPerfect's Macro Editor makes it possible for you to edit a macro that you've already created, saving you the time and trouble of deleting the faulty macro and starting from scratch.

EDITING TEXT IN THE MACRO

If you try to define a new macro by a name that already exists, WordPerfect displays a message telling you that the macro already exists, along with the options Replace, Edit, and Cancel.

If you choose Replace, the original macro is deleted and the macro definition process starts again. If you choose Edit, the cursor is placed in the Macro Editor so you can change the existing macro.

With the document MYMACRO.LRN in the typing area, follow these steps at your computer:

1. Press **Ctrl+F10** to open the Record Macro dialog box.

2. Type **myclose** and press **Enter**. Notice the prompt

        C:\WP60\MYCLOSE.WPM already exists

3. Choose **Edit**. The Macro Editor is displayed (see Figure 12.8).

Figure 12.8   **The Macro Editor**

```
 File  Edit  View  Layout  Tools  Font  Graphics  Window  Help
DISPLAY(Off!)
HardReturn
Type("Sincerely,")
HardReturn
HardReturn
HardReturn
HardReturn
PAUSE
HardReturn
Type("Macco Plastics, Inc.")
HardReturn
HardReturn
Type("Enclosure")
HardReturn
HardReturn
Type("cc:")
Tab
Type("A. Archer")
HardReturn
Tab
Type("G. Berg")
HardReturn
Tab
Edit Macro:  Press Shft+F3 to Record          Doc 9 Pg 1 Ln 2.17" Pos 1"
```

4. Move to the *R* in *R. Allen*.

5. Press **Del** eight times to delete *R. Allen*.

6. Type **A. Archer**, the new closing name.

7. Move the cursor to the bottom of the document.

8. Press **Tab**. The cursor moves one tab stop to the right. Suppose that what you wanted to do, however, was to insert a {Tab} code into the macro.

9. Press **Backspace** to erase the Tab.

10. Type **Tab** to insert the macro command for a Tab, and press **Enter**.

11. Type **Type("M. Short")** and press **Enter**. Be sure to enter the command exactly.

When editing a macro, keep in mind the following:

- Text is inserted and deleted the same way as in the typing area. For example, the arrow keys, Del, and Backspace can be used in the usual manner.

- For most features and commands, you press the corresponding key to insert the feature or command in the macro. For example, first press Shift+F3 to begin recording, and then press F10 to insert the Save command into the macro.

 SOUNDING A BEEP WHEN THE MACRO PAUSES

You can set up your macro to make your computer beep when the macro pauses. You access the Beep command through the Macro Commands dialog box while in the Macro Editor.

With the macro MYCLOSE.WPM in the Macro Editor, follow these steps at your computer:

1. Move to the beginning of the PAUSE code.

2. Press **Ctrl+PgUp** to open the Macro Control dialog box.

3. Choose **Macro Commands** to open the Macro Commands dialog box, highlight the BEEP command, and press **Enter** to insert the BEEP code into the document.

4. Press **Enter** to place the BEEP code on its own line, and then compare your screen to Figure 12.9.

5. Save your changes and return to the typing area. (Use the same method you would use for a standard document.)

Figure 12.9   **The MYCLOSE macro with a BEEP code inserted**

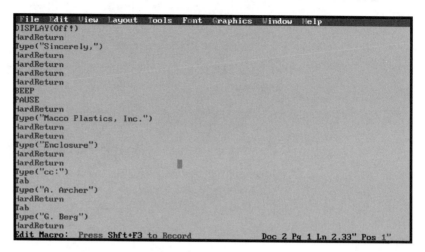

```
File  Edit  View  Layout  Tools  Font  Graphics  Window  Help
DISPLAY(Off!)
HardReturn
Type("Sincerely,")
HardReturn
HardReturn
HardReturn
HardReturn
BEEP
PAUSE
HardReturn
Type("Macco Plastics, Inc.")
HardReturn
HardReturn
Type("Enclosure")
HardReturn
HardReturn
Type("cc:")
Tab
Type("A. Archer")
HardReturn
Tab
Type("G. Berg")
HardReturn
Edit Macro:   Press Shft+F3 to Record           Doc 2 Pg 1 Ln 2.33" Pos 1"
```

EDITING THE LETTER CLOSING AND RUNNING THE NEW CLOSING MACRO

Now that you've edited the closing macro so it contains a beep, let's delete the old closing and run the macro again.

Follow these steps at your computer:

1. Move to the blank line above *Sincerely,* near the bottom of the letter.

2. Block and highlight the text designated as the closing, beginning with the blank line, through the list of names ending with *J. Murphy.*

3. Delete the closing.

4. Run the MYCLOSE macro (press **Alt+F10**, type **myclose**, and press **Enter**). The computer beeps when the macro pauses.

5. Type your name and press **Enter** to release the pause. The rest of the macro is performed. Notice the changes caused by the new macro.

6. Use **F7** to update the document; then clear the typing area.

PRACTICE YOUR SKILLS

This section gives you the opportunity to practice the skills you just learned. You will create a macro for creating a form, as shown in Figure 12.10. This macro will contain pauses to allow the user to type information from the keyboard. You can see the final form in Figure 12.11.

Figure 12.10   **The form stored in the MYFORM macro**

```
                    NOTIFICATION OF SINGLE RELEASE
     RECORD #:                      A & R MAN:
     CG #:                          DATE:
     P.O. #:                        RELEASE DATE:
     WRITER(s):                     ALBUM #:
     PRODUCED BY:                   PUBLISHER:
     ADDITIONAL INFORMATION:
```

Figure 12.11   **The completed form**

```
                    NOTIFICATION OF SINGLE RELEASE
     RECORD #:  1216               A & R MAN:  Claude Hampton
     CG #:  13456                  DATE:  (Today's Date)
     P.O. #: 1023A                 RELEASE DATE:  June 11
     WRITER(s):  Tommie Russell    ALBUM #:  S-43481
     PRODUCED BY:  Clyde Brinkley  PUBLISHER:  Royal Music
     ADDITIONAL INFORMATION:  Final cut date May 5
```

With the typing area cleared, follow these steps at your computer:

1. Start the macro recording session by pressing the Record Macro keys and naming the macro file MYFORM.

2. Change the line spacing to *2* through the Line Format dialog box.

3. While still in the Line Format dialog box, select **Tab Set**. Then do the following:

   - Press **Ctrl+End** to erase all tabs.

   - Set a left-aligned tab at Position 3.5".

   - Exit the Tab Set area and return to the document area.

4. Center and type the heading as seen in Figure 12.10.

5. Type the form, following each colon (:) with two spaces and a pause. For example: Type **RECORD #:**

   - Insert two spaces after the colon.

   - Press **Ctrl+PgUp**, choose **Macro Commands**, highlight **PAUSE**, and press **Enter**.

   - Tab to the next title.

6. End the macro recording session.

7. Clear the typing area. Do *not* save the file again.

8. Run the macro **myform**.

9. Using Figure 12.11 as a guide, complete the form.

10. Save the document as MYPRAC12.LRN.

11. Print the completed form.

12. Clear the typing area.

When you have finished this activity, you might like to try another one that requires similar skills, yet is more challenging. Create the three macros shown in Figures 12.12, 12.13, and 12.14, and name them using the Alt key (refer to the figure captions). Running the macros creates the product form shown in Figure 12.15.

Figure 12.12   **The file ALTA.WPM**

```
                          MACCO PLASTICS INC.
                        2345 Industrial Parkway
                         Nashua, NH  03060
                           (603) 223-5678

        TO:
```

Figure 12.13   **The file ALTB.WPM**

```
                                                   NEW PRODUCT RELEASE
        -----------------------------------------------------------------
        PRODUCT #:
                                    Expected Release   Price per
        Name:                       Date:              Unit: $

        Purpose/Description:
```

Figure 12.14   **The file ALTC.WPM**

```
        PREFERRED CUSTOMER PRICING INFORMATION
        -----------------------------------------------------------------
            Macco Plastics  Inc. sincerely  appreciates the patronage of
        all of our  customers   and holds  special  customers   like
        _____  in  high  regard.   Therefore, the introductory
        prices above have  been  discounted  an  additional _____
        percent.

        As always,  we encourage  your comments  and look forward to
        serving you for years to come.
```

With the typing area cleared, follow these steps at your computer:

1. Create a macro, named by pressing **Alt+A**, to store the heading seen in Figure 12.12. Insert a pause after the colon (:).

2. Clear the typing area.

Figure 12.15   **The assembled document MYOPT12.LRN**

```
                         MACCO PLASTICS INC.
                        2345 Industrial Parkway
                         Nashua, NH  03060
                          (603) 223-5678
       TO:  Bonakin Distributors
            1099 Hoffman Place
            Augusta, Georgia  30901

                                            NEW  PRODUCT  RELEASE
       ----------------------------------------------------------------
       PRODUCT #: 1
                              Expected Release    Price per
       Name: Plasti-cote Trays  Date: June         Unit: $3.20 ea.

       Purpose/Description:  These  trays  will  fill  the  need for an
       inexpensive,  durable,  attractive  tray  for  carrying food in
       cafeterias.  Color  selections  are:  orange, yellow, brown, and
       red.   The  dimensions are 18" by 24" and the  recommended  load
       limit is three pounds.

                                            NEW  PRODUCT  RELEASE
       ----------------------------------------------------------------
       PRODUCT #: 2
                              Expected Release    Price per
       Name: Chug             Date: April         Unit: $.10 ea.

       Purpose/Description:  Chugs  are  pieces  of  molded  plastic that
       hold up  shelving units,  most commonly  inside kitchen cabinets.
       Several  models  will  be  available  for  different  placements:
       corner, mid-shelf, and end, as  well as chugs that fasten a shelf
       in place versus those on which the shelf lies.

       PREFERRED CUSTOMER PRICING INFORMATION
       ----------------------------------------------------------------
            Macco Plastics  Inc. sincerely  appreciates the patronage of
            all of  our  customers  and  holds  special  customers  like
            Bonakin   Distributors   in   high  regard.   Therefore, the
            introductory prices above have been discounted an additional
            fifteen percent.

            As always,  we encourage  your comments  and look forward to
            serving you for years to come.
```

3. Create the product-announcement form seen in Figure 12.13, naming the macro by pressing **Alt+B**. As you do so:

   - Set left-aligned tab stops for the *Expected Release Date:* and *Price Per Unit: $* lines.

   - Insert pauses after each colon (:).

4. Clear the typing area.

5. Create the pricing policy seen in Figure 12.14, naming the macro by pressing **Alt+C**. Include pauses for typing the customer name and percent discounted.

6. Clear the typing area.

7. Combine running the macros and typing text to assemble the final document shown in Figure 12.15. (Hint: To run a macro named using the Alt key, press Alt plus the letter used in the macro name. You need not press Alt+F10.)

8. Print the completed document, and compare your printout to Figure 12.15.

9. Save the document as MYOPT12.LRN.

CHAPTER SUMMARY

In this chapter you learned how to create, name, run, and edit macros to help you use your word-processing time more efficiently. You also learned how to prompt the macro user by making the computer beep every time the macro pauses.

Here's a quick technique reference for Chapter 12:

Feature or Action	How to Do It
Record a macro	**Ctrl+F10** (Record Macro), type the macro name, **Enter**, press the keys you want to record, **Ctrl+F10**
Insert a Pause	While recording keystrokes, **Ctrl+PgUp**, **Macro Commands**, highlight **PAUSE**, **Enter**
Run a macro	Position the cursor, **Alt+F10** (Play Macro), type the macro name and press **Enter**; or press **Alt** and the associated letter
Stop a macro while it is running	**Esc** (Cancel)
Use Alt to name macros	**Ctrl+F10**, **Alt+letter**, continue recording the macro

Feature or Action	How to Do It
Edit a macro	**Ctrl+F10**, type the macro name and press **Enter**, choose **Edit**, perform the edits, press **Ctrl+F10**

Congratulations! You have arrived at the end of this book. You've learned to use all of WordPerfect's basic features plus some that are considerably more sophisticated. Now more than ever, it bears repeating that practice is the best way to get comfortable with everything you've learned. That's why you should feel free to review the material in this book whenever you have a question. This was the main reason for keeping the original Data Disk files intact. So, remember to keep your Data Disk in a safe place, and good luck as you continue using your new-found skills on your own WordPerfect documents.

APPENDIX A:
INSTALLING
WORDPERFECT

Using
WordPerfect's
Installation
Program

This appendix shows you how to install WordPerfect on your computer's hard disk using WordPerfect's own installation program. You will be installing the program onto a directory called C:\WP60, which will be created during the installation process.

USING WORDPERFECT'S INSTALLATION PROGRAM

WordPerfect's installation program, INSTALL.EXE, is designed to simplify the installation process by providing you with prompts and menus. If you follow these prompts and menus carefully, you will find this procedure straightforward.

Note: WordPerfect is designed so that you must run INSTALL.EXE to install WordPerfect properly. Do not attempt to install WordPerfect without using the installation program.

Follow these steps at your computer:

1. Turn on your computer.

2. At the DOS prompt, which will look something like *C:* or *C:\>*, insert the disk labeled "Install 1" in drive A (or B).

3. Type **a:install** and press **Enter**. Note: If you are using a drive other than A, use that drive letter when typing this command—for example, *b*:install. Momentarily, the WordPerfect 6.0 Installation screen will be displayed. At the bottom of the screen, the prompt

   ```
   Do you see red, green, and blue colored
   boxes?
   ```

   is displayed.

4. If the colored boxes are visible on your screen, type **Y** (or press **Enter**) for Yes; if not, type **N** for No. In the next screen that is displayed, under Installation Options, 1 - Standard Installation is currently selected (highlighted).

5. Press **Enter** to perform the standard installation. (For the purposes of performing the exercises in this book, we recommend that you perform the standard installation.) The next installation screen tells you that the program will be installed in a directory that the program itself will create, C:\WP60.

6. At the prompt

   ```
   Do you want to change these directories?
   ```

   press **Enter** for No. A screen that lists the hard-disk space required to install the program is displayed (also see the Introduction).

7. At the prompt

   ```
   Continue with installation?
   ```

   press **Enter** for Yes. The Replace Existing Files Options screen is displayed.

8. Press **Enter** to choose selection 3. At this point, you may be asked if the program should change your AUTOEXEC.BAT file.

9. If you are prompted to update your AUTOEXEC.BAT file, press **Enter** for Yes; if not, press any key to continue.

10. At the prompt

    ```
    Do you want to install any additional
    Graphic Drivers?
    ```

    press **Enter** for No. At this point, the actual installation begins. A bar showing the installation's progress is displayed. Above it, the names of the files are displayed as they are installed.

11. When prompted to insert the Install 2 disk, remove the Install 1 disk, and replace it with the Install 2 disk; then press **Enter** to continue the installation.

12. When prompted to insert the Install 3 disk, remove the Install 2 disk, and replace it with the Install 3 disk; then press **Enter** to continue the installation.

13. At the prompt

    ```
    Do you want to install any Sound Drivers?
    ```

    press **Enter** to continue the installation *without* installing a sound driver. Note: If you have installed a sound board in your computer and would like to use it with WordPerfect, type **Y**, and then continue with the sound-driver installation as prompted.

14. When prompted to insert the Program 1 disk, remove the Install 3 disk, and replace it with the Program 1 disk; then press **Enter** to continue the installation.

15. When prompted to insert the Program 2 disk, remove the Program 1 disk, and replace it with the Program 2 disk; then press **Enter** to continue the installation.

16. When prompted to insert the Program 3 disk, remove the Program 2 disk, and replace it with the Program 3 disk; then press **Enter** to continue the installation.

17. At the prompt

```
Do you want to install any Printer Drivers?
```

press **Enter** if have a printer and would like to use it to print WordPerfect documents. If you do not have a printer, press **N**; then skip to step 21.

18. If you pressed Enter in step 17, remove the Program 3 disk and replace it with the Printer 1 disk when prompted. Then press **Enter** to continue. The Printer Selection box lists all the printers currently supported by the program.

19. Use the Up and Down Arrow keys to highlight the name of your printer. Use the PgDn and PgUp keys to view more printer names. If you are selecting only one printer, highlight the desired printer name and press **Enter**. If you are selecting more than one printer, highlight a desired name and press the * (asterisk) key to mark the name, and continue in this manner until you've marked all the desired printer names; then press **Enter**. For additional printer information, press **F1** to get help (see also your printer manual). After you have pressed Enter, you will be asked whether you want the program to select the printer(s) you have chosen.

20. Check the prompt to make sure each printer name is correct, and press **Enter**. In a moment, the prompt

```
Do you want to install another printer?
```

will be displayed. If you wish to install another printer, type **Y**; if not, press **Enter**. At this point, the program will actually begin running. The first time the program is run, the Welcome WordPerfect User screen prompts you to enter your registration number, which comes with your copy of the program.

21. Type your registration number and press **Enter**. The program now completes the installation procedure. In a moment, the program will exit itself, leaving you at the DOS prompt.

22. Remove the Printer 1 disk from drive A.

23. If you instructed the program to update your AUTOEXEC.BAT file in step 9, press **Ctrl+Alt+Del** (or turn off your computer, and then turn it on again) to reboot your computer before starting the program. This allows the changes in the file to take effect.

Now, you're ready to begin learning how to use WordPerfect 6.0! Please turn to Chapter 1 to begin.

APPENDIX B: WORDPERFECT'S HELP SYSTEM

Using Help

Context-sensitive Help

WordPerfect offers a Help system that you can use when you are working on your own in the program. This Help system provides you with information on almost all of WordPerfect's commands, menus, and cursor movements.

USING HELP

To use the Help feature, follow these steps at your computer:

1. From the WordPerfect typing area, press **F1** (Help). The opening Help screen is displayed (Figure B.1). From this screen, you can move to any of the different Help areas listed under *Choose*. The *For information about* column gives a brief description of each Help area. Notice that the Index is highlighted by default; this is the most commonly used Help area.

Figure B.1   **The Opening Help Screen**

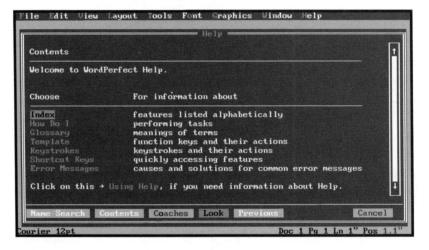

2. Press ↓ several times. Notice that the highlight moves down through the list of Help areas.

3. Press ↑ until the highlight rests once again on *Index*.

4. Press **Enter** to display the Help Index (see Figure B.2). In the Help Index, features are listed alphabetically. Included in the Help Index are the features listed in the opening Help screen.

5. Press ↓ several times. Here, too, you can use the Up and Down Arrow keys to highlight a topic about which you'd like more information.

Figure B.2   **The Help Index**

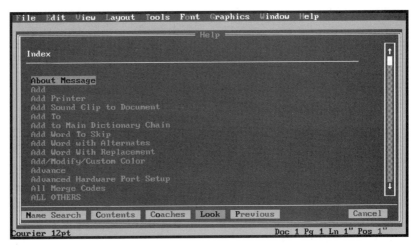

6. Press the **PgDn** key several times. Notice that each time you press PgDn, the next screen of information is displayed. Likewise, you can use the PgUp key to move backward through the list. Notice the Name Search option in the lower-left corner of the Index area.

7. Press **N** (the highlighted letter in the option) to choose Name Search, and begin typing **template**. (You won't have to type the whole word.) Notice that the Index scrolls to match the letters you have typed.

8. After *Template* is highlighted in the list, press **Enter** twice to display the WordPerfect function-key template (see Figure B.3). This template tells you at a glance what each function key is used for in WordPerfect, both on its own and in combination with the Shift, Ctrl, and Alt keys. For example, pressing Shift+F8 gives you access to WordPerfect's Format feature. Keep in mind that this template represents the use of the function keys when you press them from the typing area.

9. Press **P** to choose Previous. This option returns you to the previous Help screen, in this case the Index.

10. Press **N** to choose Name Search once again, and begin typing **keystrokes** until *Keystrokes* is highlighted in the list.

Figure B.3   **Template of function keys in WordPerfect**

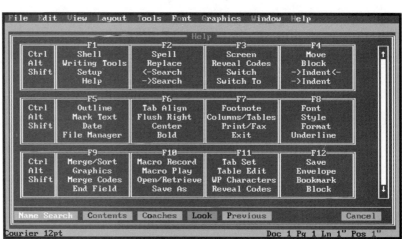

11. Press **Enter** twice to display the Keystrokes Help screen. This alphabetical listing gives you information about the uses of keys other than function keys in WordPerfect.

12. Use the same method to scroll in the Keystrokes Help area that you used in the Help Index.

13. Press **Esc** to return to the typing area.

CONTEXT-SENSITIVE HELP

Another way to obtain specific information about a feature is to use *context-sensitive* Help. Context-sensitive Help enables you to obtain help from anywhere in the program, not just from the main typing area. For example, if you have displayed a menu, press F1 to get information about that menu.

Use the same method to exit from context-sensitive Help that you would use to exit from general Help: press Esc. This brings you back to where you were before you accessed Help.

APPENDIX C: FILE CONVERSION

Converting a
Document from
Another Word
Processor to
WordPerfect
Format

Saving a File in an
Earlier WordPerfect
Format

This appendix shows you how to transfer information between WordPerfect and other programs with the ConvertPerfect 2.0 program.

CONVERTING A DOCUMENT FROM ANOTHER WORD PROCESSOR TO WORDPERFECT FORMAT

When you perform a file conversion, we recommend that you do so from the WordPerfect typing area. Therefore, before you begin the file conversion, please start the WordPerfect program (see "Starting WordPerfect" in Chapter 1).

In WordPerfect 6.0, no special procedure is required to convert a document (file) from another word processor to WordPerfect 6.0 format. When you attempt to open a file that was previously saved in another format, WordPerfect's ConvertPerfect program automatically performs the conversion. To open a document created in another format, we recommend that you use the WordPerfect File Manager (see Chapter 1) or the File Open feature (see Chapter 5).

When WordPerfect first detects that the file you are attempting to open is not in WordPerfect 6.0 format, the File Format dialog box is displayed (see Figure C.1). This dialog box contains a list of file formats. The program automatically highlights what it believes to be the file's current format, and prompts you to

```
Please select the file's format.
```

in case WordPerfect has guessed incorrectly. If necessary, use the arrow keys to highlight the correct format, and press Enter.

Figure C.1 **The File Format dialog box**

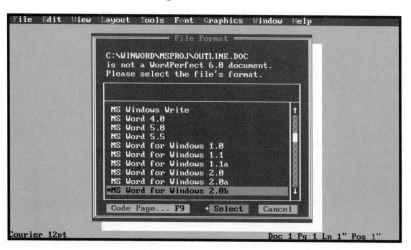

Note: Before you select a format other than the one that is automatically identified, make sure you have the right one; otherwise, the file may be misformatted, possibly resulting in lost information.

ConvertPerfect then takes over and reformats the file into WordPerfect 6.0 format. For small documents containing only text, this process takes only a few moments; for very large documents—particularly for those containing graphic images—file conversion may take several minutes (a cup of coffee, please!).

When the conversion is completed, the document appears in the typing area. At this point, it's a good idea to save the document in its new format, just in case the world comes to an end or, worse yet, your computer loses power (see Chapter 1).

Note: Use this same procedure to open a document created in an earlier version of WordPerfect; for example, to open a WordPerfect 5.1 document in WordPerfect 6.0.

SAVING A FILE IN AN EARLIER WORDPERFECT FORMAT

To save a WordPerfect 6.0 document in WordPerfect 5.1/5.2, 5.0, or 4.2 format,

- Press the F10 key or choose File, Save As to open the Save Document dialog box.

- Press Shift+F1 to display the Save Setup dialog box.

- Choose 2. Default Save Format to open the Default Save Format drop-down list box, which contains a list of all the formats in which you can save a WordPerfect 6.0 document (see Figure C.2). WordPerfect 6.0 is, of course, currently selected. (To scroll through the list, use ↑ and ↓. You'll notice that formats other than WordPerfect are also available.)

- Use ↑ (or ↓, if necessary) to highlight WordPerfect 5.1/5.2, WordPerfect 5.0, or WordPerfect 4.2.

- Press Enter.

This feature saves the document on your screen in the new format; it can then be retrieved within that version of WordPerfect.

Figure C.2   **The Default Save Format drop-down list box**

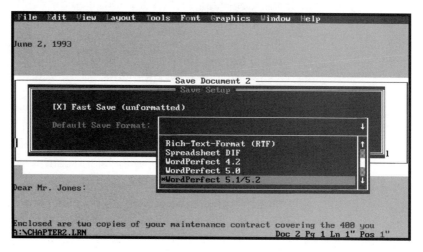

INDEX

Ziff-Davis Press Survey of Readers

Please help us in our effort to produce the best books on personal computing.
For your assistance, we would be pleased to send you a FREE catalog
featuring the complete line of Ziff-Davis Press books.

1. How did you first learn about this book?

Recommended by a friend . . . . ☐ -1 (5)

Recommended by store personnel . . . . ☐ -2

Saw in Ziff-Davis Press catalog . . . . ☐ -3

Received advertisement in the mail . . . . ☐ -4

Saw the book on bookshelf at store . . . . ☐ -5

Read book review in: _____ ☐ -6

Saw an advertisement in: _____ ☐ -7

Other (Please specify): _____ ☐ -8

2. Which THREE of the following factors most influenced your decision to purchase this book? (Please check up to THREE.)

Front or back cover information on book . . . ☐ -1 (6)

Logo of magazine affiliated with book . . . . . . ☐ -2

Special approach to the content . . . . ☐ -3

Completeness of content . . . . ☐ -4

Author's reputation. . . . . ☐ -5

Publisher's reputation . . . . ☐ -6

Book cover design or layout . . . . ☐ -7

Index or table of contents of book . . . . ☐ -8

Price of book . . . . ☐ -9

Special effects, graphics, illustrations . . . . ☐ -0

Other (Please specify): _____ ☐ -x

3. How many computer books have you purchased in the last six months? _____ (7-10)

4. On a scale of 1 to 5, where 5 is excellent, 4 is above average, 3 is average, 2 is below average, and 1 is poor, please rate each of the following aspects of this book below. (Please circle your answer.)

Depth/completeness of coverage	5 4 3 2 1	(11)
Organization of material	5 4 3 2 1	(12)
Ease of finding topic	5 4 3 2 1	(13)
Special features/time saving tips	5 4 3 2 1	(14)
Appropriate level of writing	5 4 3 2 1	(15)
Usefulness of table of contents	5 4 3 2 1	(16)
Usefulness of index	5 4 3 2 1	(17)
Usefulness of accompanying disk	5 4 3 2 1	(18)
Usefulness of illustrations/graphics	5 4 3 2 1	(19)
Cover design and attractiveness	5 4 3 2 1	(20)
Overall design and layout of book	5 4 3 2 1	(21)
Overall satisfaction with book	5 4 3 2 1	(22)

5. Which of the following computer publications do you read regularly; that is, 3 out of 4 issues?

Byte . . . . ☐ -1 (23)

Computer Shopper . . . . ☐ -2

Corporate Computing . . . . ☐ -3

Dr. Dobb's Journal . . . . ☐ -4

LAN Magazine . . . . ☐ -5

MacWEEK . . . . ☐ -6

MacUser . . . . ☐ -7

PC Computing . . . . ☐ -8

PC Magazine . . . . ☐ -9

PC WEEK . . . . ☐ -0

Windows Sources . . . . ☐ -x

Other (Please specify): _____ ☐ -y

Please turn page.

6. What is your level of experience with personal computers? With the subject of this book?

	With PCs	With subject of book
Beginner	☐ -1 (24)	☐ -1 (25)
Intermediate	☐ -2	☐ -2
Advanced	☐ -3	☐ -3

7. Which of the following best describes your job title?

Officer (CEO/President/VP/owner) . . . . ☐ -1 (26)
Director/head . . . . ☐ -2
Manager/supervisor . . . . ☐ -3
Administration/staff . . . . ☐ -4
Teacher/educator/trainer . . . . ☐ -5
Lawyer/doctor/medical professional . . . . . . ☐ -6
Engineer/technician . . . . ☐ -7
Consultant . . . . ☐ -8
Not employed/student/retired . . . . ☐ -9
Other (Please specify): _____ ☐ -0

8. What is your age?

Under 20 . . . . ☐ -1 (27)
21-29 . . . . ☐ -2
30-39 . . . . ☐ -3
40-49 . . . . ☐ -4
50-59 . . . . ☐ -5
60 or over . . . . ☐ -6

9. Are you:

Male . . . . ☐ -1 (28)
Female . . . . ☐ -2

Thank you for your assistance with this important information! Please write your address below to receive our free catalog.

Name: _____

Address: _____

City/State/Zip: _____

Fold here to mail.   1056-01-01

_____

_____

_____

BUSINESS REPLY MAIL
FIRST CLASS MAIL   PERMIT NO. 1612   OAKLAND, CA

POSTAGE WILL BE PAID BY ADDRESSEE

Ziff-Davis Press
5903 Christie Avenue
Emeryville, CA 94608-1925
Attn: Marketing

■ TO RECEIVE 5¼-INCH DISK(S)

The Ziff-Davis Press software contained on the $3^{1}/_{2}$-inch disk included with this book is also available in $5^{1}/_{4}$-inch format. If you would like to receive the software in the $5^{1}/_{4}$-inch format, please return the $3^{1}/_{2}$-inch disk with your name and address to:

Disk Exchange
Ziff-Davis Press
5903 Christie Avenue
Emeryville, CA 94608

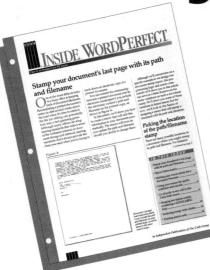